Tapestries
of Life

Tapestries of Life

Women's Work, Women's Consciousness, and the Meaning of Daily Experience

BETTINA APTHEKER

The University of Massachusetts Press
Amherst

Copyright © 1989 by
The University of Massachusetts Press

All rights reserved

Printed in the United States of America
LC 88–26715
ISBN 0-87023-658-X (cloth); 659-8 (paper)

Designed by Susan Bishop
Set in Linotron Sabon by Keystone Typesetting, Inc.
Printed by Thomson-Shore

Library of Congress Cataloging-in-Publication Data
Aptheker, Bettina.
    Tapestries of life : women's work, women's consciousness,
and the meaning of daily experience / Bettina Aptheker.
       p. cm.
    Bibliography: p.
    Includes index.
    ISBN 0-87023–658–X ISBN 0–87023–659–8 (pbk.)
    1. Women—Social conditions. 2. Feminism. 3. Lesbianism. I. Title.
HQ1154.A745   1989
305.4'2–dc19   88–26715
                                                CIP

British Library Cataloguing in Publication
data are available.

Acknowledgments for permissions to reprint material under
copyright begin on page 295.

To Kate

for sharing in the breath of life

When, with breaking heart,
I realize
this world is only a dream,
the oak tree looks radiant.
  —Anryū Suharu

Contents

Acknowledgments

MANY, many people contributed to the successful completion of this book. It has been my good fortune to be affiliated with women's studies at the University of California at Santa Cruz, with colleagues who have provided me with outstanding support, encouragement, and affection. I am particularly indebted to Donna Haraway, Diane K. Lewis, Helene Moglen, Candace West, and Patricia Zavella. I am also indebted to colleagues elsewhere in the country for their kind assistance, including Barrie Thorne, Phyllis Rogers, Maria Herrera-Sobek, Kathryn Sklar, and Kathleen Barry.

The students at Santa Cruz have been a source of inspiration, and my experiences with them infuse this book. I am particularly indebted to Shelley Shepard, Hiroko Yamano, Noelle Remington, and senior-in-residence, Ruth Chinn, for sharing their writing with me. I also thank several students for providing me with a fund of information about and access to women artists and their work, in particular Hinano Campton, Beth Collins, Alison Kim, Julie Porcella, and Alvina Quintana.

Several artists have been most helpful to me. Mayumi Oda generously shared her work with me, and her presentation in my class on women's culture in the winter of 1987 was very useful in framing my ideas. Betye Saar kindly sent me catalogs and slides relevant to her work, which made it accessible to me in ways that would otherwise not have been possible. Mary Warshaw supplied me with wonderful catalogs and books over several years, and her close reading and criticism of chapter four on imagination and survival was especially helpful.

In seeking a supportive process among writers I sent portions of this manuscript to many of the authors whose works I quote and discuss. I am enormously grateful for their support of this work, for their encouragement, and for their time in reading and sometimes correcting relevant sections of the manuscript. I wish to thank Paula Gunn Allen, Gloria Anzaldúa, Gwendolyn Brooks, Elsa Barkley Brown, Fran Leeper Buss, Victoria Byerly, Lorna Dee Cervantes, Janet Campbell Hale, Ursula K. Le Guin, Maxine Hong Kingston, Nicholasa Mohr, Bernice Johnson Reagon, Alice Walker, and Anna Lee Walters. In this connection I am most indebted to Adrienne Rich whose thinking on so many issues influenced my own, and who read this manuscript in full, offering detailed notes. Her support, and incisive criticisms and suggestions were of great importance to me emotionally and intellectually.

Meridel Le Sueur, whose work I cite and discuss, has been an inspiration to generations of women writers. Having known her since I was a child, it is with a special gratitude that I thank her both personally and professionally for her labors.

Several friends and colleagues read this manuscript in full and provided me with invaluable comment. I thank Ann Jealous, Mamie Bland Todd, Carol Whitehill, Arlene Avakian of the women's studies program at the University of Massachusetts, Amherst, who served as our consulting editor, and Richard Martin, editor of the University of Massachusetts Press. I am deeply indebted to the Press's managing editor, Pam Wilkinson, for her superb reading of the text and her extraordinary attention to detail.

I would also like to thank Nancy K. Bereano, publisher of Firebrand Books, for her cheerful assistance in locating authors, and Sherry Thomas of Aunt Lute/Spinsters publishing in San Francisco for her thoughtful correspondence with me about small press publishing, and her generous support of this project.

Birdie Flynn typed the manuscript through several revisions with expert skill. In addition, her frequent and enthusiastic comments about the work as I struggled to complete it were thoroughly uplifting. Many thanks to Leslie Simon for a splendid index.

I am indebted to the Committee on Research of the Academic Senate of the University of California, Santa Cruz, for a Faculty Research grant which helped me complete the final stages of manuscript preparation.

My lover Kate Miller read everything as I worked in all stages of incompletion and fragmentation. She gave of her time and wisdom over many years with extraordinary generosity. She is frequently acknowledged in the text because she was an integral part of its creation.

Finally, I would like to express my gratitude to the community of women scholars, writers, poets, and artists in the United States for providing all of us with such a rich and beautiful weaving of our lives. Their love for women, and their commitment to tell our stories became for me both inspiration and model.

Tapestries
of Life

Conditions for Work

No one ever told us we had to study our lives,
make of our lives a study, as if learning natural history
or music. . . .
  —Adrienne Rich, "Transcendental Etude"

The oppressed without hope are mysteriously quiet. When the conception
of change is beyond the limits of the possible, there are no words to articulate
discontent so it is sometimes held not to exist. This mistaken belief arises
because we can only hear silence in the moment in which it is breaking.
  —Sheila Rowbotham, *Woman's Consciousness, Man's World*

All of us remembering what we have heard together—
that creates the whole story
the long story of the people.
  —Leslie Marmon Silko, *Storyteller*

Things don't fall apart. Things hold.
Lines connect in thin ways which last and last
and lives become generations made out of
pictures and words just kept. . . .
  —Lucille Clifton, *Generations*

ROM the late spring until the first snows of late fall, a ferry called the *Sierra Queen* chugs its way across a windswept lake in the high Sierra, the water churning with whitecaps. The engines roar and the voices of the passengers shouting above the din are clearly audible for more than a mile. A battered blue and red boat, the *Queen* recalls its namesake of movie fame, the *African Queen* which transported Humphrey Bogart and Katharine Hepburn into adventure and romance. The waterway marking the route of this *Queen*, however, is a lake eight thousand feet above sea level. Its passengers are mostly backpackers preferring this transport across the lake to an eight-mile hike around it, bringing them to their point of entry onto the wilderness trails.

Ten-thousand-foot peaks mark the eastern and western boundaries of the lake, while more gentle ranges slope upward along its northern and southern sides. The mountains are dotted with pine, cedar, aspen, scrub oak, and manzanita ripe with its green berries. There are hearty blooms of wildflowers in the first flush of summer and an occasional expanse of alpine meadow. The ridges of the highest peaks are laced with snow, and waterfalls spiral down the steep ravines. Varieties of woodpeckers, jays, crows, wrens, chickadees, and warblers and occasionally the bright beautiful Western Tanager populate the shoreline and the sparse woods. There are deer, and infrequently the howls and barking of the coyotes can be heard at nightfall. Rocks and trees are teeming with life; white water pours into the lake from the western ridges; fish, mostly trout, can be seen leaping into the dusk, snapping up insects. But the overwhelming sense of these mountains is the sheer sweep of their gray, sparkling granite rock.

My lover and I have been coming here for many years. The skipper of the *Queen* will expect us in mid-June. He will pack us onto the ferry and eventually deposit us along the shore. A hefty climb up the rocks will bring us to a "summer residence." We stay in the "No-Man's-Land" between the boundary of a national forest and the lake, where what the guide books call "primitive camping" is permitted. For long stretches of time we will be alone and see only an occasional fisher out on a boat. We live in a tent.

We love this place, cherish the land, the rocks, the trees. I am particularly attached to a Pygmy Nuthatch whom I have never seen, but it sends out its monotonous three-toned call every morning, and I whistle back. And "Sally" is the yellow-bellied marmot who resides somewhere nearby and once consumed some very precious potato salad, before we had learned to properly secure the lids on all boxes and containers. It is in this place that Kate and I do our best and most serious work. Much of this book was written there.

Kate and I have been together since 1979. She teaches women's studies at a community college near our home. By training Kate is probably best described as a cultural anthropologist; by temperament, she is an anarchist. Her family name was Krieg, which means "war" in German. She was married to a "Miller" for six years and kept the name. She was born and raised in North Dakota, in a hard-working family. She has worked hard all of her life and has raised her daughter alone. Kate is largely self-taught. She has systematically studied a wide range of subjects. She is one of the most learned people I have ever known. She is an excellent therapist, and people come to her for (free) counseling very often. She loves the opera, most specifically because of the sound of the high note a truly great soprano will hit and hold with crystalline perfection. After we heard Leontyne Price in one of her last performances of *Aida,* Kate was breathless for hours.

In contrast, professionally I am best described as a historian, and temperamentally I am a communist (although unaffiliated). I was born into a Jewish, Communist, middle-class intellectual family and raised in New York. I have an almost irresistible urge to clown and a highly developed fantasy life. I love the opera for its larger-than-life drama. I am well versed in the Marxist texts and in political theory and history. Only in these last years with Kate have I been exposed to a wider range of readings in classical, contemporary, and science fiction, poetry, Eastern metaphysics, and murder mysteries.

Our differences produce interesting patterns. For example, I appreciate the safety of a theoretical structure when I am doing intellectual work. In contrast, Kate acknowledges the importance of structure in people's lives (whether it be theoretical, theological, or psychological) but treats these as interesting examples of how human beings process information. I gravitate toward institutional settings, whereas Kate prefers the freedom of a kind of spiritual levitation around them. In our relationship these differences work themselves into new ways of seeing.

Kate has played an integral part in the creation of this book. It is not that I could not have written a book without her; it is that this book has been fundamentally influenced by our interaction and discussion. She read (or I read aloud to her) every chapter in various stages of its formation. She often knew, intuited, or encouraged my lines of thinking. Most of all we talked, sifting and weighing experiences, stories, poems, and streams of thought. Kate is everywhere in this book, and my references to her are simply a part of the telling. Our relationship formed the emotional bedrock for this work, and the mountains provided the first and most important condition for work. It was not so much having a "mountain of one's own" as it was being completely removed from academic life in the formative stages of writing. It was having the space in which to think in new ways, without feeling bound by the requirements of academic (i.e., objective, abstract, theoretical) methods. The mountain provided a grounding, a way of seeing beauty and of gaining perspective.

In purpose and design this book is about putting women at the center of our thinking. Whether we, as women, have tried to reframe our personal experiences into new and meaningful patterns in consciousness-raising groups; to write poetry, fiction, or autobiography from a self-consciously women-centered perspective; or to write feminist theory within an academic discipline; whether we have engaged in women's studies, or the women's liberation movement which gave rise to them, the process of putting women at the center has been at the heart of the effort. This book proposes a way of doing it structured out of the dailiness of women's lives, and it attempts to put this doing into practice. The focus is on women in the United States, primarily in modern times. I draw upon the works of women writers, poets, artists, dramatists, dancers, musicians, and academics, and upon the words of women factory workers, domestics, and agricultural laborers. I look at things women create in their everyday lives. I incorporate the works of women of diverse races, classes, ages, and geographic regions. A lesbian sensibility informs my core ideas.

In purpose and design this is also a book about healing, and beauty, and balance. It is about helping to restore these things to ourselves as women. By this I mean that I am interested in questions about how to change women's consciousness of themselves, about how to help women heal from the racist and sexual violence that permeates our lives, about how to restore a sense of beauty in women whose aesthetic senses are continually assaulted, mocked, and degraded. I want to explore how to promote balance in a system that institutionalizes class, racial, and gender inequities at every level.

While the mountains provided the first condition for work, they also laid the foundation for the second. This was to break up old patterns of thinking. Most specifically, it was to change my ideas about the privileging of theory as the most important or most significant way of knowing. Those of us trained to think in the framework of traditional theories have known for some time that we needed a radical critique of them. "What we have not known," as the Canadian sociologist Dorothy Smith has observed, "is how to begin from our own centre, how to begin from our own experience, how to make ourselves as women the subjects of the . . . act of knowing."[1] We have visualized this problem as one of theoretical invention. I think, however, that the problem is one of form; that is, the problem is lodged in the nature of theory itself. I felt this for the first time when writing my last book.

Woman's Legacy is a collection of seven essays focusing on the history of Afro-American women.[2] Each essay addresses a constellation of issues around a particular moment in history, contrasting the perspectives of Black and white women, and examining the interplay between class, race, and sex. Suffrage, lynching, rape, domestic labor, and the myth of the Black woman as matriarch are considered. The central argument of the book, replayed in each moment, is that women's liberation and Black liberation are inextricably intertwined. Neither can be achieved without the other. Afro-American women, I suggest, because of their dual identity, are at the hub of this connection. I urge the formation of conscious alliance, of a coalition between the two movements. I do not disagree with the premises or the conclusions of that book. However, I began to question the methods of argument and presentation and the narrowness of its appeal for interracial unity.

The book was grounded in traditional methods of historical research, including the use of archives and other primary sources such as contemporaneous newspapers, journals, magazines, and books. It was framed in a traditional and relatively orthodox Marxist theory. This meant, in part, that I was interested in an "objective" assessment of political struggles, independent of the presumed consciousness of any of their participants, and that I gave primacy to class in that assessment. This was not so much a matter of the working-class or middle-class backgrounds of the participants, white or Black, as it was an estimate of the class alignments of those in power, e.g., slaveholders, industrialists, financiers, and politicians.

Although the book grew out of many personal experiences in the civil rights and student movements of the 1960s and seventies, its concerns were generated by what I saw as the failures of Marxist theory to adequately address women's issues. In writing the book, then, I proposed to put women at the center of my thinking *about Marxism*. The point was at once to reform the theory and to gain insight into women's position in society. This centering is most apparent in the chapter called "Domestic Labor: Patterns in Black and White."

In doing research I learned that between 50 and 60 percent of the Black women gainfully employed outside of their own homes between 1920 and 1960 were in "private service" as domestic workers. In what reflected the fierce racial and sexual segregation of the U.S. working class, these women were consigned to the lowest-paying, most menial, and least secure section of the work force. Most were employed by individual households, worked for below minimum wages, and were isolated from one another. Yet in trying to find a way to discuss domestic labor I found myself outside the framework of traditional Marxist theory which focuses its discussion of exploitation on the extraction of surplus value in the production of commodities, i.e., in industrial production. To gain more of a grip on the issue I began to read the debates among Marxist feminists ensuing then, primarily in British sociological circles, about the nature of housework. I was amazed to follow the contortions through which the theory was adjusted to accommodate women's reality. That is, these theorists were trying to show that housewives, doing domestic chores in their own homes, from cleaning, to shopping, to child care, were producing a form of surplus value in that they were reproducing the working class, which sold its "labor power" to a capitalist employer. Since "labor power" was a commodity, the argument went, the production of it, albeit "privatized" in the home, was as essential to the capitalist economy as the production of steel.[3] I saw the logic, indeed the merit, of this argument, but I feared its theoretical consequences since it appeared to violate basic premises about the primacy of class in Marxist theory. It felt important to me personally to avoid this approach. I proposed, therefore, that domestic service, whether a paid form of employment as in the case of Black women, or an unpaid form of labor as in the case of all women, was a *pre*capitalist arrangement. I did this to escape the dilemma of the Marxist categories! Women did not sell their "labor power," but, more closely, they sold themselves. This precapitalist arrangement, I argued, reflected the extent to which men owned women as property—literally as chattel slaves and legally as wives. I drew heavily upon the works of Engels and the early Marx to sustain my arguments. Clever? Perhaps. But what was

's theoretical twister? What did I (or we) learn about women's
.v did this theoretical pursuit contribute to an understanding of
..к women's lives? Who could understand what we were writing?
Moreover, in my "cleverness," I saw later, I had obscured the significance
of the relationship, the partnership, between capital and patriarchy.[4] The
experience with *Woman's Legacy* and with the chapter on domestic labor
in particular prompted these questions and conclusions.

It seemed to me that this kind of work, whether it involved Marxism
or other theoretical systems such as psychoanalysis or structuralism, was
inaccessible to the vast majority of women, including even those within
the broad spectrum of the women's liberation movement. The work was
inaccessible because it was constructed from categories of analysis that
had no immediate (and sometimes no even remote) reference to women's
actual experiences. Its matters of concern had been generated primarily by
priorities of the theory as it might be applied to women (or efforts to
reform the theory to accommodate women's reality, as I had done) rather
than by women's everyday lives. Moreover, the primary thrust was to
convince men, upon whose authority theories are accepted or rejected, of
the merit of a feminist viewpoint. Accessibility for women reading (or
trying to read) this material had not been a problem of abstraction but of
reference. If I sound harsh in this assessment it is because I am both self-
critical and frustrated. I spent years steeped in this theory spinning in the
ozone.

I have not been alone in these conclusions. Philosopher Sandra Harding, pursuing a discussion of what she called "The Instability of the
Analytical Categories of Feminist Theory," observed that feminist scholars, in using Marxism, psychoanalysis, deconstructionism, and other theoretical frameworks

> have stretched the intended domains of these theories, reinterpreted
> their central claims, or borrowed their concepts and categories to
> make visible women's lives. . . . After our labors these theories often
> do not much resemble what their nonfeminist creators or users had in
> mind, to put the point mildly. . . . it has never been women's experi-
> ences that have provided the grounding for any of the theories from
> which we borrow. It is not women's experiences that have generated
> the problems these theories attempt to resolve, nor have women's
> experiences served as the test of the adequacy of these theories.[5]

Ultimately it seemed to me that a preoccupation with fitting women into theories that subordinated them at their core was crippling. "There is," Adrienne Rich once wrote, "no such thing as an intellectual blind-spot surrounded by an outlook of piercing lucidity—least of all when that spot happens to cover the immense and complex dimensions in which women exist, both for ourselves, and in the lives of men."[6] It was easier, of course, to come to these conclusions as an abstract intellectual exercise than it was to shift the boundaries of my thinking. I was comforted by the knowledge that I was not alone. I recalled a conversation I had had with a Renaissance historian, the late Joan Kelly. She told me that every time she thought she had a foundation upon which to build her discussion of women's history, it collapsed under the weight of the evidence it itself exhumed and assembled.

After the experience with *Woman's Legacy* I knew that I wanted to approach the writing of this book in a different way. I wanted to start with women's experience and form the patterns from it. I wanted to write in a way that was more accessible, that came out of our everyday lives as women, that could be useful in changing the balance of power in each other's lives. A paragraph from a book by the socialist feminist Sheila Rowbotham hummed in my brain for a long time. It said: "In order to create an alternative an oppressed group must at once shatter the self-reflecting world which encircles it and, at the same time, project its own image onto history. In order to discover its own identity as distinct from that of the oppressor it has to become visible to itself."[7]

Part of "shatter[ing] the self-reflecting world" for me meant shattering the notion that theory—in the sense of causality, in the sense of the "scientific method" of hypothesis, prediction, verification, and replication, in the sense of constructing definitive boundary—was the best or only method for understanding women's lives. When I talked about "placing women at the center of my thinking" I meant that the structure of my thinking had to change. This was the second condition for work.

The third condition was to invent the ground upon which I could stand; that is, to find a foundation that would allow me to start with women's experiences and build from there. I felt that two things about this foundation were very important. The first was that it be stripped to the bare minimum: enough to begin, but with as little theoretical baggage as possible. The second was that it be broad enough and flexible enough to hold a range of women's experiences. I wanted a grounding upon which the center could pivot to include the experiences of Afro-American, Asian-American, Native American, Latina, Chicana, and Euro-American women, and the diversity within and between them. Essential to my purpose was the shedding of a whitened center in conception and design. The point was not to homogenize. It was not to invent one "woman" as a kind of universal iconography. The purpose was to interpret, to form patterns, to make intelligible the multiple, highly complex, and ever-changing ensemble of social relations in which women are lodged. That ensemble is multiracial, cross-cultural, of different classes, religions, work experiences, ages, and sexual preference. In defining those differences among women, I also sought connection, as long as the connection remained respectful of the difference and became a point of illumination rather than a mush of obfuscation in a white, ethnocentric, heterocentric landscape.

I began then, with this idea: women have a consciousness of social reality that is distinct from that put forth by men. That is, women have a distinct way of seeing and interpreting the world. This is not to say that all women have the same consciousness or share the same beliefs. It is to say that women of each particular culture or group have a consciousness, a way of seeing, which is common to themselves as women in that it is distinct from the way the men of their culture or group see things. All women share this *process* of distinction. I propose to take women's consciousness of social reality as it is constructed in the artifacts of daily life and represented in stories, songs, poems, and rituals enacted by women and use it to form patterns.

The idea that women have a distinct consciousness rests upon two assumptions, which, I think, are widely shared among women activists and scholars. The first is that in virtually all societies, and certainly within the United States today, there is a sexual division of labor. Women perform distinct tasks, are socialized in gender-specific ways, and must enact their gendered roles daily to continually reconstitute their identity as women. Again, the specificity of gendered roles differs between cultures, but the process of gendering, of a specific division of labor, is virtually universal.

The second assumption is that in almost all societies, and certainly within the United States today, with the possible and significant exception of certain Native American peoples who maintain a matrilineal descent, women are subordinated to men. The evidence for this is overwhelming, in everything from the discrimination against women in education and employment, to the history of marriage laws in which women in many times, places, and cultures have been and still are the property of men, to the violence against women perpetrated in a variety of forms including rape, battery, pornography, and prostitution. The subordination of women is codified in all major religions including the Jewish, Christian, Hindu, Shinto, Buddhist, and Islamic scriptures, and its practices and assumptions pervade all or most institutions including the executive, legislative, and judicial branches of government, the educational system, the medical establishment, the arts and literature, and so forth.

These two factors, the sexual division of labor and the institutionalized subordination of women to men, in combination produce a distinctly female consciousness.[8] Women give expression to this consciousness in their everyday lives by producing specific cultures. There are, for example, many work cultures that are identifiably female: among clerical workers, telephone operators, waitresses, nurses, elementary school teachers, cannery, garment, and electronics workers. Likewise, there are places in our society that are predominantly and distinctly female spaces, such as kitchens, child-care centers, beauty salons, social welfare agencies, fabric, yarn, and variety stores, department stores (at least major sections of them), and supermarkets. There are also many art forms that are specifically female (although which ones vary among ethnic groups) such as quilting, needlework, tapestry, beadwork, pottery, basketry, and weaving. Each women's culture, of course, is significantly informed by its racial, ethnic, and religious context. There is not one women's culture; there are many. There are also connecting patterns among them.

One way to understand women's consciousness is to make visible the cultures it creates. Culture may be defined as the ordered system of meanings in terms of which people define their world, express their feelings, and make their judgments. Cultural interpretation, as the anthropologist Clifford Geertz has suggested, is a process of "searching out and analyzing the symbolic forms—words, images, institutions, behaviors— in terms of which . . . people actually represent themselves to themselves and to one another."[9] It is not uncommon, for example, to hear one woman say to another, "You know what I mean," when, engrossed in sharing experience, words elude meaning. The other will nod in understanding. This communication comes precisely from a shared consciousness of ordered meanings and symbols. There are times when those mean-

ings are accessible across the racial and/or class divide, and times when
they can be shared only among women of the same ethnic, class, or religious group. (But they will not be readily or easily accessible to the men.)
This is what I mean when I speak of women's consciousness. It is really, I
think, a simple observation. It has seemed complex, elusive, invisible even,
precisely because of what Dorothy Smith has called "a peculiar eclipse" in
which women are excluded from the making of "man's culture," and
"man's culture" is accorded a universal status as Culture. Mindful of class,
as well as gendered relations, Smith writes:

> the concerns, interests, experiences forming "our" culture are those
> of men in positions of dominance whose perspectives are built on the
> *silence* of women. . . .
>
> As a result the perspectives, concerns, interests of only one sex and
> class are directly and actively involved in producing, debating, de-
> veloping its ideas, in creating its art, in the formation of medical and
> psychological conceptions, in the framing of its laws and political
> principles and its educational values and objectives. It is thus that a
> one-sided standpoint comes to be seen as natural, obvious and gen-
> eral.[10]

To name women's consciousness is to identify its webs of significance
and meaning, to make it intelligible on its own terms. This identification,
according to Geertz, is a process of cultural *interpretation:* "the analysis . . . is not an experimental science in search of law but an interpretive
one in search of meaning. . . . Culture is not a power, something to which
social events, behavior, institutions or processes can be causally attributed; it is a context, something within which they can be intelligibly—that
is—thickly described."[11]

To map women's consciousness, to give examples of women's cultures, to look at women's poems, stories, paintings, gardens, and quilts
from this point of view is to make women's actions and beliefs intelligible
on their own terms. It is to show connections, to form patterns. This is not
to invent another theory of women's oppression; it is to suggest a method
of representation, a sounding, a making visible. It is to recognize women's
strategies for coping, surviving, shaping, and changing the parameters of
their existence on their own terms, and not in contrast to predominantly
male strategies as if these were the natural, normative, or correct models.

To do this is to begin to designate the categories of analysis that mark women's knowledge of the world, women's interpretation of events, women's *standpoint*. If this designation can be achieved it will allow for a different kind of philosophical space, for an ordering of women's experience as knowledge, for an emancipatory vision rooted in our own grounds. This is the project. It is a very big one. It will take us many years of "thinking in common," as Virginia Woolf once suggested we needed to do.[12] This book is a piece of our work in progress. I want to propose a new way of seeing, a different way of thinking.

I use many examples of women's cultures in this book but I did not do field work or interviews. I read many works of fiction and poetry; I saw a lot of art and sculpture; I read plays and saw others performed. I was mindful of a multiracial exposure and consciousness. However, I have located no "new" manuscripts, discovered no "new" talent. It didn't seem to me that I needed more information so much as a new way of looking at the information already accessible to me. This way of looking, which included but did not privilege theory and which framed the particularity of women's consciousness of social reality, provided my third condition for work. It also suggested a fourth.

Trained in both academic and ideological ways of reading, I was taught to categorize, measure, critique, and slice. I needed to change how I read what women wrote. My experience with Adrienne Rich's book *Of Woman Born* will serve to illustrate this point. I first read it in 1978 when I had, as yet, only a limited awareness of feminist thinking and no knowledge of Rich's poetry. I read it again in a graduate seminar in feminist theory two years later. Neither reading was useful in the sense in which I mean it here, but the experience taught me how to read and to appreciate Rich's method of work.

Of Woman Born had been given to me as a gift by a friend who was twenty-five years my elder, a medical researcher, a World War II pilot, and the mother of three children. At the time she gave me the book, she was dying of cancer. Beset with grief, and with the sound of her labored breathing in the background, I sat near her and read. She died before I finished the book and before I had any chance to talk to her about it. The only comment she made about the book was when she handed it to me. She said: "I wish I had had this information thirty years ago."

In reading *Of Woman Born* for the first time, I didn't know what to make of it. I remember that in the margins, in pencil, I made lots of notes, trying to use a Marxist perspective as a guide. Next to a long excerpt from

Engels quoted in a context highly critical of Marxism, I had written: "There's much truth here, but I think you are too hard on Engels." I understood the history of childbirth which Rich recounted. And I felt the experience of reading this book as something new, and I knew I liked the experience. I knew too that the book had got inside my experience, as a daughter and as a mother. I thought too that it must have somehow gotten "inside" my friend. I don't mean by that that Rich knew our inner thoughts. I mean simply that she understood something about the fabric of our lives as women. I didn't understand how that was possible. I didn't understand how Rich had gotten inside. The second reading of the book in the graduate seminar clarified the first, if only by explosive contrast.

Everyone in our seminar was stimulated by Rich's main idea of separating the experience of being a mother from the institution of motherhood created by the culture, with its rules, demands, expectations, and methods of enforcement and control. By disclaiming the "natural" mother, and naming motherhood as the social prescription it was, we felt that Rich had provided us with a major breakthrough in feminist thinking. Everyone was also comfortable with the two chapters on the history of childbirth, which I had also found familiar on my first reading. Here, of course, Rich's method of work was most conventional. Women were at the center of her thinking about history, and she used traditional tools of research. The chapters were carefully documented and referenced.

We divided, wrangled, whined, and harangued each other about the accuracy of everything else in the book because it was based on Rich's personal experience. The only experience we had to contrast with hers was our own, or that of others with whom we were intimately acquainted. If this didn't fit the detail in Rich's account we disputed the truth of what she had written, by which we meant its accuracy as a general statement about the condition of women. Had Rich written the book solely as autobiography and claimed it as such, there would have been no dispute. But she had accorded it a more general status and we read it as a statement of theory. Our only experience with theory had been that which is objectively constructed, the details capable of verification and replication within the parameters it claimed to represent. Based on this way of thinking we began to attack the book, deconstructing its premises. We were destroying it. We stopped somewhere in midsentence, appalled at ourselves and at the violence we were doing to something that we all said we loved reading! We tangled with each other because we did not know how to order women's experience as knowledge, because we had no method of "thinking in common." Rich predicted the problem in her foreword:

> It seemed to me impossible from the first to write a book of this kind without being often autobiographical, without often saying "I." Yet for months I buried my head in historical research and analysis in order to delay or prepare the way for the plunge into areas of my life which were painful and problematical, yet from the heart of which this book has come. I believe increasingly that only the willingness to share private and sometimes painful experiences can enable women to create a collective description of the world which will be truly ours. On the other hand I am keenly aware that any writer has certain false and arbitrary power. It is *her* version, after all, that the reader is reading at this moment, while the accounts of others—including the dead—may go untold.[13]

What we missed in the wrangle, and what Rich herself could only begin to clarify for us, was that she was developing a new method of work. She constituted women's experience as the base of her interpretive process. She used her own experience because it was available to her. It was not, however, the detail of that experience which was important to us, but the way in which she took it and transformed it into knowledge. I will give two examples to illustrate how she did this.

First, Rich saw that what she had been told about motherhood in the 1950s by the psychological and medical experts in the United States was false. That is, her experience, and the accounts of other women's experiences, did not correspond to the established canon about motherhood. Furthermore, her archival and literary research disclosed that this canon was changeable and diverse depending upon historical period and culture. The canon changes seemed also to correspond to certain changes in women's status. Rich's research confirmed her sense that ideas about motherhood were a male invention and that those inventions served political purposes in enforcing women's subjugation. Women's actual experiences as mothers were something else again and largely unknown. These were largely unrecorded because women's ideas had never been accorded anything resembling the authority invested in men's. Rich's method of work combined this "common" sense about her own experience, including her feelings, her parenting, and her observations, with traditional research skills. Rich made no attempt to develop a theory of motherhood. Rather, she was interested in naming, in legitimating women's felt experiences and perceptions as a way of knowing.

The second example of how Rich transformed her experience into knowledge illustrates how this process may compromise widely accepted ideas in Western theory. When she was pregnant, Rich found that the fetus was not definitely "inside" her *or* "outside" her; it was both at the same time. In thinking through her body, as Rich put it, she challenged Freud's certainty of inner and outer spaces as polar opposites. This concept informs many of Freud's theoretical constructs and especially those about the ego. (Likewise, in popular culture at the time of Freud's work, women were assigned an inner space corresponding to the home-and-hearth, cult-of-true-womanhood ideology of the nineteenth century.) Rich wrote: "As the inhabitant of a female body . . . in pregnancy I [did not] experience the embryo as decisively internal in Freud's terms, but rather as something inside of me, yet becoming separate from me and of-itself. . . . The child I carry for nine months can be defined *neither* as me or as not-me. Far from existing in the mode of 'inner' space women are powerfully attuned both to 'inner' and 'outer' because for us the two are continuous, not polar."[14]

Rich builds on this rejection of polar oppositions as a way of thinking, disputing what she calls the "dualism of the positive-negative polarities between which most of our intellectual training has taken place."[15] The philosophical implications of this point are very significant. We learn almost everything on the basis of oppositional thinking. Indeed, we derive the meaning of words through oppositional contrast: death versus life; dark versus light; evil versus good; female versus male, and so on. To think about contrast as difference rather than as opposition is to think in terms of cycle rather than polarity; continuum rather than disruption and separation. (I am mindful of the fact that even to make the point I resort to oppositional contrast to make myself understood!) The Freudian model of the inevitable opposition between mothers and daughters at adolescence is an invention that derived from this way of thinking. As it was popularized it became prescriptive. It was also an invention specific to a particular historical moment and to Western European, Euro-American, middle-class culture. Once I encountered a wonderful line from a poem that a Black woman in New York City had written about her mother. She said: "Embrace difference as identity as key."[16]

Placing mothers and daughters along a continuum, Rich suggested that it is from other women that we learn, and from our mothers that we often first learn, at a subliminal and nonverbal level, the boundaries of the possible within a patriarchal, exploitative, and racist world. Rich wrote:

> The most notable fact that culture imprints on women is the sense of our limits. The most important thing one woman can do for another is to illuminate and expand her sense of actual possibilities. For a mother this means more than contending with the reductive images of females in children's books, movies, television, the schoolroom. It means that the mother herself is trying to expand the limits of her life. *To refuse to be a victim:* and then go from there.[17]

"My mother was much of a woman," reported a former slave to her interviewer in the 1930s.[18] In hearing so many Afro-American women speak of their mothers we are struck by a repeated theme which reworks the meaning of Rich's ideas: each mother worked "to expand the limits of her own life" by working herself to the bone to expand the limits of her children's lives. The struggles of these Black mothers and grandmothers, especially to ensure an education for their children, pushed back the boundaries, the limits, set by a white, racist world.

The contrast between my first and second readings of *Of Woman Born* can be mapped out this way. My first reading was problematic because I could only weigh Rich's ideas in relation to the Marxist paradigm through which I appraised various writings. I was very limited in my understanding of the book because I resisted using my own experience as a way into the text, as a method of connection and analysis. My second reading (and seminar discussion) was also problematic because we *critiqued* the book as a statement of theory using the details of our respective experiences to undermine the "universal" claims we presumed Rich to be making. What we needed to learn was how to cull a way of knowing from the interpretation of experience. The point was not to corroborate the detail of Rich's experience. It was to replicate her method of work for ourselves.

Now this way of knowing requires a different way of reading. It requires that we read and listen to each other's ideas, and to those of our foremothers, without ascribing to them ideological categories and political lines prescribed by men. Sometimes we ascribe categories by freezing

labels onto each other (or self-imposing those labels), classifying ideological camps. We read into each other's works the baggage we attribute to
particular positions, e.g., cultural feminist, lesbian separatist, radical feminist, socialist feminist, liberal feminist, academic feminist, and so on. In
academic jargon we talk about an author's claims and authorities and
sources and credentials. We are trained to slice; sometimes to devastate.

I found that these ways of thinking impeded my work. I needed to
learn how to read for information, even through major disagreements
with a point of view. I needed to learn how to find and interpret the
experience embedded within a text, even one written in a very scholarly
and objective way. My requirements were simply that a work helped me to
understand some aspect of women's lives. I tried to focus outward on an
author, respecting the cultural, political, and psychological origins of her
work. I presumed the integrity of her purpose. I think we must read each
other with tenderness, with grace, with care for the enormity of effort that
goes into forming a coherent thought. We must critically appraise each
other's work, give our best opinion. We disagree, we challenge, we are
rigorous and demanding because we want to help each other, because we
are honest with each other, because we honor women. This honest respect
was my fourth condition for work.

The fifth condition for work was to make my thinking, my interpreta-
tions, my sources, an ensemble of color and class; to make connections
among ourselves, while recognizing and respecting our differences, as an
integral way of knowing. It was to pivot the centering, to let each woman's
story or poem or experience or idea stand on its own merit, as its own
center, and in the juxtaposition of stories appreciate the complexity of our
continuum as women. What follows is an example of this method of
work.

Naming is a central motif in feminist thought. Look at the ways in
which it is represented in contemporary U.S. women's literature from this
cross-cultural perspective. Consider the connections between naming and
identity, between naming and language, between naming and silence.
Consider the separable but interconnected strands through which we
identify our cultural/racial identities and our female identity.

Chicana poet Lorna Dee Cervantes walks the streets of Oaxaca,
Mexico, all day looking for a way to name herself, for her heritage, "for
the dye that will color my thoughts." But Mexico casts doubt upon "this
bland pochaseed," this Americanized Mexican:

I didn't ask to be brought up tonta!
My name hangs about me like a loose tooth.
Old women know my secret.
"Es la culpa de los antepasados"
Blame it on the old ones.
They give me a name
that fights me.[19]

Kitty Tsui writes a poem about all the names she has been called by non-Chinese people:

> sway
> sue
> suzy
> tissue
> ha-chiew

My father pronounced it choy
so i grew up saying choy
always careful to add: t-s-u-i.

In the same poem she tells how non-Chinese people consistently mistake Chinese women for each other:

a newspaper woman thought
i was willyce kim for months.
willyce kim gets called susan kwong.
nellie wong is made nellie kim
or not mentioned by name at all.
merle woo is called merle wong
or smeared as yellow woman
in a gay male publication

it happens all the time
it's in the name.
it's in the face.

orientals so hard to tell apart.

She relates the struggle for identity:

our faces
strong, brown,

different as
the bumps
on the skin of
bittermelon.
our tongues,
sharp and fragrant
as ginger,
telling our history,
our experiences
as asian american women,
workers and poets,
cutting the ropes
that bind us,
breaking from
the silence of centuries.[20]

Think of the story of "No-Name Woman," which opens Maxine Hong Kingston's memoir and tells of the death of her aunt and illegitimate baby—a woman erased, and the silence revoked by a new woman warrior wielding a pen.[21] Think of Nessa Rapoport's short story about "The Woman Who Lost Her Names" between her Jewish and American identities, and Nellie Wong's poem about how she got lost between the names her teachers gave her in Chinese school and American school.[22] Think of Paule Marshall's widow whose praisesong is *nommo*, the African ritual of naming, as Avey Johnson becomes Avatara and claims the story Great Aunt told her about the Ibos who walked on water all the way back to Africa to escape from slavery.[23] Think of Michelle Cliff claiming her African heritage and the identity she was taught to despise[24] and of Sandra Cisneros finding her Chicana roots in *The House on Mango Street*. Cisneros writes of her name, Esperanza. She is named for her grandmother. "In English my name means hope," she says. "In Spanish it means too many letters."[25]

Jewish poet Irena Klepfisz writes in the *mame-loshn*, Yiddish, the mother tongue, even her fragmentary version of it, as an act of reclamation, to salvage what is left, "this echo of a European era and culture in which I never lived and about which I have only heard second-hand like a family story." As she combines Yiddish and English, and reads her poems aloud she tells us:

my tongue, mouth, lips, throat, lungs,
physically pushed Yiddish into the
world—as I, a Jew, spoke a Jewish
language to other Jews, Yiddish was very
much alive. Not unlike a *lebn-geblibene,*
a survivor, of an overwhelming catastrophe,
it seemed to be saying *'khbin nisht vos*
ikh bin amol geven. I am not what I once
was. *Ober 'khbin nisht geshtorbn. ikh leb.*
But I did not die. I live.[26]

Klepfisz writes of a Jewish holocaust which nearly extinguished Yiddish language and culture in Europe; Native American women speak of the genocide in which millions of their people died and which has now nearly extinguished their traditional languages and cultures. In dozens of oral histories women describe how their children, or they themselves as children, were forced to go to missionary school. Caught speaking their native languages, many were whipped or otherwise severely punished. Janet Campbell Hale, born January 11, 1947, in Los Angeles, and raised on the Coeur d'Alene Reservation in northern Idaho, writes of this loss of language in her poem called, "Desmet, Idaho, March, 1969":

At my father's wake,
The old people
            Knew me,
      Though I
            Knew them not,
And spoke to me
In our tribe's
Ancient tongue,
Ignoring
The fact
That I
Don't speak
The language,
And so
I listened
As if I understood
What it was all about,

And,
Oh,
How it
Stirred me
To hear again
That strange
    Softly
    Flowing
Native tongue,
So
Familiar to
My childhood ear.[27]

Katherine Smith, one of the elders of the Navajo people, who has led their resistance to relocation from the ancestral homeland at Big Mountain near Flagstaff, Arizona, ordered by the U.S. government, explained why they cannot go: "There is no word for relocation in the Navajo language; to relocate is to disappear and never be seen again."[28]

From this ensemble we see that language is the context within which naming is possible. Language designates meanings already assembled, and it makes meaning itself possible. For example, in the Navajo language the word for beauty also means harmony, balance, and health. The phrase "may you walk in beauty" contains all these meanings. It speaks to a way of seeing the world, a way of being in which all things, animate and inanimate, of this world and the spirit world are connected. Each must be respected, and held in balance, in harmony with one another.[29] In the Italian language, the word *luoghi* means "logic." But the word has the connotation of "the logic of space." Because of this connotation, the Italian feminist sociologist Laura Balbo began to think about the "logic of spaces" which women shared with one another in an industrial-capitalist society. Her essay on the servicing work of women in kitchens, laundries, schools, hospitals, and welfare agencies collapsed the distinction between public and private, and crossed traditional boundaries in its analysis of political economy.[30] This brought new insight into the sociology of women's work. Language, then, is not simply a matter of translation. Language is a matter of culture, of the framing of ideas according to cultural experience and nuance. To rob a people of their language is to deny them the tools of cultural continuity, of heritage, and of restoration.

In a similar yet distinct way, to deny women freedom of speech is to rob them of the possibility of expression, of establishing meaning on their own terms as women. Susan Griffin began her book, *Woman and Nature: The Roaring Inside Her* with a dedication that called attention to the connections between language, silence, and naming:

> These words are written for those
> of us whose language is not heard,
> whose words have been stolen or erased,
> those robbed of language, who are called
> voiceless or mute, even the earthworms,
> even the shellfish and the sponges, for
> those of us who speak our own language. . . . [31]

Adrienne Rich's poem, "Origins and the History of Consciousness," speaks to the same issue:

> No one lives in this room
> without confronting the whiteness of the wall
> behind the poems, planks of books,
> photographs of dead heroines.
> Without contemplating last and late
> the true nature of poetry. The drive
> to connect. The dream of a common language.[32]

Virginia Woolf, in *A Room of One's Own*, addressed the problems women writers encounter trying to establish an experiential core from which to create:

> since freedom and fullness of expression are of the essence of art, such a lack of tradition, such a scarcity and inadequacy of tools, must have told enormously upon the writings of women. Moreover, a book is not made up of sentences laid end to end, but of sentences built, if an image helps, into arcades and domes. And this shape too has been made by men out of their own needs for their own uses. There is no reason to think that the form of the epic or the poetic play suits a woman any more than a sentence suits her.[33]

These two strands of naming, of the use of language, one race culture and one female culture, are separable, but they are also deeply connected. While women and men may join together in a common struggle against the racist or anti-Semitic destruction of their language and culture, male supremacy within a race culture can operate to silence women's independent voice, women's freedom of expression, experience, and perception. Chicana poet Lorna Dee Cervantes speaks directly and forcefully to this issue in her poem "Para Un Revolucionario." Observing her exclusion from the talk of liberation politics and strategies among the men, Cervantes protests the assumption that she was to be restricted to the kitchen and the bedroom. She writes these words to her revolutionary compañero:

> You speak of your love of mountains,
> freedom,
> and your love for a sun
> whose warmth is like *una liberación*
>
> . . . .
> When you speak like this
> I could listen forever.
> *Pero* your voice is lost to me *carnal,*
> in the wail of *tus hijos,*
> in the clatter of dishes
> and the pucker of beans upon the stove.
> Your conversations come to me
> *de la sala* where you sit,
> spreading your dreams to brothers
>
> . . . .
> when I stand here reaching
> *para ti con manos bronces* that spring
> from *mi espiritú*
> (for I too am Raza)
>
> *Pero,* it seems I can only touch you
> with my body
> You lie with me
> and my body *es la hamaca*
> that spans the void between us.

Cervantes concludes her poem with a warning:

> *Hermano Raza,*
> I am afraid that you will lie with me
> and awaken too late

to find that you have fallen
and my hands will be left groping
for you and your dream
in the midst of *la revolución*.[34]

Cervantes warns that without her experience, without her knowledge structured out of the dailiness of her life, the dream of liberation will remain incomplete, will remain unrealizable.

Women of color may join together in struggle with white women against their common oppression as women. However, the racism embedded in white women's cultures may operate to silence women of color, to erase, subjugate, colonize their independent voice. The book *This Bridge Called My Back: Writings by Radical Women of Color* was, in part, impelled by this reality. In "The Bridge Poem" by Kate Rushin, with which the book opens, the poet disputes her position as "the damn bridge for everybody." People use her, she says, as mediator and translator to connect with each other, or to be "politically correct" in the women's movement, "integrating" parties and functions by her presence. Rushin protests:

I do more translating
Than the Gawdamn U.N. . . .

and ends with an affirmation of self:

I must translate
My own fears
Mediate my own weaknesses

I must be the bridge to nowhere
But my true Self
And then
I will be useful

For Rushin this usefulness is connected to both a self and a collective identity as a Black woman, an identity that is "the bridge to my own power."[35]

While Rushin's poem comes out of her experiences in the women's movement of the late 1970s, its protest addresses an old theme in the experience of Afro-American women. Part of the emotional work performed by countless numbers of Black women has been not only to sustain their own families but also to nurture those of their white employers (or masters in the slave South) in domestic service, and especially white women and children. There is nothing liberating, personally or politically, about forming alliances with white women in which old roles are simply recast in a new context.[36]

Similarly, women of color in university circles have protested the construction of what they call a "colonial discourse" in which they are marginalized or erased in feminist theory. By this process white women create "theory" in much the same way that their male counterparts create "culture" and pronounce their "universal" claims. Writing on "The Costs of Exclusionary Practices in Women's Studies," an interracial team of scholars observed:

> Until the past few years, women of color have been virtually hidden in feminist scholarship, made invisible by the erroneous notion of universal womanhood. In an effort to emphasize the shared experiences of sexism, scholars passed over the differences in women's situations. Knowledge assumed to be "universal" was actually based on the experiences of women who were white and primarily middle class.

The authors point out that the criticism directed at women's studies for its myopia resulted in some acknowledgment of diversity among women but that this work "is often tacked on, its significance for feminist knowledge still unrecognized and unregarded."[37] The inclusion of minority women, as these authors suggest, is not merely a problem of addition but of synthesis, changing the way in which problems are both named and analyzed.

In this discussion of naming as a central motif in feminist thought, women's poems and stories, art, and scholarship are juxtaposed in a cross-cultural arrangement. Through this juxtaposition, patterns within and between the two strands of cultural and female identity form braids of meaning. Each plait is identifiable and useful in itself. Likewise, in the crossing of plaits we also see how women's experiences touch each other. This way of pivoting the center of our thinking on women clears a space in which difference provides meaning. It provides a way of knowing how we are connected. The point is not whether this connection can lead to theoretical generalization. The point is not whether this connection is positive. The point is simply to know the attributes, tensions, dimensions, depths of the connection; to reconnoiter and step carefully from there. This was my fifth condition for work. Only with this process could my thinking become more of an ensemble of color and class.

My sixth condition for work was to honor poetry alongside traditional materials of research as a way of knowing about our lives. In search of new avenues of interpretation, poetry and, by extension, many short stories, novels, oral histories, plays, dances, paintings, and sculptures provide tools to forge women-centered patterns. This is not a new form of literary or art criticism. It was not so much interest in the construction of the text as text, but, rather, in how the text—the painting, poem, story— structures our understanding of women's lives; it was an interest in how to learn from the shape, the texture, the rhythm of the telling. Consider the power of poetry to name and define women's experiences.

"My mother pieces quilts," wrote Teresa Paloma Acosta:

they were just meant as covers
in winter
as weapons
against pounding january winds
but it was just that every morning I awoke to these
October ripened canvasses
passed my hand across their cloth faces
and began to wonder how you pieced
all these together. . . .[38]

Remember the "Woman Work" wrote the Native American poet Paula Gunn Allen:

Some make potteries
Some weave and spin
remember
the Woman/Celebrate
webs and making
out of own flesh
earth
bowl and urn
to hold water
and ground corn
balanced on heads

and springs lifted
and rivers in our eyes
brown hands shaping
earth into earth . . .[39]

Remember the women of my mama's generation, counseled Alice Walker:

Husky of voice—Stout of
Step
With fists as well as
Hands
How they battered down
Doors. . . .
How they led
Armies. . . .
How they knew what we
Must know
Without knowing a page
Of it
Themselves.[40]

Remember to weave real connections, wrote Marge Piercy:

create real nodes, build real houses
Live a life you can endure; make love that is loving
. . . .
Connections are made slowly, sometimes they grow underground
You cannot tell always by looking what is happening
More than half a tree is spread out in the soil under your feet. . . .[41]

"Ripen on the ancient root" wrote the elder, working-class poet Meridel
Le Sueur, to the young poet still wading in the safe waters of her rational,
statistical, pedantic voice. In her eighty-third year, Le Sueur wrote:

I am luminous with age
In my lap I hold the valley
I see on the horizon what has been taken . . .
In my breast I hold the middle valley . . .
Like corn I cry in the last sunset . . .
        My bones shine in fever
Smoked with the fires of age.[42]

Lorna Dee Cervantes grew up "Beneath the Shadow of the Freeway" in San Jose, California, a witness to her grandmother's suffering and to her enduring joy in the simple pleasures of life. Grandmother waters her geraniums every morning and

> She likes the ways of birds,
> respects how they show themselves
> for toast and a whistle.
>
> She believes in myths and birds.
> She trusts only what she builds
> with her own hands.[43]

Hiroko Yamano went to interview her mother, to take down her oral history, to represent the story of a Japanese-American woman's internment in a concentration camp during World War II. The mother did not want to tell her story. Hiroko Yamano wrote a poem in her mother's voice. It was called "My Mother's Stories":

> I don't want to tell her my stories
> I am old.
> I don't remember.
> My stories were of long time ago.
> I locked my stories in a box.
> I buried the key.
>
> My daughter wants my stories.
> Her soul is too restless.
> I can't keep her quiet.
> She wants to know about my past,
> about the old,
> about something that is gone.
>
> I don't want her to come home.
> She's here.
> She waits endlessly,
> in my garden
>> in my dreams
>> for my answers.
>
>> I know
>> someday

she'll be knocking
at my grave
she'll stand there
wanting my stories

I can only tell her,

> I am old
> I don't remember
> My stories were of long time ago.
> I locked my stories in a box.
> I buried the key.
> Now you must go.[44]

Poetry is not a luxury for women, explained Audre Lorde. It is the distillation of our experience, the moment of interpretation, the intuitive leap transcending the boundaries of the conventional coordinates on the official map designating our place in the world:

> The distillation from which true poetry springs births thought as dream births concept, as feeling births idea, as knowledge births (precedes) understanding. . . .
>
> For women, then, poetry . . . is a vital necessity of our existence. It forms the quality of light within which we predicate our hopes and dreams toward survival and change, first made into language, then into idea, then into more tangible action. Poetry is the way we help give name to the nameless so it can be thought. The farthest horizons of our hopes and fears are cobbled by our poems carved from the rock experiences of our daily lives.[45]

Poet and critic Norma Alarcón tells us that "poetry has been the single most important genre employed by Chicanas in order to grasp and give shape to their experience and desire."[46] Puerto Rican poet Rosario Morales writes:

> Poetry is
> something refined in your vocabulary
> taking its place at the table in a
> silver bowl:
> essence of culture[47]

Muriel Rukeyser's first poem in her first book of poetry published in 1935 begins: "Breathe in experience, breathe out poetry."[48] And in her tribute to the German graphic artist Käthe Kollwitz, Rukeyser asked: "What would happen if one woman told the truth about her life?" And answered: "The world would split open."[49] This is not the poetry of contrivance; this is the poetry of naming, of philosophy, framing a set of ideas through which to interpret our realities as women.

"From the body of the old woman," Susan Griffin wrote in a prose-poem called "The Anatomy Lesson," "We can tell you something of the life she lived." Griffin chronicled the life of the old woman, the evidence culled from the physical residue of her body:

> We can catalog her being: tissue, fiber, bloodstream, cell, the shape of her experience to the least moment, skin, hair, try to see what she saw, to imagine what she felt, clitoris, vulva, womb, and we can tell you that despite each injury she survived. That she lived to an old age. (On all the parts of her body we see the years.) By the body of this old woman we are hushed. We are awed. We know that it was in her body that we began. And now we can see that it is from her body that we learn. That we see our past. We say from the body of the old woman, we can tell you something of the lives we lived.[50]

Consider the stories the poems tell, the images they portray. They tell of women's work in specific and concrete detail, counseling us to remember the value intrinsic to that work in nurturing, sustaining, and re-creating the human community endlessly, through time. Often there is a sense of resistance built into the poetry reminding us of the integrity of women's power. From each cultural motif, themes of connection and ways of knowing are told; even, as in the case of Hiroko Yamano's mother, we are reminded that silence too has meaning.

Walk the ground between the stories and the images in the same way you might walk through a garden. Do not make categories of species. See the individuation, the beauty in each flower, "blooming gloriously for its Self" as in the world of Alice Walker's revolutionary petunias.[51] Walk away from the argument and jargon in a room, as Adrienne Rich advised in her poem "Transcendental Etude," pulling the tenets of our lives together with "care for the many-lived, unending forms" in which we, as women, find ourselves.[52] Women's poems are a gift of sight. They provided my sixth condition for work.

The fact that such a poetry has existed, that it has been recovered and is being written again, speaks to the particular moment in which we are living. The women's liberation movement of the 1970s and eighties has changed the conditions in which many of us now labor. This change was wrought through very, very hard struggle. It has changed the balance of power allowing for a renaissance in women's art and literature which has not existed for us in modern times. We can see this shift in balance with historical hindsight. When Judy Grahn wrote of the Greek poet Sappho, she suggested that she was not the first woman poet in Western civilization, not a solitary female voice rising out of an otherwise barren plain. On the contrary, Grahn said, hers was the surviving voice, the last voice in a long line of women poets and artists—Sappho's works so badly fragmented because they were systematically destroyed. Grahn wrote:

And what was the nature of Sappho's wealth? She praised it often enough: love, beauty, grace, flowers, appropriate behavior to the gods, lovely clothing, intelligence, tenderness. Her poems are filled with the color purple, the color gold, the sun, flowers, especially the violet and the rose, and altars, deer, groves of trees, and the stories of the gods. Love, she said, is a tale-weaver. Wealthy? We own no kind of money that would buy us Sappho's wealth. In her world, women were central to themselves; they had to have been to write as she did. She lived on an island of women, in a company of women, from which she addressed all creation. And oh, how they listened.[53]

Of the modern writers, Virginia Woolf is one who consistently attempted to place women at the center of her thinking. But she did not do it with the bold and inclusive sweep of Sappho. She did it awkwardly and with apology, with a tone of self-deprecation. This is apparent, for example, in A Room of One's Own, in its style and tone and in its apparent random "female" ambience of thought hither and yon, an innovation to mask the real power of her intellect. Writing of Woolf, Adrienne Rich observed that:

No male writer has written primarily or even largely for women, or with the sense of women's criticism as a consideration when he chooses his materials, his theme, his language. But to a lesser or greater extent, every woman writer has written for men even when, like Virginia Woolf, she was supposed to be addressing women. If we come to the point when this balance of power might begin to change, when women can stop being haunted, not only by "convention and propriety" but by internalized fears of being and saying themselves, then it is an extraordinary moment for the woman writer—and reader.[54]

We are at the beginning of such a moment. We have begun to place women at the center of our work, of our thinking, of our interpretive flow without camouflaging either our purpose or our content. We have begun to write from the core of our own experiences as women without apologizing for it, with less fear of humiliation or annihilation. We are rebuilding a literary and artistic tradition, making possible the potential for handing on a collective female vision, weaving corroborative threads, allowing each other the luxury of a self-consciously created women-centered community in which to sift through our ideas, tell our stories, read our poems, dance our songs, play out the fantasies of our imagination. What is new about many of the works of the present period is that they are being written and performed for women, with less or no regard for the male critic. The material is of women's lives, depicting dailiness from an interior space of lived experience. "Martha and Mary raise Consciousness from the Dead," Michele Roberts called her short story:

> We carry the memory of childhood like a photo in a locket, fierce and possessive for pain and calm; everybody's past is inviolate, separate, sacrosanct, our heads are different countries with no maps or dictionaries, people walk vast deserts of grief or inhabit walled gardens of joy. "Tell me about your past," I began to urge other women and they to urge me. The women sit in circles, they are passing telegrams along battle lines, telling each other stories that will not put them to sleep, recognising allies under the disguise of femininity, no longer smuggling ammunition over back garden walls.[55]

These stories and plays, paintings and poems relentlessly, collectively commit to tell the truth, to tell as much of the whole story as can be told, revealing the dimensions of the struggle to change our lives. These "truths we are salvaging from / the splitting-open of our lives"[56] are the connecting links, the nexus in which experience is transformed into meaning, into a way of knowing. None of this is possible without community. A community of women now exists, however tenuous its roots and conflicted its elements. It must be held with patient care. These are the conditions that make our work possible.

The Dailiness
of Women's Lives

Dandelions were what she chiefly saw. Yellow jewels for everyday, studding the patched green dress of her backyard. She liked their demure prettiness second to their everydayness; for in that latter quality she thought she saw a picture of herself, and it was comforting to find that what was common could also be a flower.

—Gwendolyn Brooks, *Maud Martha*

We are still learning to recognize what we see.
Traces erased. Details removed.
Letters sewn into quilts—or burned.
Self-portraits hidden in trunks—or burned.
The perishable nature of so many of our artifacts.

. . .

If in our remembrance we find the depth of our history
Will we opt for description only
or choose to ignite the fuse of our knowledge?

—Michelle Cliff, *Claiming an Identity They Taught Me to Despise*

All of life in the grain, the seed; all of time in the second. One does not have to look at the horizon for meaning.

—E. M. Broner, *A Weave of Women*

My whole life is in that quilt. . . . All my joys and all my sorrows are stitched into those little pieces. . . . I tremble sometimes when I remember what that quilt knows about me.

—Marguerite Ickis, quoting her great-grandmother, in Mirra Bank, *Anonymous Was a Woman*

OMEN'S everyday lives are often fragmented and dispersed, caught up short between a job, dinner, and the laundry. They are often episodic. That is, they are often determined by events outside of women's control, such as the opening or closing of a factory in which most of them and/or their husbands are employed. Likewise, women are frequently required to move from city to city or country to country, uprooting family and community, because their husbands' corporate, professional, or military assignments are relocated. Women are continually interrupted. Projects, especially their own, are put aside to be completed on another day or in another year. In the course of a day, a week, women carry the threads of many tasks in their hands at the same time. Poet Deena Metzger once wrote: "Each day is a tapestry, threads of broccoli, promotion, couches, children, politics, shopping, building, planting, thinking interweave in intimate connection with insistent cycles of birth, existence, and death."[1] Some of these things also happen to men, but not all of them, and they don't happen in the same ways because most men in the United States are not ultimately responsible for maintaining personal relationships and networks. They are not primarily responsible for emotional work. They are not primarily responsible for the children, the elders, the relatives, the holidays, the cooking, the cleaning, the shopping, the mending, the laundry. Their position as men, even as working-class men and men of color, gives them access to more resources and status relative to the women and families of their communities because the society institutionalizes a system of male domination.

By the dailiness of women's lives I mean the patterns women create and the meanings women invent each day and over time as a result of their labors and in the context of their subordinated status to men. The point is not to describe every aspect of daily life or to represent a schedule of priorities in which some activities are more important or accorded more status than others. The point is to suggest a way of knowing from the meanings women give to their labors. The search for dailiness is a method of work that allows us to take the patterns women create and the meanings women invent and learn from them. If we map what we learn, connecting one meaning or invention to another, we begin to lay out a different way of seeing reality. This way of seeing is what I refer to as women's standpoint.[2] And this standpoint pivots, of course, depending upon the class, cultural, or racial locations of its subjects, and upon their age, sexual preference, physical abilities, the nature of their work and

39

personal relationships. What is proposed is a mapping of that which has been traditionally erased or hidden.

To find a starting point for this map we may turn back to our mothers, as Susan Griffin suggested we do in her book *Woman and Nature*. We turn back to our mothers for clarity, Griffin said. We turn back to them not only personally, to see what their individual lives were like, but also to them collectively for the shared memories of women. Griffin wrote:

> We listened for the stories of their lives. We heard old stories re-told. . . . We heard again the story of the clean house, we heard the story of the kitchen, the story of mending, the story of the soiled clothes. . . . of the cries of birthing, the story of waking at night, the story of the shut door, the story of the voice raging. . . . [3]

In this turning we see that many of our mothers sacrificed, worked hard, nurtured, did the best they could to "make do," to improve the quality of our daily lives. We also know that some of our mothers died before we were grown. We see that others of our mothers were alcoholic, abusive, emotionally distant. We see that some of our mothers abandoned us as children. We see that some of our mothers were materially privileged but spiritually impoverished. From all of these stories we learn about the reality of women's lives, about the suffering, the failure, the struggle to nurture well. We learn about how other women took care of children who were not their own—grandmothers and aunts, friends and older sisters—women who just took over the child care and did the best they could to raise us. In the conflict between mothers and daughters we learn about the ways in which women are divided from each other, about how we are taught to compete with each other. All of this speaks to women's social condition, to women's social reality enforced by class, by race, by the prescription of gendered roles, inscribed in the dailiness of women's lives.

Many of women's stories have never been written. They form an oral tradition, passed on from one generation to the next. Sometimes they are just seen as anecdotes about family "characters" and their antics. Sometimes they are teaching stories. They are about having respect, about having decent values, about how to live properly, about how to survive.

Cultures shape stories in different ways, and stories pass on women's consciousness as it has been shaped by specific cultural, racial, and class experience. Central to women's consciousness, of course, is an understanding of the ways of men. Sometimes we have heard these stories so often we don't think they are important. Then a situation arises, and we need help, and we remember a story because the help we need is embedded in it. We hear the voice of the teller again, and we remember the details. The story is useful.

Some of the stories I remember from my childhood were not told, they were enacted. And it was only when I was older and learned other things that I could interpret how my mother acted. For example, my mother had a very good friend whose name was Helen West Heller. She was an artist. She was a very elderly woman when I was a child. I can remember going with my mother to visit this woman. She lived in an apartment in lower Manhattan. It was in a very poor neighborhood. She lived, I think, in what were called cold-water flats. I remember that the apartment was relatively dark except for the focused light of special lamps. I remember the smell of oil paints, canvases stacked everywhere, heavy bags of sand which the artist could still lift. I remember that two of her oil paintings hung in our living room, that there were many women shown working in the paintings, and animals too, like cows and monkeys, and that the overriding colors of those paintings were oranges and browns. I remember the artist preparing tea for Mother and me, and serving it in small, rose-petaled tea cups. What I remember most, though, is that Mother never visited Helen West Heller without bringing her bags of groceries.

Some of us cannot remember women's stories. We think we must have heard stories from our mothers, grandmothers, or aunts. But when we think about it we can't remember anything or we can remember family jokes, or the repetition of stories about hurt feelings, or feuds. These do not feel like teaching stories, although sometimes later we realize that we have learned from them. Sometimes we better remember stories by our fathers, grandfathers, and uncles. And sometimes, too, in those stories, women are made to seem incoherent or unreasonable or frivolous. The fact that some of us cannot remember the women's stories—the fact that some women may never have told stories to their children—is a symptom of our oppression as women.

The "thealogian" Carol Christ, in her book *Diving Deep and Surfacing,* wrote of the importance of stories as a way of knowing:

Without stories there is no articulation of experience. Without stories a woman is lost when she comes to make the important decisions in her life. She does not learn to value her struggles, to celebrate her strengths, to comprehend her pain. Without stories she cannot understand herself. Without stories she is alienated from the deeper experiences of self and world that have been called spiritual or religious.[4]

In the context of her book, Christ was writing especially about women's need to create stories now from our own experiences so we can pass these on.

Leslie Marmon Silko, storyteller and poet of the Laguna pueblo in New Mexico, wrote down stories she could remember from her childhood, many of them told to her by a woman she knew as Aunt Susie—Susie Marmon—who was her father's aunt:

Around 1896
when she was a young woman
she had been sent away to Carlisle Indian school
in Pennsylvania.
After she finished at the Indian School
she attended Dickinson College in Carlisle.

When she returned to Laguna
she continued her studies
particularly of history

. . . .
From the time that I can remember her
she worked at her kitchen table
with her books and papers spread over the oil cloth.
She wrote beautiful long hand script
but her eyesight was not good
and so she wrote very slowly.[5]

She was, Silko continued, "a brilliant woman, a scholar of her own making who cherished the Laguna stories all her life."

From Silko, as she was taught by Susie Marmon and others in her family and pueblo, we begin to understand the importance of stories in a more systematic and coherent way, of the connection between oral tradition, storytelling, the invention of meaning, and the preservation of cultural identity:

She was of a generation
the last generation here at Laguna
that passed down an entire culture
by word of mouth
an entire history
an entire vision of the world
which depended upon memory
and retelling by subsequent generations.[6]

In the context of the history of the physical and cultural destruction
of American Indian peoples brought about by the European and Euro-
American conquest, storytelling became central to the struggle for cultural
integrity and physical survival. Near the end of her book, Silko tells "The
Storyteller's Escape." She begins with these words:

the storyteller keeps the stories
          all the escape stories
          She says "with these stories of ours
          we can escape almost anything.
          With these stories we will survive."[7]

Women's stories serve a purpose that is analogous to those of tribal
peoples. And many tribal stories are also, of course, specifically women's
stories. They serve an analogous purpose because in male-dominated
society women's ways of seeing, women's culture both in an artistic sense
and in the sense of beliefs and values, are systematically erased, denied,
invalidated, trivialized. In some cases, as in Europe between the thirteenth
and seventeenth centuries during the witch trials, as in the United States
during slavery, the physical survival of many thousands of women has
been very tenuous. Women's stories locate women's cultures, women's
ways of seeing; they designate meaning, make women's consciousness
visible to us. Stories transform our experiences into ways of knowing—
about ourselves as women and about ourselves as women looking at the
world.

     After reading the stories, poems, and essays by Silko and by other
Native American women I began to understand storytelling as a powerful
tool for teaching and learning. I saw this in practice when I attended Kate's
classes at the community college and her "storytellings" on Friday nights
at the Y W C A in Monterey. She sits on the floor, the class in a circle around

her, and she tells the stories of women's lives as she has researched them from autobiographies, biographies, ethnographies, histories, and elsewhere. From this the women (and men) who are listening learn something about their own lives, and about courage, patience, devotion, love, beauty, grief, strife, resourcefulness, failure, survival, and struggle. The stories, accumulated over weeks and months, and now years, form a legacy of strength, of endurance, of astonishing will.

Stories are one of the ways in which women give meaning to the things that happen in a lifetime, and the dailiness of life also structures the telling, the ordering of thought, the significance allocated to different pieces of the story. In studying a "theory of form in feminist autobiography," the literary critic Suzanne Juhasz suggested that "the concept of dailiness [is] a structuring principle in women's lives":

> When you ask a woman, "what happened?" you often get an answer in style that [is] . . . circumstantial, complex, and contextual. You hear a series of "he saids" and "she saids"; you are told what they were wearing, where they were sitting, what they were eating; and slowly the story unrolls. The woman is omitting no detail that she can remember, because all details have to do with her sense of the nature of "what happened." A man, on the other hand, will characteristically summarize: give you the gist, the result, the *point* of the event. . . . In their form, women's lives tend to be like the stories that they tell: they show less a pattern of linear development towards some clear goal than one repetitive, cumulative, cyclical structure. One thinks of housework or childcare: of domestic life in general. . . . Dailiness matters to most women; dailiness is by definition never a conclusion, always a process.[8]

Probably all of us have heard stories told in this way, although it is also important to recognize that cultures shape the way stories are told as much as their content. Juhasz's description is only one of several possible modes, but her general points are important: dailiness is a process rather than a conclusion; it structures thought. Women's stories are different from men's in content and form.

Women use stories in their everyday lives, and especially as a way of doing emotional work. Discussing the significance of talk among women friends, sociologists Fern Johnson and Elizabeth Aries showed the ways in which stories are shared. Disputing the dominant culture's trivialization of women's talk, Johnson and Aries described the intimacy among women friends and the compelling, therapeutic, tactical, and emotional support women provide for each other. As one woman put it, a close friend "makes you feel like a worthwhile human being—that you are capable of loving and sharing."[9]

Some of the stories I use in this chapter (and in this book) are part of women's oral histories; some have been stitched into quilts or planted in gardens or painted or sculpted or written in letters and journals. Some are stories from my own life; others have been published by women in the United States at different times. Some are from academic sources, which I have read as though they were stories but in a different form—stories about the women who wrote them and about the women who were the subject of their study. Women's stories evoke distinct meanings, distinct spacial and temporal arrangements. They have been crafted in or out of the artifacts of daily life, beckoning us to see. These stories reveal that women have not been exclusively or primarily victims, crushed by circumstances, but survivors and creators, their artifacts of beauty arising as it were from nothing.

The act of knowing from our own experience "is so simple," Alice Walker tells us, "that many of us have spent years discovering it. We have constantly looked high, when we should have looked high—and low." She continues:

For example; in the Smithsonian Institution in Washington, D.C., there hangs a quilt unlike any other in the world. In fanciful, inspired, and simple and identifiable figures, it portrays the story of the crucifixion. It is considered rare beyond price. Though it follows no known pattern of quiltmaking and though it is made of bits and pieces of worthless rags, it is obviously the work of a person of powerful imagination and deep spiritual feeling. Below this quilt I saw a note that says it was made by an anonymous Black woman from Alabama a hundred years ago.

If we could locate this anonymous Black woman from Alabama, she would turn out to be one of our grandmothers—an artist who left her mark in the only materials she could afford and in the only medium her position in society allowed her to use.[10]

The dailiness of women's lives pervades our literature, and our history, and our art. It was deposited for us in the course of living done by ordinary women, our grandmothers, and great-great grandmothers. Alice Walker learned a way of knowing from the quilt she saw at the Smithsonian. Describing Walker's method of writing, literary critic Gloria Wade-Gayles observed that she pieces "bits and pieces of used material rescued from oblivion into a profound and terrifying picture of black suffering in the South."[11] Moreover, in remembering her mother's garden as she had seen it in childhood, Walker also saw her mother's artistry and presented its meaning to us. The garden was an act of renewal, a way to transcend the limits of poverty, to nurture children and neighbors, to make life aesthetically bearable. Walker recalls:

> My mother adorned with flowers whatever shabby house we were forced to live in. And not just your typical straggly country strand of zinnias either. She planted ambitious gardens—and still does—with over fifty different varieties of plants that bloom profusely from early March until late November. . . . Because of her creativity with flowers even my memories of poverty are seen through a screen of blooms—sunflowers, petunias, roses, dahlias, forsythia, spirea, delphiniums, verbena . . . and on and on.[12]

From this search for her mother's garden, Walker saw many of women's everyday labors in a new light. She learned to think in new ways. The quilt gave her a new way of seeing. The search for her mother's garden inspired her own, but Walker's gardens are filled with poems. *Revolutionary Petunias* is one such collection, and from it we can see also the cumulative effects of women's gardens over years of patient care—the gardens of floral beauty, and the gardens of child work. "The Nature of This Flower Is to Bloom" Walker titles her last poem:

> Rebellious. Living.
> Against the Elemental Crush.
> A Song of Color
> Blooming Gloriously
> For its Self.
>
> *Revolutionary Petunia.*[13]

Because of my own experiences as a mother, this poem made me think about the work women do with children, and it reminded me of a story about my youngest child.

When Jennifer was seven I observed her in a densely wooded park near our house. She, however, did not see me. Cypress, pine, and oak trees, many of them dripping with lichen, fill this wood, and dirt paths weave a criss-crossed pattern through it. Jenny's bike was tossed carelessly into a bush, and she was squatted on the ground in silent concentration. The object of her gaze was a squirrel. In its paws it held an acorn. It broke it open, and rapidly consumed its center. Then it threw the shell away and darted off. Jenny searched the ground, found another acorn, and broke it open. She examined its inside in minute detail. Satisfied finally with her search, she tossed the acorn away, stood up, slapped the dirt from her hands onto her Levis, gathered up her bicycle, and pedaled on her way.

As independent beings, children change in subtle and autonomous ways. They learn things on their own, as Jenny did in the woods, and draw their own conclusions. Women are witness to these changes, but we are not always the instruments for them, and we don't always approve of them. Mothers, and women who work intimately with children, have ideas about change that are shaped by the dailiness of their labors rather than by the conventions of a highly industrialized and technologically sophisticated society. For example, we see that change is not necessarily or inherently a matter of control, or prediction, or of the effects of production. Change can also be seen as a matter of curiosity, of freedom, of balance, of growth, of dignity, of an inner sense of being. This was surely the concept of change that Alice Walker learned in the gardens of her childhood. It was, I think, this idea that empowered the creation of Celie in *The Color Purple,* a revolutionary petunia cast years after the poem, healed and blooming.

I remember a line from one of Adrienne Rich's poems about a "red begonia perilously flashing from a tenement sill six stories high" in New York City[14] which brought back memories of my own childhood in Brooklyn and my mother's potted plants everywhere in our sixth-floor apartment, their lush, green foliage draped over books and tables and lamps. An appreciation for how things grow marks a parallel between potted plants, gardens, and children, from which a point of view, a way of knowing, emerges. Writing of "Gardens, Growth, and Community," poet Bernice Mennis detailed this point of view by explaining the lessons she learned from watching the plants in her garden over the course of a season. She wrote:

First, potential life is everywhere. Land that looks barren and wasted, branches that look dead, a bush that looks scraggily, all of a sudden explode into life. . . .

Second, life takes many different forms . . . of size and shape and color and smell and texture . . . forms of movement and growth. . . . Judgment about . . . how different forms of life declare their being seems arrogant, presumptuous.

Third, there are different stages of life. Each is part of a whole process. . . . Growth is the process, not the product. . . .

Fourth, when living things are uprooted, there is danger that they won't survive. . . . it's hard to go from one environment, even a bad, cramped, stuffy chaotic environment to another, even if the other is open and roomy and sunny. . . . Exposed roots are very, very vulnerable.[15]

The need for beauty, for art, is everywhere in the dailiness of women's lives: in plants and gardens, in the textile arts, in the linen tablecloths and ritual dinners prepared with elaborate care, sometimes for days in advance, sometimes collectively, the pieces of it eventually brought together—Thanksgiving, Christmas, the Chinese New Year, the Jewish Passover. Carrying the feelings of what she had learned about life and growth in her garden, Bernice Mennis describes the preparation for a Passover *tsimmes** in her mother's kitchen. The dailiness of women's labors is given new meaning:

We worked together   my mother and I
in her kitchen of forty-five years
where the water drips cold
and the hot water never gets
really hot   where the oven
must be watched and the re-
frigerator strapped closed.
I was to grate 20 carrots.
And I   the jogger basketball athlete
invested in my woman's body strength

*Literally the Yiddish word *tsimmes* means "to make a big deal over something" that shouldn't warrant it. The idea of carrot *tsimmes* is a big fuss over making carrots, a simple vegetable made into an astonishingly wonderful treat.

grated 6 carrots with great
difficulty   my arm exhausted
my fingers grated
And you   my 4' 11"
74 year old mother
grated 14 carrots
without stopping
evenly
not easily or quickly
but calmly
silently
providing again
the dark coarse uneven ground.[16]

In a similar way, Paule Marshall described the poets in the kitchen of her childhood, her mother and her mother's friends who taught her about language as art. They worked as domestic servants in the Flatbush section of Brooklyn by day, and in the early evening gathered together to talk before going home to cook dinner for their husbands and children:

The basement kitchen of the brownstone house where my family lived was the usual gathering place. Once inside the warm safety of its walls the women threw off the drab coats and hats, seated themselves at the large center table, drank their cups of tea or cocoa, and talked. While my sister and I sat at a smaller table over in a corner doing our homework, they talked—endlessly, passionately, poetically, and with impressive range. No subject was beyond them.[17]

In a vein similar to Alice Walker's thoughts about art and creativity in women's lives, Marshall tells of these women who made of language an art form that "in keeping with the African tradition in which art and life are one—was an integral part of their lives." Language was the resource they had available to them, and they used it to express the many subtleties of life they observed. For example, Marshall said that nothing, no matter how beautiful, was ever described as simply beautiful: "It was always 'beautiful-ugly': the beautiful-ugly dress, the beautiful-ugly house. . . ." Pondering this paradox in the linking of opposites, Marshall concluded: "My mother and her friends were expressing what they believed to be a fundamental dualism in life: the idea that a thing is at the same time its opposite, and that these opposites, these contradictions make up the whole. . . . Using everyday speech, the simple, common-place words—but always with imagination and skill—they gave voice to the most complex ideas."[18]

This complex of ideas reflects much of what is experienced in the dailiness of women's lives—the way, for example, a domestic worker has to be able to see inside her employer's mind and feelings in order to keep her job, regardless of the external posture that employer may assume. Moreover, experiences with children confirm the contradictory nature of their psychology, the vagaries of mood, the distinct patterns of growth and personality in each one, the ways in which you can love them passionately and dislike them intensely and all at the same time. Additionally, many of us who have witnessed a birth, or given birth, know how much its power is like the power of death: the same moment of transcendence moving in opposite directions. The thrust toward life is fierce, and yet the moment of life is terribly perilous.

Like Paule Marshall, Mohawk writer Beth Brant described her memory of the women from her childhood home in Detroit. She was the child of a white mother and an Indian father, and all her father's sisters married white men. Still, they preserved pieces of the Mohawk culture:

> After marrying white men, my aunts retired from their jobs. They became secret artists, putting up huge amounts of quilts, needlework, and beadwork in the fruit cellars. Sometimes, when husbands and children slept, the aunts slipped into the cellars and gazed at their work. Smoothing an imaginary wrinkle from a quilt, running the embroidery silks through roughened fingers, threading the beads on a small loom, working the red, blue, and yellow stones. By day, the dutiful wife. By night, sewing and beading their souls into beauty that will be left behind after death, telling the stories of who these women were.[19]

From these stories set in basements, in kitchens, we can see that although these are places of hard work—some have called it drudgery— they are also places of conversation, art, learning, light, warmth, and comfort. In many homes the kitchen is the hub of social intercourse while the "living room" is a misnomer because either it is too formal for such a purpose, or it is the "men's room" in which television, football, and beer prevail. A women's standpoint emerges from these scenes and stories suggesting ideas, feelings, and sensibilities about the nature of beauty, about personal and social change, about the conditions necessary for life and growth, about the importance of interpersonal communication and friendship. These ideas, and certainly the feeling of dailiness from which they emanate, contrast sharply with those of the dominant culture.

Tillie Olsen's short story "I Stand Here Ironing" shows the ways in which a woman's ideas about change and progress and growth may be interpreted through her own experience. "I stand here ironing, and what you asked me [about my daughter] moves tormented back and forth with the iron."[20] The story appears in a collection of Olsen's work called *Tell Me A Riddle* and was originally published in 1961, well before the women's liberation movement. It was given to me by a woman who had worked in a kitchen hospital for twenty years washing dishes and preparing food trays. She was a union organizer and a Communist. She gave me the book on the occasion of my twentieth birthday, before I was married and before I understood very much of anything about the oppression of women. On a little note my friend wrote: "If you haven't read Tillie Olsen's book, I know you'll appreciate her tender understanding of women's problems." The book lay unread until many years later because in my male-identified world of the sixties I didn't think it was important to understand women's problems. I return now to the scene of the mother ironing with a kind of awe at the sheer power of the image churning out of my own childhood.

It is through the voice of the mother in Olsen's story that we hear an accounting of the daughter's childhood in the tangle of urban poverty. The mother is talking in her imagination to the daughter's teacher (or social worker or whomever) who has written a note home to the mother asking for a conference: "She's a youngster who needs help and whom I'm deeply interested in helping." The mother says:

> She was a beautiful baby. She blew shining bubbles of sound. She loved motion, loved light, loved color, and music and textures. She would lie on the floor in her blue overalls patting the surface so hard in ecstasy her hands and feet would blur. She was a miracle to me, but when she was eight months old I had to leave her daytimes with the

woman downstairs to whom she was no miracle at all, for I worked or looked for work and for Emily's father who "could no longer endure" (he wrote in his good-bye note) "sharing want with us."[21]

The mother was nineteen. It was during the Depression. She got whatever jobs she could and eventually put Emily in nursery school. "It was the only way we could be together, the only way I could hold a job." They struggled on, these two women, mother and daughter, bonded, embattled, and battling with each other, with the other children who came later, with poverty. The mother tells us, near the end of her thoughts:

> I will never total it now. I will never come in [to the teacher] to say: She was a child seldom smiled at. Her father left me when she was a year old. . . . She was dark and thin and foreign-looking in a world where the prestige went to blondness and curly hair and dimples, slow where glibness was prized. She was a child of anxious, not proud, love. . . . She kept too much to herself, her life was such she had to keep too much in herself. My wisdom came too late. She had much in her and probably nothing will come of it. She is a child of her age, of depression, of war, of fear.[22]

This is a personal story of a woman's problems, as my friend wrote. But it is also a political overture orchestrated out of the dailiness of Olsen's life and of the women she knew. This story tells us that change comes slowly, across the generations; that there is often damage in growth, some of it irreparable; that men, self-absorbed in their own turmoils, often abandon women and children; that help, however well-meaning, is often steeped in privileges of class (or race), and may in any event, as in this case, be too late. The mother in this story has an estimate of the potential for progress: it is an estimate rooted in experience, in her stubborn will to survive, in her knowledge of the connection between growth and change in the human spirit. Women's stories often contain these kinds of estimates.

Another story, Alice Walker's "Everyday Use," suggests the ways in which beauty and heritage can be misunderstood by women when they move into male-dominated, and white-dominated, education, and about the ways in which racism can work a devious curve. Like Tillie Olsen's story this one reflects upon the relationship between mothers and daughters, and upon the separations between them inflicted by the dominant culture. Unlike Olsen's story, this one is set in the poverty of the rural South; Walker's story is also narrated by the mother: by "Mama," who is Black.

Mama has two daughters. One is still living at home and the other, older daughter, is away at college. Mama tells us of herself: "I am a large, big-boned woman with rough, man-working hands. In the winter I wear flannel nightgowns to bed and overalls during the day. I can kill and clean a hog as mercilessly as a man. . . . I never had an education myself. After second grade the school was closed down. Don't ask me why; in 1927 colored asked fewer questions than they do now."[23]

The college daughter comes home for a brief visit. It is the sixties. We recognize the times in the way she and her male escort are attired and groomed. Mama is not pleased with their appearance. The daughter has assumed an African name so that she will "not bear the name of the people who oppress me." Mama doesn't strenuously object, but she tries to tell her daughter that she was named after her aunt, who was named after her Grandma, and she thought that if she had to she could "probably have carried [the naming] back beyond the Civil War through the branches."[24] From Mama's point of view this naming also endows a lineage, and these ancestral roots hold as much meaning as those of African origin. That meaning is not only one of subjugation, but also one of survival, of work, of the raising of children, as she herself has done. It is hard for her, perhaps, not to see in the rejection of her naming, a repudiation of her life. But she does not speak to this directly.

The daughter is home with Mama only a few hours. Her primary purpose is to appropriate her heritage and take it with her back to school so that she can display it: the top of the butter churn, whittled by her uncle, which she wants as a "centerpiece for the alcove table," and the quilts made from pieces of Grandma's dresses, for hanging on the wall. Mama objects to the taking of the quilts. She has promised them to the younger daughter for her "everyday" use after she is married. The college daughter is devastated. She tells Mama, "You just don't understand. . . ." "What don't I understand?" Mama asks. "Your heritage," the college daughter replies.[25]

But Mama has an understanding of her heritage, and she chooses to express her understanding by protecting the interests of her younger daughter. The college-educated daughter wants the butter churn and the quilts as objects of display in order to announce her southern Black roots and enhance her status among her fellow students, in an academic and politically hip milieu in which such evidence would accrue to her benefit. From Mama's point of view, however, a heritage is not an object for display. Rather, it pulses with life and beauty, with instructional purpose and practical use. There is knowledge and skill and family memories and love passed on in what the women and men of her family had made. Heritage is for everyday use. To appropriate a heritage by displaying it to garner status makes it into just another "thing," inert and useless.

In affirming the values and sensibilities intrinsic to the consciousness of the women of Mama's generation, Alice Walker's story holds important lessons for us in the women's movement and in women's studies regardless of our cultural or racial origins. The claiming of our women's heritage, of our matrilineage, has become an essential part of our work. How this reclamation is done, however, is a significant issue. We live in a society in which the commodity structure penetrates every area of life, in which women themselves are made into sexual objects for male consumption and gratification.[26] The appropriation of our matrilineage, of our heritage as an object of display and status, makes of it just another commodity to be perverted, marketed, and consumed. Moreover, in the process of making it into an object, it is easy to romanticize our matrilineage, to make of it a projection of our own desire for heroines who are flawless—perfect in their suffering, their resistance, and their redemption. It is, on the contrary, in the everyday use we make of that heritage in understanding women's lives in the fullest possible range of their complexity, and in the everyday use we make of that understanding in changing our own lives, that the act of knowing from our own experience becomes possible.

This knowing is hard. Part of overcoming our internalized oppression as women is making our heritage visible and celebrating its vitality. Part of overcoming the social conditions of our oppression as women is vigorously and critically learning from the experiences that heritage endows. Not all of those experiences are worthy of emulation. However, all of them are understandable within the bounds of the general roles and cultural codes that have defined women's existence. We learn as much, if not more, from those actions we would not wish to emulate as from those we do. Two short stories, one by Susan Glaspell published in 1917 and one by Shelley Shepard written in 1981, are highly illustrative of these roles and codes and their consequences. In both stories women's actions are understandable, though not necessarily strategies we would want to engage. Both stories are set in the Midwest.

Glaspell's "Jury of Her Peers" tells the story of a murder investigation. It is a husband who has been murdered, a farmer in a rural community found strangled to death in the master bedroom. His wife, Minnie Foster, has already been arrested for the murder. The sheriff and his men have come back to the house in order to look for clues. They want to establish Minnie Foster's motive for the murder, without which they do not believe there will be a conviction. They are accompanied by their wives who have come ostensibly to put together a few things Minnie Foster might need while she is in jail. In fact, as the story unfolds, the sheriff and his men are unable to find any clues because these are gender coded. The men search the bedroom, the barn, the surrounding grounds. The women remain in the kitchen, the center of Minnie Foster's world, and here they reconstruct the dailiness of her life and, ultimately, the reasons for her crime.

The women see the emotional distress of Minnie Foster in "some fine, even sewing" which suddenly goes awry, "as if she didn't know what she was about!"[27] They see the drabness of the kitchen, the ill-repair of things, her old and worn-out clothes. They see the remnants of kitchen chores left half done, and, finally, they find a canary with its neck broken. They conclude that the husband has been strangled by his wife to avenge the strangling of the canary. This is the evidence the men do not see because they do not know where or how to look. And, in Glaspell's final telling, the women are "a jury of her peers," so that they hide the evidence in a silent, swift, and stunning solidarity.

From their standpoint we come to understand, as literary critic Annette Kolodny put it, that:

> the husband . . . had systematically destroyed all beauty, and music in his wife's environment. . . . The essential crime in the story, we come to realize, has been the husband's inexorable strangulation, over the years, of Minnie Foster's spirit and personality; and the culpable criminality is the complicity of the women who had permitted the isolation and the loneliness to dominate Minnie Foster's

existence: " 'I wish I had come over to see Minnie Foster sometimes,' " declares her neighbor guiltily. " 'I can see now—' " She did
not put it into words.[28]

Minnie Foster was driven to kill by the physical brutality and spiritual impoverishment of her life, and her act symbolizes the desperation to
which women have been driven. Glaspell presents us with a moral verdict
of justifiable homicide—a verdict that was in fact to be legally tendered by
a jury sixty years later in the Detroit trial of Francine Hughes. But Glaspell
is also interested in the moral consequences of Minnie Foster's act for
women in general. By failing to provide sisterly support and intervention,
her neighbors, once part of her high school crowd in the small community,
are also responsible for the circumstances that led to this killing. This
story teaches us that the need for connection between people is not a fetish
of female psychology but a reality that exists independent of our intentions. The neighbors in Glaspell's story did not intend neglect; they did not
intend to abandon Minnie Foster to the cruelties of her husband; they did
not intend to contribute to the circumstances that drove Minnie Foster to
murder. But they *feel* responsible. "Oh, I *wish* I'd come over here once in a
while!" one of the women cried. "That was a crime! That was a crime!
Who's going to punish that?"[29] Glaspell has shown us that when we
abandon our own, we abandon ourselves.

The second story, by Shelley Shepard, illustrates the very harmful
consequences of institutionalized motherhood when that role is internalized by women as the defining purpose of their lives. This story is called
"Myrna."[30] It is set in the Midwest in a very small town in the early 1970s.
Shepard drew upon her experiences as a sales clerk in the lingerie section
of the town's only department store. "Myrna" is an imaginative, com-
posite drawing of what Shepard saw and felt. Reconstructing the dailiness
of the lives of the women in the department store in simple and apparent
innocence, the story reaches its climax with a subtlety that is as surprising
as it is devastating.

The story is written with much humor. The midwestern, small-town
culture is reproduced in great detail. Myrna, having lived in this town all
her life, remembers when the store was built, and she has worked in it
since it opened twenty-five years or so before. She is a fund of local gossip
and lore, hard-working, with apparent compassion for her coworkers and
all the members of her family. She is especially generous in providing gifts

for her daughter and grandchildren. Slipping her arm through that of our narrator, Myrna leads her through many a tour of the store's counters in search of appropriate gifts for them.

Then we learn that Myrna has no children and never has. She buys gifts but always returns them a day or so later, we are told. Upon each return she says the gift was the wrong size or the wrong color. We come to understand that Myrna has invented her children and grandchildren in order to fit into the women's culture of which she is a part. If you don't have children you just aren't anybody, Myrna's friend informs our astonished narrator. We are left to ponder definitions of sanity, the institution of motherhood, tactics for survival, and the ways in which women bond. In fact, we come to see that Myrna is sane in the sense that she knows she has invented her children, and she knows she is acting out a fantasy of their existence. If we take one definition of the loss of sanity to be the inability to distinguish between reality and fantasy we can see that Myrna is quite sane, however desperate her need for inclusion. Moreover, all of her coworkers know that she has no children, but as an act of sisterly compassion they indulge her fantasies, allowing her to share whatever stories she wishes to invent.

Myrna needs to connect, to be part of this circle of friends, to share in their network of support. All anyone ever talks about, she explains, are her children and grandchildren. Without them she felt herself to be a "nothing," a "nobody," an outcast. She can be admitted into the circle as an imaginary mother because she thinks that none of her coworkers can imagine a woman who isn't (or wasn't) a mother. Motherhood has been institutionalized by a whole cluster of social expectations, by forced and arranged marriages, and by men's legal control over women's access to contraception and abortion. How many children a woman has, at what intervals, and under what social conditions for their provision, determine virtually every other aspect of her life. This is central to the dailiness of women's lives.

From the dailiness of this child work, women have also accumulated a lot of knowledge about the ways of human nature, about what is called psychology, because they have focused so much of their attention on children, on the ways in which they grow, and on the formation of personality. This is what Sara Ruddick meant, in part, when she wrote about what she called "Maternal Thinking" in a provocative essay first published in *Feminist Studies:*

I am increasingly convinced that there are female traditions and practices out of which a distinctive kind of thinking has developed.... I speak about a mother's *thought*—the intellectual capacities she develops, the judgments she makes, the metaphysical attitudes she assumes, the values she affirms....

Mothers not only must preserve fragile, existing life. They must also foster growth and welcome change.... Women are said to value open over closed structure, to eschew the clear-cut and unambiguous, to refuse a sharp division between inner and outer self and other. We are also said to depend upon and to prize our private inner lives of the mind.[31]

Further, in treating mothering as a form of *labor*, and in affirming that "*all* thought arises out of social practice," Ruddick proposes a material (or objective) basis for what is widely and sometimes amusingly referred to as "women's intuition." It is, she suggests, a particular way of knowing. Describing the attention that mothers must focus on infants and children as a condition for their survival and adequate growth, Ruddick argues that this attention is "an *intellectual* capacity connected ... by definition with love, a special kind of 'knowledge of the individual.'"[32] This intuitive process, growing out of the particularity of women's labors, can be applied to virtually any endeavor if sufficient attention is focused upon it. It is a way of knowing that can be learned by anyone willing to attend.

Although Ruddick focuses on maternity as the source for intuition as a way of knowing, women also exercise a great deal of intuition about men. For many women, men are at the center of their daily lives. A lot of women's stories are about men, and men are the brunt of jokes in many of them. Not infrequently these jokes have explicit sexual content. In a marvelous essay on the bawdy humor of southern women, folklorist Rayna Green described the stories she remembered from her childhood and especially those told by her grandmother. Commenting more broadly on this humor Green wrote:

Southern or not, women everywhere talk about sex—sex with young boys, old men and handsome strangers—sexual errors, both good and bad. Newly married couples are some of their favorite characters along with prostitutes, preachers, rabbis, nuns, Easterners, country boys and girls, foreigners, and traveling salesmen. In general, men are more often the victims of women's jokes than not. Tit for tat, we say. Usually the subject for laughter is men's boasts, failures or inade-quacies ("comeuppance for lack of uppcomance," as one of my aunts used to say).

Green also noted the differences between men and women's bawdy hu-mor, observing that women—whether they are Black or white—are rarely as deeply derogatory or racist in their sex tales as men. "Southern men," she concluded, "tell stories about many of the same characters as women, but their emphases and inferences are, I believe, quite different." Finally, Green observed the ways in which these stories are sometimes really about women's anger and, as such, a form of social criticism which is socially acceptable:

> the bawdy lore itself is a form of socialization to the hidden agenda in Southern women's lives and thoughts. The tales and sayings tell young women what they can expect in private out of the men and the institutions they are taught to praise in public. . . . Poking fun at a man's sexual ego . . . might never be possible in real social situations with the men who have power over their lives, but it is possible in a joke. The hilarity over the many tiny or nonperforming tallywhack-ers, or the foolish sexual escapades of drunken, impotent men forms a body of material over which women vent their anger at males and offer alternative modes of feeling to the female hearers.[33]

There are many other kinds of stories about men, about ways around them, about comforting them, attracting them, paying attention to them, manipulating them, controlling them, pleasing them. There are also sto-ries about "holding onto your man" and some of these are made into lyrics and sung by women as, for example, in the blues. These are survival stories. They tell us how it has been and often still is very hard for a woman to survive in our society without a man. It is hard to find adequate employment, decent housing, good medical care, an auto mechanic who won't rip you off, a way to feed the children on a single (already inade-quate) income; it is hard to have the gas and electricity and water turned on in your apartment without proper employment and proper credit, to have a telephone installed, to furnish a house, to get credit established with banks and merchants.

It is perhaps hardest for women to overcome the internalized message drummed into us that we are nothing without a man. "i wish i could have convinced you how beautiful you are," wrote Ana Castillo to her friend Alicia in her epistolary novel, *The Mixquiahuala Letters*. But, she despaired, "they were only the words of another woman," and "meanwhile [you felt] you bore no resemblance to the ideal of any man you encountered anywhere."[34]

These stories tell us how far we will have to travel before women are at the center of our own lives, before our thinking is changed enough to allow us to live with integrity, meaning with wholeness, with no sense of guilt, disloyalty, shame for living and being ourselves. These stories tell us how far we will have to travel before we, as women, are able to "think in common" and so shape our own lives collectively, with respect for our different cultures and experiences. They tell us how far we will have to travel before we can articulate collectively a way of ordering human affairs so that women have at least as much to say about them as men.

The dailiness of women's lives reveals these paradoxes: how women are strong and resourceful and inventive and competent; how they see and know in distinct and important ways; and, yet, how they also internalize their sense of nothingness without a man and are weak and deferential and petty and competitive and incompetent. One woman (or many women) can display many or all of these attributes and deformities, depending on context, in the same week, in the same day, literally even in alternating moments. These paradoxes come from the imbalance in the relationships of power between women and men, from racial hierarchies, from the investment in class status. The point is to correct the imbalance. Women often strive to do this in their daily lives, to circumnavigate the powers of gender and race and class, to build decent relationships, to live well, to invest dailiness with meaning.

A novel by Gwendolyn Brooks illustrates the significance of the everyday from this point of view. Literary critic Gloria Wade-Gayles aptly characterized *Maud Martha* as

> a hymn to the beauty of "everydayness" and the beauty and character of ordinary black people. Maud Martha is neither a heroine nor a victim. . . . Her life is not all "candy buttons," but it is a life of flowers because Maud Martha plants them in her vision of possibilities. . . . [And] as wife and mother Maud Martha is incorporated into a community of women she admires and respects. In her "everyday-

ness" she is a tribute to her own dreams of life. Brooks imbues her portrait of Maud Martha with genuine admiration for the character's humanity, humility, intelligence, and ability to see the beauty in small things.[35]

Set in Chicago in the 1930s and 1940s, Gwendolyn Brooks fashioned one of the earliest portraits of urban, working-class Black womanhood published in the United States. Earlier novels by Afro-American women such as Jessie Fauset and Nella Larsen, for example, tended to focus on light, middle-class heroines whose ambitions were thwarted due to race prejudice. Until the publication of Brooks's *Maud Martha*, only Zora Neale Hurston had populated her fiction and folklore with ordinary people. Hurston's works, however, were southern and rural, and although they have been vastly important in the development of a literary self-portraiture of Afro-American women, it was Brooks's novel (and poetry) that launched a genre embedded in northern, urban, ghetto experience which encouraged the subsequent works of Paule Marshall, Ann Petry, and Alice Childress, among many others.

Maud Martha is distinguished by its brevity, its focus on the mundane, and its reconstruction of dailiness. Maud Martha grows up in Chicago, and the novel tells the story of her life, the evolution of her consciousness of self, and of her experiences as she moves through maturity, marriage, and motherhood. Brooks celebrates the courage of the commonplace. Maud Martha is not desolate or tragic; she is not chic or stunning. She is an ordinary Black woman, living her life. It is here, in Maud Martha's very ordinariness, that Brooks establishes her point: everyday Black women create their own destiny, carve their own way through the sludge of a racist and sexist world, and set their own standards of value and self-worth. We see this sense of the everyday as beautiful created again and again in Brooks's poetic grace. The texture of life is put simply and directly in small vignettes harmonizing humor and philosophy into a joyful vision for everyday use by those who read it. The story of "Maud Martha's Tumor" exemplifies Brooks's style and process.

Following the birth of her daughter, Maud Martha feels "a peculiar pain in her middle" and upon touching the spot discovers a hard knot. Weak with fear she diagnoses cancer, and her mind races in panic to her death. En route to the doctor, whom she has urgently called for an appointment, however, she assesses her life in a calm and systematic light:

Decent childhood, happy Christmases; some shreds of romance, a marriage, pregnancy, and the giving birth, her growing child, her experiments in sewing, her books, her conversations with her friends and enemies.

"It hasn't been bad," she thought. . . .

She looked at the trees, she looked at the grass, she looked at the faces of the passers-by. It has been interesting, it has been rather good, and it was still rather good. But really, she was ready. Since the time had come, she was ready. Paulette would miss her for a long time, Paul for less, but really, their sorrow was their business, not hers. Her business was to descend into the deep cool, salving bark, to be alike indifferent to the good and the not-good.[36]

The doctor charged three dollars for his examination, and pronounced Maud Martha very healthy. The supposed tumor was the pain and swelling from an over-exercised muscle:

"You mean—I'm not going to die."

She bounced down the long flight of tin-edged stairs, was shortly claimed by the population, which seemed proud to have her back. An old woman, bent shriveled, smiled sweetly at her.

She was already on South Park. She jumped in a jitney and went home.[37]

There is an absence of anger about how she has lived her life that allows Maud Martha to approach death with less anguish than we would expect. There is here also, a poking fun, perhaps, at the "Soap-Opera" self-importance and drama that might attend such episodes in "real" life as opposed to the novelist's license. There is a sober reflection by Maud Martha about her relationship to those in her immediate family which reinforces this more matter-of-fact approach to death. There is a letting-go of worldly things. In the relief that follows the doctor's pronouncement, however, Maud Martha merges easily back into the stream of life, with people "proud to have her back." From this everyday enclosure, in this ordinary way, Brooks makes us think about death as part of the stream of life. It is a small vignette that twirls playfully in the mind, settling finally on its own profound conclusions.

In another story Maud Martha goes to the beauty parlor. While she is there the proprietor, Sonia Johnson, engages in a conversation with Miss

Ingram, who is white and who sells cosmetics. Miss Ingram wants Mrs. Johnson to buy a new line of lipstick:

> Maud Martha looked at Miss Ingram's beautiful legs, wondered where she got the sheer stockings that looked like bare flesh at the same time that they did not, wondered if Miss Ingram knew that in the "Negro group" there were many complexions whiter than her own, and other complexions, brown, tan, yellow, cream, which could not take dark lipstick and keep their poise. . . .
> "What's the lipstick's name?" Sonia Johnson asked.
> "Black Beauty," Miss Ingram said, with firm-lipped determination. "You won't regret adding it to your line. . . ."[38]

The sale is made easily because Sonia Johnson tries to be accommodating and pleasant to the white salespeople who come into her shop. She doesn't believe in giving them a hard time just because they are white. Mrs. Johnson is courteous and attentive: "She was against this eye-for-an-eye-tooth-for-tooth stuff." Miss Ingram is delighted with her sale. She is putting her things together. She chats aimlessly, casually, pleasantly as she prepares to leave—about the weather, about how hard her job is, although she confides to Mrs. Johnson:

> "People . . . think this is a snap job. It ain't. I work like a nigger to make a few pennies. A few lousy pennies."
> Maud Martha's head shot up. She did not look at Miss Ingram. She stared intently at Sonia Johnson.[39]

But Mrs. Johnson's smiling expression does not change, and in another few moments Miss Ingram is gone. Maud Martha decides that she must have misheard Miss Ingram because otherwise Mrs. Johnson's manner surely would have changed. Maud Martha is relieved. She is feeling too comfortable, too relaxed to deal with this today. "Sometimes fighting is interesting," she muses. "Today it would have been just plain old ugly duty," to come to the aid of the race.

Sonia Johnson turns her attention to Maud Martha after Miss Ingram has left. Speaking "in a dull tone," because she senses Maud Martha's disapproval she explains why she didn't challenge Miss Ingram. Maud Martha realizes with a sinking feeling that she hadn't misheard the language after all. Mrs. Johnson says: "Our people is got to stop feeling so sensitive about these words like 'nigger' and such. . . . Why make enemies? Why get all hot and bothered all the time?" The story ends with these words: "Maud Martha stared steadily into Sonia Johnson's irises. She said nothing. She kept on staring into Sonia Johnson's irises."[40]

In this story we see the dailiness of racism, the casual, thoughtless way in which white people incorporate it into their speech, without noticing it, the way, I think to myself, I once heard a gentile woman describe how she successfully bargained with a shopkeeper to reduce the price of a dress she bought: "I Jewed him down," she reported, not hearing the word, its meaning, its history. Brooks contests the innocent in everyday speech, in everyday encounters. She forces us to think about the times we've heard racist comments and let them slide, and the consequences of our silence for ourselves on the inside, in the lining of our stomachs, in the light of the irises of our eyes.

Most important, Brooks's vignette penetrates to the core of internalized racism showing how it operates as a mechanism of denial. In this case, Sonia Johnson heard what Miss Ingram said but denied her feelings of anger by denying the actual meaning of the word "nigger," ascribing to it a sort of benign quality. Maud Martha, on the other hand, thought she had heard the word, although she wasn't sure. She measured its meaning, and decided she probably hadn't heard it. At the moment of acknowledgment from Sonia Johnson, Maud Martha realizes the implications of their denial and silence. She stares into the irises of Sonia Johnson's eyes, into the interior damage they have both sustained.[41]

Much of Maud Martha's dialogue is an internal one with herself. This is the wisdom of experience interpolated through the poet's eye, constructed, as the literary critic Barbara Christian has suggested, "from the world of the home, the world of emotional relationships—worlds that have traditionally been seen as woman's domain."[42] As many critics have observed, the interior dialogue is also a literary device announcing that Maud Martha's observations will not be accorded much significance by the dominant culture so they are rarely spoken. Disarming in its apparently innocuous style, *Maud Martha* penetrates and haunts, as does much of Brooks's poetry: rhymes and scenes, sonnets and long narratives, the whir of life drawn from everyday things providing a running commentary on Black life as seen through the eyes of a woman. It is a style sometimes reminiscent of Langston Hughes but infused with a female sensibility. For many, Brooks's works in general, and *Maud Martha* in particular, were a touchstone, inscribing Black womanhood, as Paule Marshall once observed, "in all the wonder of her complexity."[43]

Maud Martha, published in 1953, presaged the literary outpouring by Black women since the early 1960s. A comment by the literary critic Dexter Fisher illuminated the continuity between these two generations of writers. She suggested that modern Black women writers—she was thinking of Toni Morrison, Alice Walker, and Toni Cade Bambara in particular—have emphasized relationships within the Black community rather than the confrontation between Black and white more characteristic of their male counterparts: "what the women writers emphasize is the importance of place and community as a character. By defining their landscapes of action to the community and examining the routines of daily life and feeling under a magnifying glass, black women writers accomplish two things: they highlight the art of daily living and give back to the community a mirror of itself."[44] The pioneering achievement of Gwendolyn Brooks's *Maud Martha* was that it offered a mirror, inviting Black women to look at themselves and their urban, working-class community through the eyes of one of their own. In its emphasis on relationship, in its attention to community, in its relentless probing of the consequences of racism, in its conjuring of the intimate through interior dialogue and the interior space of Maud Martha's home, Brooks's novel expressed precisely both a female sensibility and the wisdom and insight drawn from everyday life.

*

When I am too sad and too skinny to keep keeping, when I am a tiny thing against so many bricks, then it is I look at the trees. When there is nothing left to look at on this street. Four who grew despite concrete. Four who reach and do not forget to reach. Four whose only reason is to be and be.[45]

The street is called Mango. *The House on Mango Street* is a prose-poem by Sandra Cisneros etched from the dailiness of childhood memory. Forty-four vignettes are cut in sparse and vivid language, their effect reminiscent of Gwendolyn Brooks's *Maud Martha.* These vignettes, however, come out of the barrio rather than the ghetto, in the late fifties rather than the thirties. They are not so much a "hymn to the beauty of 'everydayness'" as they are a testimony to the sufferings and small joys of those who live on Mango Street. A sensitive, compassionate witness, Cisneros re-creates the neighborhood in which she grew up, evoking the smells and tastes and feelings. The effects of sexism, poverty, racism, and the loss of culture and language are told with searing simplicity. Esperanza is the narrator of these stories.

One story is about the psychological effects of poverty on a small child. When she is still a very little girl, Esperanza and her family live on Loomis Street, in a neighborhood which is poorer still than Mango Street where they will soon move:

> a nun from my school passed by and saw me playing out front . . .
> Where do you live? she asked.
> There, I said pointing up to the third floor.
> You live *there?*
> *There.* I had to look where she pointed—the third floor, the paint peeling, wooden bars Papa had nailed on the windows so we wouldn't fall out. You live *there?* The way she said it made me feel like nothing. *There.* I lived *there.* I nodded.[46]

At the end of the book Esperanza vows that one day she will have a "House of My Own": "Not a flat. Not an apartment in back. Not a man's house. Not a daddy's. A house all my own. With my porch and my pillows, my pretty purple petunias. My books and my stories. . . . a house quiet as snow, a space for myself to go, clean as paper before the poem." The vow stands against the memory of the nun's indictment. It stands also against the memory of the girl Cathy who will be Esperanza's friend "only till next Tuesday. . . . when we move away. . . . She says the neighborhood is getting bad." It stands against the memory of Geraldo who bleeds to death in the emergency room of a hospital when the surgeon doesn't come: "Just another *brazer* who didn't speak English. Just another wet-back. . . . His name was Geraldo. And his home is in another country. The ones he left behind are far away. They will wonder. Shrug. Remember. Geraldo. He went north . . . we never heard from him again."[47]

The vow stands against the memory of Mamacita who comes to Mango Street from Mexico with her baby boy. She is a large, beautiful woman. But she misses her real home and doesn't want to be on Mango Street where her oldest son has brought her. She speaks no English. She wants to go home. This is not home. She does not want to learn English. The baby though, listening to television, begins to sound out and sing the foreign words: "No speak English, she says to the child who is singing in the language that sounds like tin. No speak English, no speak English, no speak English, and bubbles into tears. No, no, no as if she can't believe her ears."[48]

The vow stands. It is Cisneros's only reprisal. She will tell the stories. She writes: "When you leave you must remember to come back for others. A circle, understand? You will always be Esperanza. You will always be on Mango Street. You can't erase what you know. You can't forget who you are."[49]

The stories of women predominate, each a portrait forming a mosaic of daily life in the barrio:

> my mother's hair, my mother's hair, like little rosettes . . . is the warm smell of bread before you bake it, is the smell when she makes a little room for you on the side of the bed still warm with her skin. . . .
>
> Marin, under the streetlight, dancing by herself. . . . Is waiting for a car to stop, a star to fall, someone to change her life. Anybody.
>
> Rose Vargas' kids are too many and too much. It's not her fault, you know, except she is their mother and only one against many.
>
> Alicia, whose mama died, is sorry there is no one older to rise and make the lunchbox tortillas, is young and smart and studies for the first time at the university. Two trains and a bus, because she doesn't want to spend her whole life in a factory or behind a rolling pin.[50]

Cisneros's telling is relentless, clear in its simplicity. Her anger is palpable, but no words of anger are actually written. Experiences about race and class and sex are put into word pictures. The entrapment of women is drawn in big, thick lines across the page. *Sobreviviendo*, bearing witness, out of love, so that what has been (and still is) will not be erased. The stories are pieced together like a quilt, arranged so that women can see how it is and has been, can see the lines of connection between themselves as women, as Chicanas, as poor people in the barrio, can think about how they might want it to be, how they could get there. That Cisneros, like Alice Walker and Gwendolyn Brooks, chose to piece her stories like a quilt speaks to the significance of the quilting process as a way of thinking. "Each day is a tapestry," Deena Metzger has written, the piecing a reflection of the structure of daily life.

In thinking about the meaning women invest in daily life I have been frequently drawn to quilts both as the embodiment of dailiness and as a metaphor for the way in which we as women might piece the diversity of our experiences into meaningful and useful patterns. Elaine Hedges writes of the importance of quilts in understanding women's history. Hedges sees the quilts "as a vehicle through which women could express themselves; utilitarian objects elevated through enterprise, imagination and love to the status of an original art form. . . . In 1845, a Lowell, Massachusetts woman described quilts, as ' . . . the hieroglyphics of women's lives.' And so they were."[51]

Quilting was introduced into the United States because of the harsh climate and the scarcity of cloth in the colonies and on the frontier, and by a sexual division of labor that made it female-centered in origin, continuity, and practice. Quilting in a variety of forms is evidenced in many places throughout the world. It is an ancient tradition. In the United States conditions of slavery, of the special oppression of women, of the practical needs for warmth and beauty and for a cultural form that did not require literacy (since few women until modern times could read or write), produced the quilting tradition.

Quilting was done predominantly in rural areas and after the day's chores had been completed. It was sometimes done collectively and for "talking and visiting" among the women: "People would get out the frame after the chores in summertime," recalled one elder, "and how the word would fly that we had the frame up. Had to have a screened porch 'cause sometimes you'd quilt and visit until midnight by lamplight with the bugs battin' against the screen."[52] One woman usually conceived, designed, and directed these collectively made projects. Quilting was also taught to children as young as four and five, both boys and girls, as exercises in patience, manual dexterity, mathematical skills, family and community traditions, and as a form of play and amusement. The women prided themselves on the intricacy of their designs and the smallness of their stitches. I recall seeing at an Oakland exhibit one quilt made out of thirty-three thousand individual pieces of silk, stitched in a diamond pattern. It had taken the quilter seventeen years and one day to complete her project.

Quilts reflected every theme of everyday life—religion, family history, community setting, plant and animal life, children's toys and fairy tales, friendships and love, death and mourning, weddings and other celebrations, and all manner of work from the construction of log cabins to production in the cotton gins. Quilts were sold to raise money for churches, charities, and political protest movements. Sometimes they were sold to supplement a family's income. One woman, eighty-three years old at the time she was interviewed, recalled her earliest memories of quilting:

> When I was about four years old the neighbor's baby died, and all the women was called in to help. Mama knew what her part was because right away she took some blue silk out of her hope chest. I remember that silk so well because it was special and I got to carry it. . . . Mama and three other women set up the frame and quilted all day. First they quilted the lining for the casket and then they made a tiny little quilt out of the blue silk to cover the baby.[53]

Another woman described the way in which she quilted despite all the work she was required to do on the farm:

> I was dreaming on havin' all kinds of pretty things in my home after I married. Well, I found out right quick that livin' out on a farm, what with all the chores that had to be done, a person didn't have a whole lot of time for makin' pretty things.
>
> But let me tell you, I got it all worked out with a little thinking. I had to drive one of them big wheat trucks during harvest. I would just take my piecin' or crochet to the truck with me in the morning. Then that way when I had to wait for the men to load and unload the truck, I would just be piecin' on my quilt top. They would all look into the truck and laugh. I'd laugh with 'em. That way I got my quilts done.[54]

Women designed their quilt patterns with the tools and materials on hand: "I keep figuring with my materials, and thinking about my colors a long time before it feels right," explained one Texas quilter.[55] Amish women of eastern Pennsylvania were forbidden by the church men to work with patterned fabric or too brightly colored cloth. The women emphasized instead shapes, contrast of color, shading, and stitching to produce astonishingly complex and beautiful quilts. "For innumerable nineteenth-century women," as Elaine Hedges observed, "quilting became, unlike mere clothing construction, not only necessary work but also a creative outlet . . . [that] enabled women to transcend the limiting daily routine."[56] In this way women gave meaning to their daily lives, the cumulative effects of their quilts finally transforming the ragged and the mundane into discernible patterns, beautiful, sturdy, enduring. Explaining where the ideas for her intricate quilts come from, a South African woman told the Black poet Audre Lorde, "I write my thoughts down on little scraps of paper . . . a quilt is like a book of many stories done up together, and many people can read it all at the same time."[57]

Linda Otto Lipsett, in her study of women and their friendship quilts, described what happened when she brought one such quilt to a family gathering in a small town in Kansas in 1981. Ten years earlier she had found and purchased the quilt at a flea market in Pasadena, California:

> In perfect condition, the quilt was composed of thirty blocks of the *Chimney Sweep* pattern, each embroidered in red cotton floss with a person's name, his or her relationship to the quiltmaker, a town and state, a month and year (ranging from 1891 to 1894). The quilt-maker had not included her name on the quilt, but from the relationships indicated, I was determined that her maiden name was Harris, and I hoped to find out her first name soon.[58]

Her first name turned out to be Fannie, and she had come from a town called Golden, Kansas, which was no longer even on the map. Through diligent effort, and with the help of the Kansas Historical Society, Lipsett eventually located the family in Ulysses, Kansas, and arranged a reunion, returning with the quilt. She spread it out on a large table so all could view it:

> It was one of the most moving, most memorable experiences of my life when the elderly and the young alike, with glistening, teary eyes and smiles of wonderment on their faces, gazed upon the embroidered names of their grandmothers, great-aunts, even great-great-grandmothers. One white-haired, crippled, feeble little lady, nearly one hundred years old, who had appeared unable to see or hear the afternoon's program, was carefully and ever so slowly helped to a chair at the table's edge. . . . As she jerkily began moving her crooked fingers over the names, joy lighted up her face, as if she were seeing her friends again right there in that quilt.[59]

Using quilts as a resource in reconstructing women's history has proved invaluable because women often left no "written" evidence of their lives. Quilts have provided details of community and a record of women's cultural and political heritage. A good example of this process is described by Michelle Cliff in an essay discussing the history of Afro-American artists. Cliff detailed the stories and themes told in the *Second Bible Quilt* made by Harriet Powers, circa 1890. Mrs. Powers was a well-known artist in her time. She was born in Georgia in 1837. Her parents had been brought from Africa as slaves. Only two of her pictorial quilts are known to have survived. The *Second Bible Quilt* was a ceremonial quilt commissioned by a group of Black women to decorate a wall at Atlanta University, a Black college. In examining the quilt frame, Cliff demonstrated that it was drawn from both the Judeo-Christian Bible and from African symbolic and spiritual iconography. On the one hand, she wrote, "it embodies a journey from suffering to redemption: beginning with Job and ending with Jesus." And, on the other hand, layered into the Christian story are many African ones. There are, for example, representations of the Kongo cross, the Dahomeyan deity Moses who used his magic serpent as an instrument of healing, and Mawu-Lisa, the highest deity of the Fon, a figure that represented moon and sun, female and male—their union a Fon ideal. Cliff showed the ways in which Mrs. Powers's quilt became a text representing in rich, symbolic detail the ways in which Black women retained and passed on elements of their African cultural heritage. Moreover, a strong antislavery theme predominates, the quest for freedom manifest in the scenes of several pieces.[60]

The work of the quilt historian Cuesta Benberry also provides us with examples of how Black women recorded their feelings and experiences in the quilts they made. Benberry explains that the majority of those quilts that were made by slave women and are still available for viewing today were made for their masters' households. "I believe," she explains, "that most utilitarian slave-made quilts were used up long ago."[61] Benberry, however, also looked for quilts made by free Black women before the Civil War. She found that many of these were auctioned or sold and the funds used for the antislavery movement and the Underground Railroad. One such quilt, for example, was sold by the Boston Female Anti-Slavery Society in December 1836. In its center block is inscribed in ink the following words:

Mother! when around your child
You clasp your arms in love
And when with grateful joy you raise your eyes to God above

Think of the negro-mother
When her child is torn away
Sold for a little slave—oh, then
For that poor mother, pray![62]

In keeping with the spirit of this quilting tradition, Cuesta Benberry organized the collective making of a quilt in 1979 in which each block was a representative sampler from a quilt of significance in Black women's history. It was a deeply moving experience to see this quilt—the 1836 call to mothers its centerpiece—on display, bringing history alive, as it were. The Benberry quilt was part of a stirring exhibit of political quilts called *The Power of Cloth,* offered at the Euphrates Gallery, De Anza College in Cupertino, California, in March 1987. The exhibit traced the historical and contemporary use of quiltmaking as a tool of political expression by women. All together, twenty-two quilts were exhibited, each one an example of women's involvement in political movements. Sometimes these quilts had been sold as fund-raisers, as in the case of the abolition quilt; there were others sold for woman suffrage, and the Women's Christian Temperance Union. Sometimes they were also political statements in themselves ranging from a patriotic eagle motif in 1845 to the *National Peace Quilt* of 1984. Among the most memorable quilts in the exhibit was the *Hudson River Quilt* (1969–1972) coordinated by Irene Preston Miller. It was protesting the pollution of the Hudson River in New York and the fatal impact on much of the wildlife in that region. The intricacy of its design was a quilting marvel. *Cherokee Trail of Tears* (1979) by Chris Wolf Edmonds depicted the forced removal of the Cherokee people from their homeland in Georgia in the 1830s. Thousands of men, women, and children perished on this forced winter march. It was an astonishing quilt. In the apparent simplicity of its figures and subdued colors it conveyed a sense of enormous grief.

The Purple Quilt (1986) by Faith Ringgold was inspired by Alice Walker's novel *The Color Purple.* This quilt was representative of a series by the well-known Afro-American artist which she has called story-quilts. Each of the characters in Walker's novel is visually represented around the border of this quilt, and each piece represents the artist's visioning of the story. Ringgold's story-quilts allow her to "successfully bridge the gap between painting and quilt making . . . between image and language and between the personal and the political," as one art critic put it.[63] She has created a new art form in which to more adequately express both her own personal experience and the dailiness of Black women's lives. The intimacy of a quilt, lodged as it is in the bedroom, affirms the intimacy of feeling in Ringgold's quilts. This is evident too, in her choice of subject: *Echoes of Harlem, Slave Rape Story Quilt,* and the *Lover's Quilt* series.

The ritual and healing qualities of the quilting tradition can be seen in the quilt sewn for those who have died in the AIDS epidemic. This quilt, made without borders and consisting of more than two thousand individual blocks, each one three by six feet, was first displayed at the National March on Washington for Gay and Lesbian Pride in August 1987. An entire national community of gay men and lesbians—drawing upon this women's tradition—has stitched an emblem of personal and collective grief.[64] Likewise, some of the most compelling political needlework by contemporary women has come from Chile in the years since the military coup d'etat overthrew President Salvadore Allende's popularly elected socialist government in 1973. The women of that country have produced literally thousands of *arpilleras,* a form of applique in which they have depicted the brutalities committed by the junta. An apparently simple and innocuous art form uniquely suited to women and made from the everyday resources available to them, the *arpilleras* have come to symbolize the Chilean resistance. *Arpillera* means burlap in Spanish. Since the backing cloth for this applique is most often burlap or other feed or grain sacks, the finished work has come to be called by that name. They are, as Marjorie Agosín reported after a trip to Chile, "small wall hangings with figures super-imposed on the cloth to create scenes full of vitality and movement, whose principal effect is that of political denunciation." The *arpilleras* are examples of the ways in which women in many times and places have made political statements, using the resources available to them as women and integrating their actions with their everyday lives.[65]

Likewise, dailiness provided the informative thread for a collaborative exhibition between thirty-two women artists from Brazil and the United States, in January 1987. Exhibition themes included war, race, food, spirit, birth, the body, and shelter. In addition to the contributing artists, what was called "a radiating circle of 150 women artists from the two regions" participated in the project which also included the creation of collaborative books on each of the exhibition themes, a letter-writing project between women, and an exploration of the relations between art and cultures. All of the exhibition materials were published in both English and Portuguese.[66]

In studying women's quilts, and by extension the many specifically female artifacts produced in the course of a lifetime, we are able to construct a more detailed understanding of the dailiness of women's lives. Moreover, we can see the ways in which that dailiness has structured women's ways of thinking. We see that the quilts, the stories, the gardens, the poems, the letters, the recipes, the rituals are examples of women's ways of knowing. They mark the evidence that there is and always has been another point of view, another record of social reality, a women's standpoint. This standpoint has always existed, but for thousands of years it has not been valued. Because it has not been valued, it has often not been seen, even by ourselves. It has certainly not been seen as anything "important." Friendship, family, children, ritual, community, connection to the earth, a belief in life, the need for beauty and art are some of the most evident of women's values. There is also a focus on the practical, an integration of the abstract and the practical, a continual analysis and reworking of context, which comes out of the particularity of women's labors and consciousness. This is the meaning of daily life.

"No more snickering," Alice Walker counseled, at "the stiff, struggling, ambivalent lines," of the first published African-American poet, Phillis Wheatley. This kidnapped and enslaved Black woman wrote in the only materials available to her, in the only language in which she could write, and in the only cadence she knew as song. Of Wheatley, Walker also wrote: "It is not so much what she sang, as that she kept alive . . . *the notion of song.*"[67]

Under conditions of enslavement, persecution, and subordination women have had no way of articulating and handing on a systematic, collective, sustained way of knowing. Women's ideas, artifacts, writings, heritage have been fragmented, uprooted, interrupted by these conditions.[68] Many things have been deliberately destroyed. Yet, many fragments have been and are being recovered. And in daily life women have always labored to give meaning to their experiences. In these ways the notion of an alternative way of seeing has been kept alive. In the dailiness of women's lives is preserved the evidence that there is and always has been an alternative to the beliefs, priorities, and values of the dominant cultures we have endured.

The Lesbian Connection

You say I am mysterious
Let me explain myself
In a land of oranges
I am faithful to apples.
  —Elsa Gidlow, "Makings for Meditation"

I am a wind-swayed bridge, a crossroads inhabited by whirlwinds. . . . What am I? *A third world lesbian feminist with Marxist and mystic leanings.* . . . Think of me as Shiva, a many-armed and legged body with one foot on brown soil, one on white, one in a straight society, one in the gay world, the man's world, the women's, one limb in the literary world, another in the working class, the socialist and occult worlds. A sort of spider woman hanging by one thin strand of web.

  Who, me confused? Ambivalent? Not so. Only your labels split me.
  —Gloria Anzaldúa, "La Prieta"

Wild Nights—Wild Nights!
Were I with thee
Wild nights should be
Our luxury!

Futile—the Winds—
To a Heart in port—
Done with the Compass—
Done with the Chart!

Rowing in Eden—
Ah, the Sea!
Might I but moor—Tonight—
In Thee!
  —Emily Dickinson, #249 (1861)

AM IN my mother's house. It is early in the morning. I have spent the night. It has been a good visit. I am helping my mother make the bed. We are tucking the bedspread in under the pillows. I know that a week before she has had a conversation with my son in which he has inadvertently told her the nature of my relationship with Kate.

My mother says: "I understand you are gay."

My heart pounds furiously. "Yes," I say, as calmly as I can.

She sighs and sits down on a chair in the bedroom. I sit on the bench with the antique needlepoint. Her dresser, a beautifully crafted curly maple wood inherited from my father's mother, stands between us. We peer around its corners at each other.

"Why didn't you tell me sooner?" she asks.

"Well, you know, Mama, some people get very upset about these things."

"Ach!" she says. "I've lived such a long time. Nothing upsets me anymore. Besides I've known since you were sixteen."

"Mama," I fairly shriek, "why didn't you tell me?"

"Oh," she says, "I hoped for the best."

And, of course, she thought she had. I had never doubted for a moment how much she loved me. And I remembered, too, how beautifully and thoughtfully she had welcomed Kate "into the family," as she had put it, lifting her wine glass in salutation at our first dinner together.

We talk. It is very easy now that the secret is out. She tells me about all the women friends in her life; about how much they meant to her, and how much she loved them. She tells me stories. Some are so funny my sides are splitting from our laughter.

"You know, Bettina, I think Kate is a wonderful person, just a wonderful person! She's a real *mentsch!** But if you should ever fall in love again and get married it would make me very happy."

I roar with laughter. I love her so much, and what am I going to say? How can I reply to such a contradictory set of assumptions? How did it happen that my mother can, on the one hand, acknowledge my connection with Kate and our obvious joy in one another, and, on the other hand, think that my love for her is not the Real Thing? And, more important,

---

* *Mentsch* is a Yiddish word. Literally translated it means fully human, a real human being, which is my mother's meaning here. It is meant to be highly complimentary.

why did it happen, and how is it connected to forming a women-centered vision?

This chapter has a threefold purpose. First it will discuss the ways in which the lesbian connection informs a women-centered perspective. Second it will show the ways in which contemporary lesbian feminists (and, indeed, the whole gay movement) are seeking to construct an identity stripped of Freudian ideology which saw homosexuality as a perversion. Third it will explore the philosophical and political implications of the fusion of lesbian and feminist perspectives for women's liberation.

Even the definition of the word "lesbian" is elusive. Feminist philosopher Marilyn Frye explains:

> If you look up the word "lesbian" in the *Oxford English Dictionary* you will find an entry that says it is an adjective that means *of or pertaining to the island of Lesbos,* and an entry describing at length and favorably an implement called a lesbian rule, which is a flexible measuring device used by carpenters. Period.
>
> If you have picked up enough gossip to suppose that a lesbian is a homosexual, *Webster's Third International* will inform you that "homosexual" means *of or pertaining to the same sex.* The elucidating example provided is the phrase "homosexual twins" which means *same-sex twins.* The alert scholar can conclude that a lesbian is a same-sex female.[1]

We are reassured, however, when Frye reports that in *Webster's Collegiate Dictionary* a lesbian is defined as a woman who has sex, or sexual relations with other women. She continues: "Such a definition would be accepted by many speakers of the English language." But this definition too collapses into nonsense if one looks up the word "sex" or "sexual" in the same or other dictionaries, all of which

> generally agree that "sexual" means something on the order of *pertaining to the genital union of a female and male animal,* and that "having sex" is having intercourse—intercourse being defined as the penetration of a vagina by a penis with ejaculation. . . . When the dictionary defines lesbians as women who have sex or sexual relations with other women, it defines lesbians as logically impossible.[2]

From feminist literary critic Catharine R. Stimpson we learn that the word "lesbian" as a sexual designation did not come into the English language until 1908. When it did make its appearance it was associated with a specifically Freudian meaning, designating a sexual inversion in women. The public, Stimpson concluded, "used its new language with pity, hostility and disdain."[3]

An example of this definitional erasure may be measured by the fact that I did not learn the word "lesbian" until 1973, when I was twenty-eight years old. I saw the book by Del Martin and Phyllis Lyon, *Lesbian Woman*, with its lavender-colored cover in a bookstore. I suspected its contents. It took me weeks to build the courage to surreptitiously purchase the book, after locating it again in a store in which I was reasonably sure I would not be recognized.

Women who used the word "lesbian" to define themselves in the early part of the twentieth century, some of whom were clustered in Paris—women for the most part from the upper classes, like Djuna Barnes, Radclyffe Hall, Una Trowbridge—generally accepted the Freudian terms of inversion to explain their sexual preference. These women internalized the psychological consequences of this definitional framework and displayed its predictive (or prescriptive, if you will) patterns. The idea that the homosexual woman had not successfully shifted her primary attachment from mother to male lover, and therefore remained both developmentally immature and emotionally crippled, has informed much of the popular consciousness on the subject in Western society for most of this century. This had certainly shaped my mother's thinking and went a long way to explain her contradictory feelings about my relationship with Kate.

A study by the literary historian Lillian Faderman, appropriately titled *Surpassing the Love of Men*, reveals thousands of romantic friendships and intimacies between women of the upper and middle classes in European and Euro-American society from the Renaissance to the present. Nearly five hundred pages of text based upon women's letters and journals, court and church records, local newspapers, and county or village documents recount the stories of these women who shared devoted, lifelong, and passionate engagements with each other. These women were "lesbians" in any meaningful emotional sense, but in the centuries in which they lived the word did not exist. In the eighteenth and nineteenth centuries in European and Euro-American culture, female sexuality was generally muted, and homosexuality was subsumed under the definitional umbrella of masturbation. The homosocial world characteristic of women's lives before the twentieth century placed these relationships along a sympathetic and widely shared continuum. One story Faderman tells illuminates the shift in conceptual framework between the nineteenth and twentieth centuries in the United States, as the word "lesbian" made its entrance into the public discourse.

The nineteenth-century poet and novelist Sarah Orne Jewett lived for thirty years with Annie Fields in what was, in that century, called a Boston Marriage. It was considered a respectable arrangement, and friends and community acknowledged the life-companion relationship as a genuine article of devotion. When Annie Fields, however, intended to publish the letters between her and Jewett in the 1920s and after the latter's death, her close friend Mark De Wolfe Howe counseled against inclusion of any mention of their love for each other. This meant deleting four-fifths of the correspondence. Howe's objections stemmed from his fear of accusations of "perversity" against his friend in the sexually charged world of Freudian analysis. Faderman concludes that while the love between Jewett and Fields "was common and appropriate behavior in the century in which the two women had spent most of their lives (and Howe himself saw it as common and appropriate at the time) . . . it suddenly became "abnormal" in a twentieth century context, although nothing about the nature of the relationship had changed."[4]

From this and other similar examples, Faderman draws an extremely important conclusion. Namely, that sexuality is culturally constructed, and that definitions of its normative expression shift from one historical period to another.[5] Noting that the prevailing patriarchal culture of Western Europe and the United States (in the eighteenth and nineteenth centuries, at least) asserted that females, and certainly those of repute, had little sexual passion, Faderman observed that "women might kiss, fondle each other, sleep together, utter expressions of overwhelming love and promises of eternal faithfulness and yet see their passions as nothing more than effusions of the spirit."[6]

Feminist historian Leila J. Rupp casts a helpful light on the subject by suggesting that "lesbian identity" as a core sexual identity is a historical development of the twentieth century. Furthermore, Rupp observes: "the nineteenth century permitted a great deal of freedom in moving along the sexual and emotional continuum that ranges from heterosexuality to homosexuality. The twentieth century has not. . . . Passionate love between women has always existed, but it has not always been named."[7]

Indeed, as Adrienne Rich has pointed out: "The fact is that women in every culture and throughout history *have* undertaken the task of independent, non-heterosexual woman-connected existence, to the extent made possible by their context, often in the belief that they were the only ones ever to have done so."[8] This suggests, of course, that the significance of the lesbian connection to women's liberation lies not only in women's passions but also in the reasons for its definitional erasure and its systematic repression.

Embedded in the struggle to define lesbian existence divested of its Freudian limits is another, much broader philosophical struggle; that is, that the lesbian connection provides us with a way of seeing women in relationship to each other, women's work, consciousness, and culture examined on its own ground and not in subordinated contrast to the normative models of male action. It provides an essential ingredient in our understanding of the dailiness of women's lives, both in terms of the social construction of gender and in the ways in which women vision themselves. Looking at the world through a lesbian lens allows us to expand "the meaning of our love for women," as Adrienne Rich once eloquently expressed it,[9] in new dimensions and directions. In a deeply misogynist culture this love may be a source of potential transformation and of healing women's internalized oppression not infrequently expressed in self-loathing and a distrust of women in general. Let us first briefly examine some of the writings by historians reconstructing examples of woman-centered existence in order to devolve both a definition of the word "lesbian" and at least a partial explanation for the erasure and suppression of lesbian life.

Appropriately enough the feminist scholarly journal *Signs* inaugurated its first issue with an essay by the historian Carrol Smith-Rosenberg which reconstructed a female world of love and ritual in nineteenth-century white, middle-class America. Refusing either to trivialize or to sexualize these women's relations with each other, Smith-Rosenberg challenged traditional academicians who had erased women's history, either because they considered the bonds between these women to be of secondary or no historical significance or because they themselves were personally embarrassed by the intensity of the love which the women expressed for each other and wished to save them from posthumous scandal.

From Smith-Rosenberg's wide-ranging search through these women's diaries and letters we learn "that women's sphere had an essential integrity and dignity that grew out of women's shared experiences and mutual affection," and that "despite the profound changes which affected American social structure and institutions between the 1760's and 1870's," these women's relationships "retained a constancy and predictability." They were often the most important, indeed the primary, emotional and intellectual ties in their lives, their marriages notwithstanding:

> Most eighteenth and nineteenth century women lived in a world bounded by home, church and the institution of visiting—that endless trooping of women to each other's homes for social purposes. . . . Women helped each other with domestic chores and in times of sickness, sorrow and trouble. . . . Rural women developed a pattern of more extended visits that lasted weeks and sometimes months, at times even dislodging husbands from their beds and bedrooms so that dear friends might spend every hour of every day together.[10]

Smith-Rosenberg's research discloses that the women's friendships "were normally part of highly integrated networks" in which kin formed an inner core and in which "an intimate mother-daughter relationship lay at the heart of this female world." Hostility and criticism of other women was discouraged, Smith-Rosenberg tells us, so that "women could develop a sense of inner security and self-esteem."[11]

One of the most important studies of this homosocial world in American society was done by the historian Nancy F. Cott. *The Bonds of Womanhood* focused on women's relationships in eighteenth- and early nineteenth-century New England, its title conveying a double meaning. Namely, these women saw their bonds in their dual aspect of bondage and sisterhood. What tied them down in a subordinated position to men also bound them together in women's homosocial sphere. Cott argues that this homosociality was the precondition for the emergence of the woman's rights movement in the nineteenth century. "Thine in the bonds of Womanhood," the abolitionist and woman's rights advocate Sarah Grimké signed her letters. Women's sphere was of the heart, it was believed, portending friendships of fierce devotion. While Cott's study is not focused on personal relationships, it confirms Smith-Rosenberg's analysis of women's homosocial existence and exemplifies the female-centered social structure of eighteenth- and nineteenth-century Euro-American middle-class society.[12]

Likewise, publication of selections from the personal correspondence of free Afro-American women in the same time period suggests that this homosocial pattern extended into those communities as well. Female anti-slavery networks, work on the Underground Railroad, club and church activities, and literary associations reflected a significant homosocial world. Some letters also reveal intimate, lifelong friendships that crossed racial lines. The Afro-American abolitionist, educator, and woman's rights advocate Sarah Mapps Douglass had such a relationship with Sarah Grimké; and Emma V. Brown, also an educator and an early graduate of Oberlin College, corresponded with Emily Howland, a white abolitionist and Quaker educator, for more than forty years. Given the taboo against interracial friendships, these personal alliances, and others like them, are notable.[13]

The work of these historians shows that within this homosocial world women provided each other with crucial avenues of emotional support, especially in times of birth, sickness, and death.[14] This also extended into the women's club movement, the Women's Christian Temperance Union, and like organizations in communities and churches.[15] In this supportive environment, ideas about women's rights, education, suffrage, and abolition were safely harbored. Later in the nineteenth century, this homosocial world was evident in the cultural mores of the women's colleges and assumed other personal and political implications. Historian Nancy Sahli, for example, describes the practice of "smashing" among young college women. Quoting an 1873 letter, Sahli prepares us with this description of it at Vassar: "When a Vassar girl takes a shine to another, she straightaway enters upon a regular course of bouquet sendings, interspersed with tinted notes, mysterious packages . . . locks of hair perhaps, and many other tender tokens, until at last the subject of her attentions is captured, the two become inseparable, and the aggressor is considered by her circle of acquaintances as—smashed." Some women, as this letter writer confirms, kept "score" of their "smashing" successes, and not a few hearts were broken in the process. Some of these relationships, however, were more sustaining of emotional and intellectual maturity, and Sahli reports that these "committed homosocial relationships among women [began] to take on a counter-cultural aspect."[16]

An essay by the archivist Judith Schwarz on the relationship between two Wellesley college professors in the early half of this century illustrates this countercultural dimension.[17] Katharine Lee Bates and Katharine Coman were lovers and lived together for twenty-five years. Bates was a professor of English, and a poet of considerable renown, the author of "America the Beautiful." Coman was a professor of economics, a social reformer, and one of the founders of Denison House in Boston—a settlement house for poverty-stricken immigrant women and children patterned after Jane Addams's Hull House in Chicago. Although Bates was more politically conservative than Coman, she respected and supported her lover's work, and they shared a wide circle of women friends who formed an activist network spread among Boston, New York, Philadelphia, and Chicago. The love between Bates and Coman was powerful and enduring, joyous and wholesome. And it radiated outward from them, embracing within its fold an ever-increasing circle of friends and coworkers. Their relationship ended with Coman's death from cancer when she was fifty-eight. Upon her death Katharine Lee Bates wrote a series of love poems published in a small private edition and called *The Yellow Clover*. One of these poems, "If You Could Come," contains these grief-stricken lines:

> My love, my love, if you could come once more
>   From your high place,
> I would not question you for heavenly lore,
> But, silent, take the comfort of your face.
> One touch of you were worth a thousand creeds.
>   My wound is numb
> Through toil-pressed day, but all night long
>   It bleeds
> In aching dreams, and still you cannot come.[18]

In a related study, Schwarz excavates for our public appraisal the workings of the Heterodoxy Club of radical feminists who met for biweekly luncheons in Greenwich Village between 1912 and 1940. More than a hundred women were members of this club, almost all of them suffragists, labor organizers, peace activists, educators, and/or professional women. What bound them together was precisely that they were "unorthodox women" for their time and place. The club served as both a support network and a source of intense intellectual stimulation. A significant number of club members were lesbians. Club member Elizabeth Gurly Flynn, famed organizer for the Industrial Workers of the World, and later a leading member of the U.S. Communist party referred to her membership in Heterodoxy as "an experience of unbroken delight!" She added, "It has been a glimpse of the women of the future, big spirited, intellectually alert, devoid of the old 'femininity' which has been replaced by a wonderful freemasonry of women."[19]

The significance of Judith Schwarz's account of the love between Coman and Bates and her history of the Heterodoxy Club is accentuated when placed in the context of the work of another historian, Blanche Wiesen Cook. In her essay "Female Support Networks and Political Activism" Cook explores the work of Jane Addams and Lillian Wald, co-founders of the settlement house movement in Chicago and New York, respectively, and the wide homosocial reform network they supported.[20] Activists like Florence Kelley, Alice Henry, Julia Lathrop, and Elizabeth Morgan frequented Hull House using it as a meeting hall, occasional residence, and political oasis. When Florence Kelley fled an abusive husband with her daughter, she fled to Hull House where shelter and work were provided. Struggles for urban sanitation, health and safety regulations in factories, child-labor laws, women's trade union organization, woman suffrage, and struggles against lynching and for the integration of the Chicago public schools engaged the energies of these women.[21] In addition to providing a center for social activism, Hull House, Wald's Henry Street Settlement, and Katharine Coman's Denison House provided countless sources of relief for impoverished, usually immigrant women and children. Classes in subjects ranging from English to dance were offered, libraries furnished, and cultural events of all kinds sponsored.

Cook's essential point is that the love and support these women provided for each other was the bedrock for their social activism. Furthermore, Cook contends, a lesbian sensibility was at the center of the rock. Jane Addams lived with Mary Rozet Smith for forty years in what was widely recognized by their own circle of friends as a Boston Marriage. Although Smith was only a periodic resident at Hull House, her wealth, generously bestowed, was essential in financing Hull House, and she and Addams spent most summers and holidays together, sharing a home in Bar Harbor, Maine. Likewise, Cook suggests, Lillian Wald lived in a lesbian connection with Lavinia Dock and had affairs with other women during her long tenure at the Henry Street Settlement, being less monogamous but every bit as energetic as her counterpart in Chicago. Other women's historians, including Estelle Freedman and Kathryn Kish Sklar, have explored these and similar communities, and Freedman developed an analysis of the politics of what she has called "female institution building" to describe the women's work.[22]

As Cook acknowledges, there is no way of knowing whether these women (or others, as for example many of those described in Lillian Faderman's book) had sexual relations with each other. Cook argues, however, that the "insistence on genital evidence to 'prove' lesbian identity derives from a male model that has very little to do with the love, support, and sensuality that exist between women." Based upon the lived experiences of these women and others among their contemporaries as reconstructed through correspondence, journals, and autobiographical writings, Cook suggests that "even if we were to assume that Addams and [Mary Rozet] Smith never in 40 years in the same bed touched each other, we can still argue that they were lesbians because they chose each other. Women who love women, who choose women to nurture and support and to create a living environment in which to work creatively and independently are lesbians."[23]

The importance of Cook's insights into the political significance of the lesbian community is further evidenced in the history of working-class organization among women in the same time period. Some of the women who led the "Uprising of the Twenty Thousand" garment workers in New York City in 1910–11, for example, acknowledged themselves as lesbians; and, some of those who helped form both the national and the New York Women's Trade Union League were likewise. Sara Schulman, providing us with a thoroughly documented "Walking Tour Through Radical Jewish Women's History on the Lower East Side," reports that:

> Pauline Newman and her lover had a life-long lesbian relationship and adopted a child together. Mary Dreir lived for many years with Frances Keller and then with organizer Lenora O'Reilly, providing her with a house and life income. Helen Marot lived all her adult life with organizer Caroline Pratt. . . . It has taken over 65 years for historians to reacknowledge what the community knew all along, that lesbians were at the center of radical organizing on the East Side, and that their relationships influenced radical politics and strategy.[24]

The women-centeredness of their politics was evidenced in the long years of union organizing which followed the garment workers' strike. At the heart of this organizing between 1916 and 1925, these women pioneered in the formation of all-female "Unity houses." Within the relative safety of this homosocial world the women endeavored to instruct the workers in sisterhood, the powers of collective action, and the history of the labor movement of which they were so vital a part. The Unity houses also served as social, emotional, and recreational centers for work-wearied women. Historian Nancy MacLean detailed this "culture of resistance," explaining that the Unity houses

> embodied new visions of social organization and human relationships and transformed roles for women. [The] culture of resistance generated energy for the [union] movement on two fronts. On the one hand it furnished a supportive environment in which working women were able to break free from traditional gender roles, redefine what it meant to be a woman, and gain the skills and confidence to engage in ongoing activism. On the other hand, to break down the isolation of women and challenge their oppression, female organizers realized it was necessary to bring a host of non-workplace issues into the labor movement. They sought therefore to create a new labor culture, based on institutions which participants experienced as models of the sexual egalitarian socialist society they were struggling to bring into existence.[25]

What is also crucial here is that in both Cook's analysis and MacLean's example the forging of a lesbian identity was a *collective* process and tied to a specifically political consciousness about how to effectively organize to meet women's needs.

Cook's definition of lesbians and her vision of the connection between lesbian identity and independent political action by women invite a deeper understanding of the connection between the general status of women in patriarchal society and the erasure and/or suppression of lesbian existence. Indeed, in the contemporary period there has been a felt need among lesbian feminists to constitute a heritage indigenous to themselves, in part to counter the continuing persecution of lesbians and in part to counter the erasure of homosocial, woman-loving traditions.

Working from Cook's insight and this historical record, I would define lesbians as women whose primary emotional, intellectual, and erotic relationships are with other women. I would affirm that what constitutes primacy and what constitutes "erotic" must be understood within the framework of the historical period and cultural setting in which particular women lived. Some lesbians were (and still are) married. Indeed, until the most recent period it has been very difficult for most women to exist without economic support from a male provider. Those women who have survived without male support, lesbian or not, were most often forced to do so by pressures of race and/or class. They have endured great impoverishment and survived primarily through the support of extended families and female-centered support networks. Some lesbians were (and still are) celibate, including at least some who have devoted themselves to convent life, precisely to avoid marriage and remain economically solvent.[26]

In a world in which male power is pervasive, the lesbian has existed to the extent made possible by her context: her economic resources and psychological strength; her religious and cultural affiliations; her class position and racial identity. I use the term lesbian to name the primacy and intensity of women's relationships with each other, and I place their sexual aspect in context. In the United States today, sexuality is explicit and defining of the lesbian connection. A hundred years ago it wasn't, but its absence doesn't mean that those earlier women didn't have the primary emotional connections characteristic of lesbians.

The question of whether the women in the studies by Cott, Sahli, Smith-Rosenberg, Schwarz, and Cook were lesbian in the Freudian sense of that word, with its exclusive emphasis on sex, misses the point: the significance of their connection was not in their sexual habits but in their love for each other, in the networks of support, struggle, and condolence that they forged, in the bonds of kinship and solidarity that were at the center of their work. In the post-Freudian, post-sixties generation, such bonds as these women exhibited frequently have an explicitly sexual component; and in our context that component is both personally definitive and politically potent. The crushing of this sexual component by male authorities is not an act of moral purification but an enforcement of patriarchal privileges and powers. It has, as its purpose, the effect of shattering or limiting women's bonds, in general. The disruption of such bonds—in order to prevent significant numbers of women from acting in concert, independent of male supervision and approval—becomes most urgent when economic and political conditions shift. For example, in the United States it was precisely after the victory of woman suffrage in 1920, when large numbers of women entered the paid work force and thereby gained a modicum of political and economic independence from men, that the homosocial world of the nineteenth century was effectively dismantled. Official pronouncements held that this homosocial arrangement was emotionally unhealthy, and the taboo on sexual relations between women was rigidly enforced.[27] We see precisely the same pattern repeated in the 1950s when lesbian persecutions were part of a concerted drive to force women back into their homes and into dependence on a male provider after their relative freedom as employed heads of households, union members, and antifascist activists during the Second World War.[28]

Crucial to our definition of lesbian identity today is the fact that in acknowledging their sexual preferences, women face severe persecutions, including the loss of their children, and a variety of economic, religious, and social sanctions. This persecution is consistent with the historic pattern because in contemporary society the assertion of a lesbian sexuality is emblematic of women's independence, threatening men's conventional claims to manhood. A story related by the lesbian-feminist poet Judy Grahn illustrates this point.[29]

Grahn reports that she has been paranoid for years about random violence by men directed at "butch" women. She has consciously changed her appearance to travel with a greater sense of security. She does not look particularly different from other women in hairstyle or dress. She does, however, ride a motorcycle. One day she had driven to a hamburger stand. She parked her bike and approached the counter. She was accosted by a drunk young man who did not like the way she looked. He called her a "queer." When she failed to respond he punched her in the face and broke her nose. Grahn's conclusions from this experience are useful to us:

> I believe he was not so much punching out a lesbian as he was punching out a woman who was carrying a motorcycle helmet. He didn't give a damn about my choice of sexual partners. . . . What upset him was my intrusion into two of his manly territories: machinery and action. . . . I had antagonized him not as a pervert, but as a somewhat liberated woman—capable of thinking and acting on my own.[30]

Grahn is exactly right. But, I think if the man had known her choice of sexual partners, he would have added this to his list of her offenses. This too would have been seen as an intrusion upon his territory. That is, her choice of sexual partner would also have been seen as an expression of her independence from men, and/or her "unnatural" impersonation of a man. In our culture, sexual access to women is a primary symbolic representation of manhood. Manhood and womanhood are encoded in relationship to each other. The lesbian, by stepping outside the code, cracks it. Many people—in my experience, particularly men—find this terrifying at a nonrational, gut-wrenching level because it threatens their core identity. A lesbian presence signals a potential for female independence that is as despised as it is feared. This potential is not only for an individual, personal escape from the conventional female subordination, but also for a far more general, structural challenge to the social relations between the sexes.

Men's fear of women's independence is not only politically motivated; it is also inspired by psychological need. An examination of the ways in which the dominant culture encodes the social relations between the sexes reveals the extent to which men's core identity is constructed in relationship to a subordinated womanhood. Although most men generally allow that women have rights of employment, education, citizenship, proprietorship, and so on, a presumption of possession, which was enforced as literal ownership in earlier centuries, still persists. This presumption deeply affects women's daily lives, as for example in the laws governing rape and domestic violence.[31] And men, to varying degrees depending on class, culture, and experience, may still presume to "permit" their wives to work, or go to school, or visit with friends and colleagues. I can remember, for instance, our efforts to organize electronics workers in what is called Silicon Valley, in San Jose, California, in the early 1970s. Mostly women worked the assembly lines. They worked long hours, for minimal wages, and safety and health regulations were grossly violated. Many of the women were willing to attend union meetings or see union representatives at their homes in the evenings, but many of their husbands objected and could not be persuaded otherwise. Angered that they could not adequately provide for their families on their income alone, threatened by their wives' potential independence and advancement, and jealous of alliances and friendships formed outside the purview of their control, the men inhibited the union efforts. These women were primarily of Philipina and Mexican heritage, but their experience is enacted across many class and cultural lines.[32]

The core of male possession in modern times pivots on an emotional axis that is not so much possession in a literal sense of ownership, as "possessiveness." That is, men require (and expect) that women will focus continual, soothing, adoring, and altogether undivided attention upon them. From women, men expect support, and praise, and self-sacrifice. They expect women to see their work as all-important (certainly as more important than anything in which the women are engaged). They expect women to perform the mundane tasks of domesticity, service their emotional needs, raise their children, and execute those social amenities necessary to their careers. These social amenities are codified among officers in the military, and presumed in professional, corporate, academic, political, and religious life. In working-class families men's work and their social, political, sports, church and/or community connections are given the same precedence. Likewise, working women, especially those in clerical, staff, and auxiliary positions, are expected to perform many of these same amenities in the workplace, smoothing their superior's day and way. Not infrequently those amenities are presumed to include sexual favors. This presumption has been so pervasive that one historian referred to sexual harassment as a more or less general condition of female employment.[33]

Although the details of the male expectations may vary, women's position as satellite orbiting their men is at the center of gendered roles in the United States regardless of race, ethnicity, or class. It is this that is at the emotional heart of men's privilege and women's servility. It is this that makes it difficult for professional women to develop and sustain intimate relationships with men. It is this that makes some Black men rail against writings by Black women when those writings reveal the abuse women have endured at their hands as an integral part of the constellation of violence and oppression that informs their existence. It is this that impels many white working-class women to continually defer to their husbands' judgment, and especially on questions perceived as political or as matters of public policy. And it is this that forces or encourages women to manipulate behind the scenes as it were, to get their way in domestic and financial matters. The extent to which these gendered expectations are emotionally embedded may be illustrated by the following story, revolving in this case around the issue of women's autonomy.

Having given a lecture once on feminism for the freshman "core course" at the college with which I am affiliated on the University of California Santa Cruz campus, I retired to the provost's house, accompanied by my colleagues for an informal discussion and social hour. What I expected to be a respite turned into a very intense and not altogether sympathetic exchange. The atmosphere stayed cordial, but the issues were highly charged. In the course of my presentation I had offered what I called a "working definition" of feminism—"working," as in the sense of working draft—something that remains open-ended, changeable, according to experience. The definition was this: "Feminism means the collective empowerment of women as autonomous (independent, self-defined) human beings who shall have at least as much to say as men about everything in the arrangement of human affairs."

I had intended this as a definition of feminism as a social movement, but the male faculty had interpreted it as a code for the conduct of their personal relationships. They registered their upset and zeroed in on the word "autonomy" with a defensive ardor cloaked in philosophical discourse. Crudely summarized, the philosophical dictum they espoused was that "no man is an island" and no one can exist "autonomously," i.e., without connection. But the debate proceeded on the philosophical ground set by the men, its logic closed in on itself. Finally, Carol Whitehill, a psychologist for the counseling services at the college, pointed out in a gentle, resolute manner that she thought the word "autonomy" resonated with different meaning for women because they had so little of it in their personal lives, revolving as they did around men. Shortly thereafter, one of the more distinguished elders among us rose abruptly from his chair and announced his departure. The expression on his face left no doubt that he, for one, had absolutely gotten the point. "I must leave," he said briskly, "to be home on time for dinner, prepared, of course," he continued, peering intently at his colleagues, "by my wife."

Coming from my Marxist background I had used the word "autonomy" with a specific political intent: as, for example, a racial minority's "autonomy," meaning its right to self-determination. The emphasis in my definition is on collective, the point being that women constitute a distinctively oppressed group whose interests, needs, and so forth must be first collectively and autonomously assigned by them. Equality means that this collective voice then shares equally with men in determining all aspects of human affairs, in proportion at least to their numbers in society. (I would affirm precisely the same rights for each racial minority, providing women of color with a double collective voice.) Such autonomy is not to be confused with "separation," although it often is in the mistaken belief that any political action undertaken by women on behalf of themselves without men's prior knowledge and approval is deceptive, if not inherently divisive. It is a measure of how much personal autonomy we have lost when we understand that women who remain pleasant, even amiable, toward men, but who refuse them a certain kind of emotional, nurturing "juice," are perceived as unfeminine, remote, and even angry.

I could see from our discussion at the provost's house that my male colleagues were not about to give up their personal, daily privileges. I had used the word "autonomy" as a political concept in a social setting; they had used the word "autonomy" as a personal concept in a psychological setting. The political and the personal are, of course, intertwined, and Carol Whitehill was exactly right: on a personal level the word "autonomy" does resonate with different meaning for women. Moreover, most women, in our culture at least, would see themselves as having to personally choose between autonomy and attachment. Posed in this dichotomous and individual way, most will choose attachment over autonomy, and with excellent reasons.

In her book *In a Different Voice,* which traces the contours of women's psychological development, Carol Gilligan observed that women invariably "flunked" developmental tests. This happened because the tests were designed according to normative male patterns of development in which the assertion of autonomous need signified a growing maturity in the progression toward adulthood. But, Gilligan maintained: "Illuminating life as a web rather than a succession of relationships, women portray [personal] autonomy as the illusory and dangerous quest. In this way women's development points toward a different history of human attachment, stressing continuity and change, rather than . . . replacement and separation."[34] The problem, of course, is that for women autonomy and attachment have been posed as oppositions by men having the power to assert one over the other, and women have had to choose between them. Despite personal losses most women have chosen relationship (attachment), or juggled the two in agonizing tension because in terms of most women's everyday lives—their emotional needs, the economic feasibility of remaining single or raising children on one income, the willingness of men to be in relationship with them—there has been no real choice.

A lesbian presence, especially a *community* of lesbians, can potentially change the grounds upon which women have been compelled to juggle these choices. The settlement house women of whom Blanche Cook writes, in choosing to nurture each other, and, in Cook's words, "create a living environment in which to work creatively and independently," were taking a crucial political step. They were, in fact, moving outside the normal, conventional patterns of the social relations between the sexes as these have been historically and culturally constructed in the United States. These women had cordial and collegial relationships with men, but they were female centered in politics, outlook, energy, and achievement.

The real difference in perceptions between lesbians and heterosexual women turns on this point. Most heterosexual women see that their personal self-interest requires them to act within the cultural ground rules governing their relations with men. Moreover, in order to maintain viable, intimate relationships they have to collaborate in establishing those ground rules and participate daily in their enactment. Sociological literature confirms in myriad detail the elaborate structure of sex-role socialization which reproduces these rules. Most women know that unless they abide by them, their relationships with men will founder.[35]

In a culture in which "having a man" presumes a woman's completion, normality, and success, and in which male approval and love is emotionally central to female self-esteem, the social relations between the sexes have remained fixed and apparently unassailable. They are all the more complicated by the fact that an authentic and intimate love between individual women and men may exist, however "unbalanced" its foundation. Having fulfilled the needs of their men, it is very difficult for women to direct energy to themselves or other women. More important, these personal, psychological factors shaping a core identity invariably and indelibly mark women's political, intellectual, and societal views. The social relations between the sexes, the encoding of (a privileged) manhood and (a servile) womanhood are personally enacted, but they are also entrenched in the economic and social fabric of society as a whole.

A lesbian presence has the potential of rupturing this system because a lesbian's emotional needs are not focused on men in the same way. She stands outside the established norms. It is precisely for this reason that the fusion of a lesbian and feminist perspective is so potent. Moreover, unlike previous historical periods, the basis for women's economic survival independent of male provision exists to an unprecedented degree in the United States today. Women are not wealthy; access to power is limited; racism is rampant; raising children is demanding. But surviving, even flourishing in modest ways, is possible. To live a women-centered life is feasible, providing a potential political base from which to renegotiate the social relations between the sexes on a mass scale. This is new. In addition, because those relations also stand as a mirror of and as an integral part of the hierarchical, exploitative relations of power that frame society as a whole, a questioning of the one challenges the viability of the others. For these reasons the fusion of lesbian and feminist perspectives potentially revisions the character of all social relations. Finally, in utilizing the understanding of privilege in race conscious and class conscious ways, lesbian feminists have defined heterosexual *privilege* for the first time, coming to understand that sexual preference is a choice that invests personal decisions with social and political consequences.

Women of color who are lesbian feminists have been particularly clear about the difficulties in changing established ideas about relations between women and men. From their experiences with white people coveting a race privilege, they have a sober estimate of the upheavals necessary to shake privileges loose; and from their particular vantage point in society they have also seen the ways in which the social relations between the sexes are connected to everything else. Their writings reflect a multiple consciousness of the ways in which race, class, and sex intersect. In her essay challenging us to reconsider "the master's tools" in disassembling his house, the poet Audre Lorde brought these connections into sharp focus:

> Those of us who stand outside the circle of this society's definition of acceptable women; those of us who have been forged in the crucibles of differences—those of us who are poor, who are lesbians, who are Black, who are older—know that *survival is not an academic skill.* It is learning how to stand alone, unpopular and sometimes reviled, and how to make common cause with those others identified as outside the structures in order to define and seek a world in which we can all flourish. It is learning how to take our differences and make them strengths. *For the master's tools will never dismantle the master's house.* They may allow us temporarily to beat him at his own game, but they will never enable us to bring about genuine change. And this fact is only threatening to those women who still define the master's house as their only source of support.[36]

The growth of the lesbian-feminist community, geographically spread, racially diverse, and with an emerging working-class articulation, has extended its energies through the component layers of the women's liberation movement. Lesbians have initiated and/or helped to staff many of the movement's most immediate needs, like battered women's shelters, rape crisis and rape prevention centers, abortion clinics, and women's health centers. Likewise, many women-centered academic associations and political and trade union caucuses have been inspired and/or staffed by lesbian feminists. Lesbian feminists have also flooded the movement with literature, poetry, music, and theater. This highly visible, women-centered, and women-loving culture has influenced and nourished tens of thousands of women regardless of their sexual identity. In turning now to a more detailed consideration of a lesbian-feminist perspective, I review some of this work. In establishing itself as a community, lesbian feminists have been about the business of creating a collective self-portraiture rooted in the dailiness of life and without the fetters of a Freudian-based psychoanalysis.

The physical establishment of lesbian archives, the largest of which is the Lesbian Herstory Archives in New York City, serves to create and preserve a significant heritage. Each photograph, story, manuscript, each piece of memorabilia, confirms the existence of a women-loving tradition. From these records we learn something of the boundaries of endurance. "The Lesbian Herstory Archives," wrote its founders in a retrospective in 1986, "is a concrete expression of a people's refusal to lose their memory. For 13 years, we have been nurturing and sharing a collection alive with voices that the larger society has judged obscene, sick, or inconsequential. . . ."37 In 1986 the New York archive was still housed in a private apartment and included over five thousand books, more than one thousand individual biographical files, and thousands of slides, photographs, and periodical listings. Lesbian elders, such as Mabel Hampton, Elsa Gidlow, and Barbara Deming, whose lives span the twentieth century, have been particularly crucial in both inspiring and organizing the archival resources in New York and elsewhere.

Mabel Hampton, born in 1902, says she's "been in the life" as long as she can remember. She has been, in the words of one biographer, an "ambassador extraordinaire" for the New York archive. As a Black woman from Harlem, honored in that community and within the gay and lesbian movement, she is a survivor whose memory and experience "touch the hearts of those fortunate enough to meet and listen to her everywhere she goes."38 Likewise, the memoirs of poet Elsa Gidlow (1891–1986) and civil rights and peace activist Barbara Deming (1917–1985) evidenced the struggle with which so many have engaged for a lesbian identity rooted in self-esteem and dignity. In publicly affirming who they were, each encouraged the sense of continuity and tradition central to the formation of lesbian archives.

Deming, writing in 1971 to her "dear brother and dear sister," Ray Robinson and Cheryl Buswell-Robinson, southern civil rights activists with whom she had worked in the 1960s, confronted her own oppression as a lesbian and the anger and agony of her feelings of powerlessness: "The bottom I write about of course is the bottom of being a homosexual. Facing always the threat of being despised for that. . . . And as I write this, the tears begin to gush from my eyes, and I know I'm writing the truth of it." Deming's lover, faced with losing custody of her children, literally ransomed them from her ex-husband. "But how it hurt to resolve things that way," Deming continued in her letter, "not daring to an open struggle because the children were hostages."[39]

Elsa Gidlow, largely self-educated, was a poet and dramatist with ten published works and one unpublished manuscript to her credit. Raised in Quebec Province in Canada in a working-class English family of seven children, Gidlow was especially devoted to her mother and sisters all her life. For many years she struggled to earn a living doing secretarial and then editorial work. She lived in New York City, traveled in Europe, and eventually settled in San Francisco. Later she moved to Marin County just north of the city. From then on—even through the very hard times of the Depression—she earned her living as a free-lance journalist and editor. Through the generosity of friends she was able to buy what she described as "a decrepit summer 'cottage' in the hills north of Golden Gate. [I] learned amateur carpentry and organic gardening, and transformed it into a pleasant home," which she shared for ten years with one of her lovers.[40]

Gidlow's autobiography provides us with an account of her own feminist conclusions in the 1920s about women's need for economic independence and her own lifelong struggle to sustain this for herself and for other women, including her sisters, when she could share her meager resources. Gidlow also had a strong sense of social justice and opposed war. Her autobiography provides us with a vivid sense of her lesbian experience. She is frank about her feelings and draws several excellent portraits of the women with whom she had the longest and most significant relationships. Gidlow's choice to be a lesbian, to live a full, creative, and long life without the fetters of Freudian psychology and internalized homophobia, and her experiences provide us with an important model of independence, health, self-love, and endurance.

Central to Gidlow's life was its spiritual focus: an affinity with the natural world and an intense appreciation for what she believed was the oneness of all things. Her life was marked by ritual and poetry and beauty. In the last decades of her life she became a student of the Tao and other Eastern philosophies, a close friend of Allan Watts, and cofounder with him of the Society for Comparative Philosophy. A gentle, gifted, and extraordinarily generous woman, Gidlow had a wide range of friends— women and men—from all over the country. She died in the summer of 1986 on the land where she had made her home and which she named "Druid Heights." In a poem read on the occasion of her eightieth birthday, Gidlow celebrated her personal liberation in "Creed for Free Women":

> I am Child of every Mother
> Mother of each daughter,
> Sister of every woman
> And lover of whom I choose or chooses me.[41]

The reconstruction of lesbian history through the archives, and as evidenced by the work of Blanche Cook, Lillian Faderman, Carrol Smith-Rosenberg, and Judith Schwarz discussed earlier, has been central in forging a sense of continuity and heritage. In drawing intimate portraits of two Black literary figures of the early twentieth century, the literary historian Gloria T. Hull concluded that both Angelina Weld Grimké (1880–1958) and Alice Dunbar-Nelson (1875–1935) had significant lesbian connections. Hull based her conclusions upon their respective writings, including Grimké's poetry and Dunbar-Nelson's diary. In both cases the women had gone to considerable lengths to hide their relationships, which made the posthumous revelations a difficult editorial decision. Hull decided in favor of it so that the works of these women writers "would be presented without the lies and distortions which have marked far too many of us."[42]

Angelina Weld Grimké, poet, playwright, short story writer, whose great aunts were the famed southern white abolitionists, was buried, as Hull shows us, under the crushing weight of racism, sexism, and homophobia. Her poetry resonates with the poignant despair of unrequited love. Her most well-known play, *Rachel,* published in 1920, "dramatizes the blighting effect of American racism on a sensitive young Black woman who, like her creator, vows never to bring children into this ugly world."[43] Another of her works, a short story called "The Closing Door," tells of a young woman shattered by the lynching of her brother in Mississippi. Overwhelmed with despair, she kills her infant son rather than provide a future victim for the mob, afterwards going mad and dying herself. Reproducing one of Grimké's poems of quiet desperation, Hull concludes that this Black lesbian poet "had no spirit left to send us. . . . We have to struggle to connect with her." Crushed by the isolation and the denial of her lesbian identity, "she is a lesson whose meaning each person will interpret as they see fit and are able." Writes Hull: "What she says to me is that we must work, write, live so that who and what she was never has to mean the same again."[44]

In contrast, Alice Dunbar-Nelson lived a full, rich, and relatively joyous life. In publishing her diary, *Give Us Each Day*, Gloria Hull makes available to us an important gift. It is only the second such diary by a Black woman to be published in the United States (the other being *The Journal of Charlotte Forten*, a leading abolitionist and teacher in the Georgia Sea Islands during and after the Civil War). Dunbar-Nelson was a teacher, journalist, poet, short story writer, and political activist. She published widely, encouraged younger writers during the Harlem Renaissance, and was a pillar of support in the Black women's club movement, the woman suffrage movement, and the antilynching crusades of the 1920s. She worked in the White Rose Mission in Harlem in the late 1890s with its founder Victoria Earle Matthews. The mission was modeled after Hull House in Chicago but fitted to the special needs of young Black women entering New York City from a childhood in the rural South. Her associations spread throughout the political and literary network of Black America and included close personal friendships with Edwina B. Kruse, founding principal of Howard High School in Washington, D.C., Georgia Douglas Johnson, one of the most popular of Black poets in the 1920s, and Mary McLeod Bethune, educator and founder of Bethune-Cookman College in Daytona Beach, Florida, and later of the National Council of Negro Women. Dunbar-Nelson is perhaps most widely known as the widow of the celebrated poet Paul Laurence Dunbar with whom she had, Hull reports, a "storybook courtship" and a "tempestuous marriage." They were separated after only a few years, and Dunbar died shortly thereafter. Dunbar-Nelson made a second marriage some years later to

Robert J. Nelson (1873–1949), a journalist, and their relationship lasted for the rest of her life. Her diary also reveals two significant lesbian affairs, and "despite cryptic and hesitant allusions . . . the existence and operation of an active Black Lesbian network." Hull continues: "All of these women were prominent and professional, and most had husbands and/or children. Somehow they continued to be themselves and carry on these relationships in what must surely have been an extremely repressive context—with even more layers of oppression piled on by the stringencies of their roles as Black women."[45]

Dunbar-Nelson's diary was kept, as Hull explains, in the "ordinary way" and especially at times of personal crisis. In this regard it is unselfconscious and gives many insights into Dunbar-Nelson's life and the political and social network in which she was a central figure. While it reveals the strengths of women's bonds and Dunbar-Nelson's considerable energy and commitment, it also frames an important view of the jealousies, self-doubts, and personal intrigues that informed Dunbar-Nelson's inner world. The lesbian connections were forged in secrecy and through a labyrinth of personal and political hazard.

Gloria Hull's decision to reveal Dunbar-Nelson's lesbian relationships also reveals how often the reclamation of lesbian history involves significant struggles of conscience and political clarity by researchers. Friends, coworkers, and/or relatives have obscured, denied, and deliberately attempted to erase evidence of a deceased's lesbian connections. Nancy Manahan, in a paper presented to a panel on "Lesbian Survival Strategies, 1850–1950" at the 1981 National Women's Studies Association Convention, also illustrated this when she presented the story of Tracy Mygatt (1885–1973) and Frances Witherspoon (1886–1973). Writers, suffragists, and pacifists, Mygatt and Witherspoon fell in love with each other while both were students at Bryn Mawr College early in this century. They lived together from the time of their graduation from college in 1908 until their deaths within less than a month of each other in 1973.

Mygatt and Witherspoon led full and productive lives as political activists. They were the first organizers of the Woman's Suffrage party in eastern Pennsylvania, joined the Socialist party in 1913, were founding members of Jane Addams's Women's Peace party, and actively opposed the U.S. entrance into World War I. They were early members of the War

Resisters League and for nearly fifty years they devoted themselves to radical pacifist activities. Nancy Manahan explains:

> During the War in Vietnam Witherspoon, then in her eighties, organized a project which got over 1,000 Bryn Mawr alumnae to sign a full-page ad in the *New York Times* and in the *Philadelphia Evening Bulletin* calling for an end to the war. Mygatt and Witherspoon received the War Resisters League Peace Award in 1961 and served as honorary chairs of the organization from then until their deaths. . . . During the Civil Rights movement, Witherspoon, the daughter of former Mississippi Senator Witherspoon, wrote an open letter supporting civil rights struggles. Her letter appeared in four Mississippi newspapers and brought a torrent of abuse. "Several people told me never to show my face in Mississippi again," she said.[46]

Both women were prolific writers, producing articles, short stories, plays, and books. Sometimes they collaborated and sometimes they wrote individually.

At the memorial service held in their honor by the War Resisters League their relationship was never acknowledged, much less celebrated, as the half century and more of love that it was, and in other works in which they are discussed there is likewise no mention of Mygatt and Witherspoon's lesbian connection.[47] This kind of erasure is typical, and particularly for those of their vintage and politics. Writers, educators, suffragists, civil rights and peace activists who were lesbian couples in the United States within this century, and have not been previously mentioned in this chapter, include, for example, Katharine Anthony and Elizabeth Erwin, Jeanette Marks and Mary Woolley, Lena Madesen Phillips and Marjory Larey-Barker, Alice Morgan Wright and Edithe Goode, Mabel Vernon and Consuelo Reyes, Alma Lutz and Marguerite Smith, and Grace Hutchins and Anna Rochester.[48]

Looking at this roster, even the partial version offered here, in conjunction with the lesbian participation in organizing the International Ladies' Garment Workers' Union, the suffrage and peace movements, the Black women's clubs, and the founding of the settlement houses, one sees that this contingent was not incidental to, but a cornerstone of, women's social activism. When Adrienne Rich refers to the "blazing lesbian energy" in these movements she is not making a rhetorical gesture. The historical verification of this lesbian presence is fundamental to an understanding of the role of women in social movements. Most specifically, it is crucial to an understanding of the intrinsic connections among radical social change, women's self-determination, and lesbian existence. This connection was lived by these women in the first half of the twentieth century, and it is consciously pursued by us as the century draws to a close.

Central to this pursuit has been the work of lesbians of color in the United States. Caught between the sexism of their own racially oppressed communities and the racism within the still predominantly white women's liberation movement, it has been of prime importance to them to assemble a continuity of tradition between themselves and the women of their respective communities. In establishing this continuity, we see again that the lesbian presence is fundamental to an understanding of those communities and cultures, and the position of women, in general, within them. Paula Gunn Allen, of the Laguna and Sioux peoples, writes of "Beloved Women" in tribal life:

> It is not known if those
> who warred and hunted on the plains
> chanted and hexed in the hills
> divined and healed in the mountains
> gazed and walked beneath the stars
> were Lesbians
> It is never known
> if any woman was a Lesbian. . . . [49]

In an essay accompanying this poem, Allen establishes the lesbian connections among tribal women. Documenting the power, independence, dignity, and respect that women had in many cultures, she speaks of the time spent together, outside of the company of men; of the special words like *Kouskalaka* in the Lakota language, which designated women who chose not to marry. Allen writes: "These women were said to be daughters (the followers, the practitioners) of *wiya numpa* or Doublewoman. Doublewoman is a Spirit/Divinity who links two women together making them one in Her power."[50]

Allen defines the lesbian connections within the concepts of tribal culture in which balance, wholeness, interconnection, and spiritual life are crucial, and she suggests that these connections were not only widespread but central to the formation of a cultural identity that was founded on sisterhood as the prototypical community:

> Because traditional American Indian women spent the preponder-
> ance of their time with women, and because attitudes toward sex
> were very different from modern Western views, it is likely, in my
> opinion, that Lesbianism was an integral part of American Indian
> life. . . . Lesbianism must be viewed in the context of the spiritual
> orientation of tribal life.
>   The prototypical relationship in this sphere was that of sister to
> sister. [Leslie Marmon] Silko makes this apparent in her account of
> Indian myth: Is'ts'tsi'n, Thought Woman, thought of her sisters, and
> together they created the universe, this world and the four worlds
> below. This concept posits that the original household, the proto-
> community was founded on sisterhood. It was based on the power of
> Creative Thought, and it was that Thought—of three sisters united—
> which gave rise to all creation.[51]

Similarly, Audre Lorde writes of the lesbian connections in some African cultures. In her essay first published in the *Black Scholar* designed to dispel sexist and homophobic currents in the Black community, and subtitled "Notes on Barriers to Women and Loving," Lorde summoned authority from an African tradition in which "women have always bonded together in support of each other, however uneasily and in the face of whatever other allegiances which militated against the bonding." She continued:

> On the West Coast of Africa the Fon of Dahomey still have twelve
> different kinds of marriage. One of them is known as: "giving the
> goat to the buck," where a woman of independent means marries
> another woman who then may or may not bear children, all of whom
> belong to the bloodline of the first woman. Some marriages of this
> kind are arranged to provide heirs for women of means who wish to
> remain "free," and some are lesbian relationships. Marriages like
> these occur throughout Africa, in several different places among
> different peoples. Routinely the women involved are accepted mem-
> bers of their communities, evaluated not by their sexuality but by
> their respective places within the community.[52]

From an ethnography, cited by Lorde, we find the oral history of a
ninety-two-year-old African woman of the Ibibio people of southwestern
Nigeria. This story is contained within it:

> I had a woman friend to whom I revealed my secrets. She was very
> fond of keeping secrets herself. We acted as husband and wife. We
> always moved hand in glove and my husband and hers knew about
> our relationship. The villagers nicknamed us twin sisters. When I ran
> low of funds she would be the only person to render help. When I am
> out of gear with my husband, she would be the person to restore
> peace. I remember one day when I was beaten by my husband out of
> the house, I ran to take shelter in her place, and she gave me a dress
> and food to eat. I often sent my children to go and work and in return
> for her kindness to me.[53]

Likewise, recovery of the writings of Agnes Smedley, and the reissue
of a collection of her work, *Portraits of Chinese Women in Revolution,* led
to the rediscovery of the sisterhoods among silkworkers in Canton in the
early part of this century. The sisterhoods, economically viable because of
the women's employment in the silk industry, were formed for the express
purpose of resisting marriage. The sisterhoods also led to successful actions by the workers for shorter hours, higher pay, and better working
conditions. Smedley's young male escort had nothing but contempt for
these women, she reported, "because they were notorious throughout
China as Lesbians." But, Smedley affirmed, what marked them off for her
was their independence and joy in a country where bound feet, the toes
literally crushed under the ball of the foot, forced marriages, and female
infanticide shaped the lives of millions. It was this independence which the
escort found intolerable, and which Smedley found utterly thrilling:

> The hatred of my escort of these girls became more marked when we
> visited the filatures. Long lines of them clad in glossy black jackets
> and trousers, sat before boiling vats of cocoons, their parboiled
> fingers twinkling among the spinning filaments. Sometimes a remark
> passed along their lines set a whole mill laughing. The face of my
> escort grew livid. . . .
>   One evening the two of us sat at the entrance of an old family
> temple. . . . On the other side of the canal rose the high walls of the
> filature, which soon began pouring forth black clad girl workers,

each with her dinner pail. All wore wooden sandals. . . . Their glossy
black hair was combed back and hung in a heavy braid to the waist.
At the nape of the neck the braid was caught in red yarn, making a
band two or three inches wide—a lovely sash of color.

As they streamed along in long lines over the bridge arching the
canal and past the temple entrance, I felt I had never seen more
handsome women.[54]

It is not known, of course, how many of these women may, in fact,
have been lesbians. That some were is certain. The sisterhoods, however,
which existed also in Shanghai and in Kwangtung in the 1920s and 1930s,
were striking because they demonstrated female independence and female-centered bonds in much the same ways that Blanche Cook described
the liaisons of the Settlement House women in America. The women in
China used the sisterhoods as a way of re-creating the cultural pattern of
filial devotion divested of its patriarchal content, the sisterhoods replacing
their families of birth.[55]

For many women of color, the struggle to claim a lesbian identity
without abandoning a racial one has led to a re-visioning of the women in
their cultures of origin. Born into a racist society that shuns and ridicules
nonwhite cultures and exerts enormous pressures toward assimilation (of
values and beliefs, at least, even when color prevents "passing"), their
poems, essays, and stories form a litany of race pride, self-affirmation, and
healing. The struggle to sustain this lesbian identity, informed by a race
consciousness which is women-centered, women-loving becomes the gate-
way to a fuller recognition of the cultural values and complex labors of the
women in their families and communities.

This dynamic informs Cherríe Moraga's *Loving in the War Years*, an
autobiographical collection of poetry and prose rooted in her Chicana
heritage. Attending a concert in which the Afro-American poet and choreographer Ntozake Shange read from her works, Moraga recognized a part
of herself which she had long denied: "I have acclimated to the sound of
white language," she wrote in her journal after the event, "which . . . did
not speak to the emotions in my poems—emotions which stem from the
love of my mother." Moraga continued:

Sitting in that auditorium chair was the first time I had realized to the
core of me that for years I had disowned that language I knew best—
ignored the words and rhythms that were the closest to me. The

sounds of my mothers and aunts gossiping—half in English, half in Spanish—while drinking cerveza in the kitchen. And the hands—I had cut off the hands in my poems. But not in conversation; still the hands could not be kept down. Still they insisted on moving. The reading had forced me to remember that I knew things from my roots.[56]

Writing with new voice and purpose, Moraga's poem "For the Color of My Mother" repeated the refrain "I am a white girl gone brown to the blood color of my mother speaking for her . . ." and concluded with this impassioned sense of collectivity in the breaking of silence:

dark women come to me
                    sitting in circles
I pass thru their hands
the head of my mother
painted in clay colors

    Touching each carved feature swollen eyes and mouth

they understand the explosion, the splitting
open   contained   within the fixed expression
they cradle her silence
                    nodding to me[57]

"A woman lies buried under me," wrote Gloria Anzaldúa, in a poem that speaks directly to this process of reclamation:

interred for centuries, presumed dead
A woman lies buried under me
I hear her soft whisper
the rasp of the parchment skin
fighting the folds of her shroud.
Her eyes are pierced by needles
her eyelids two fluttering moths.[58]

Merle Woo wrote a letter to her mother, stating her pride in being a Chinese-Korean-American woman: "We have such a proud heritage, such a courageous tradition." It is a tradition Woo sees rooted in the heritage of her mother's daily life:

When I look at you there are images: images of you as a ten-year-old Korean girl, being sent alone from Shanghai to the United States . . .

then growing up in a "Home" run by white missionary women. Scrubbing floors on your hands and knees, hauling coal in heavy metal buckets up three flights of stairs, tending to the young children, putting hot bricks on your cheeks to deaden the pain from the terrible toothaches you always had. Working all your life as a maid, waitress, sales-clerk, office worker, mother. But throughout there is an image of you as strong and courageous and persevering. . . . [59]

Kitty Tsui wrote of her grandmother, "Kwan Ying Lin: Kwan Yuen Sheung," who was an actress and traveled widely:

you were renowned for your acting
your beauty and the power of your voice.
my grandmother, you have endured
eighty years of work and struggle
taking the songs and legends of china
to your people in the chinatowns of vancouver,
seattle, san francisco, l.a.,
new york, chicago, hawaii; to vietnam,
hong kong, macao; to shanghai
and provinces in southern china
my *poa poa,* i burn incense and make offerings.
i write this poem for all to know
your life
your work.[60]

Lesbians of color have been among those feminists who have most consistently pursued the deepest analysis of the interconnections between class exploitation, racial oppression, and homophobia, and have demonstrated the greatest need for solidarity among peoples of differing cultures within the women's movement. Insisting upon an integrated analysis and politics that recognizes that the major systems of oppression are interlocking, Barbara Smith observed that "the concept of simultaneity of oppression is . . . the crux of a Black feminist understanding of political reality and, I believe, one of the most significant ideological contributions of Black feminist thought."[61] Lesbian feminists of color have been the decisive element "moving the mountain" of consciousness in the women's movement as a whole, as well as within their respective communities. Theirs is a virtue born of necessity. There has been no other ground on which to stand. Further, an understanding of this "simultaneity of oppression" encourages coalition; that is, it encourages the formation of political alliances between groups sharing the consequences of these interlocking oppressions, however diverse their respective experiences and cultures.

It is no coincidence then that some of the most significant dialogue between Black and Jewish women at least since the 1940s has taken place among lesbian feminists. In setting the guidelines for this dialogue, the women affirm difference as a condition for unity. The dialogue has addressed both racism in the Jewish community and anti-Semitism in the Black community. It has explored the sensitive issues of Jewish/white privilege in a racist society, and Black/gentile assumptions in a Christian one. And it has addressed major differences in our respective histories: for Black people, the overwhelming majority brought here in chains from Africa and enduring slavery's horrors; for Jews, America as sanctuary from the pogroms of Eastern Europe and, later, the Hitler terror. "Between a Rock and a Hard Place," one group of women called their exchange. They carved a common ground in the sheer determination to forge a coalition that is, by definition, fraught with discomfort, believing, however, that coalitions such as these are crucial to the survival of the women's movement. They have certainly been crucial in allowing many Jewish women, myself included, to claim their identity.

In this dialogue, Jewish contributor Elly Bulkin wrote of the debt Jewish feminists owe to "women of color, especially lesbians, [who] have been in the forefront of creating a theory and practice that insist on the importance of difference among women and on the positive aspects of cultures and identities."[62] Bulkin writes of an "identity politics" that allowed her and many others to embrace their Jewishness and confront anti-Semitism as a crucial component of their feminist consciousness. Bulkin's essay spoke very personally to many of my own experiences. Embracing my Jewish heritage, with all of its contradictions, has been part of a general process of naming myself and claiming all aspects of my identity. Likewise, and to the point of this discussion of identity and dialogue, it was this process of reclamation and naming that opened the door to a much deeper understanding of the dynamics of my own racism and to a way to fend consciously against it.

In reading Evelyn Torton Beck's lesbian anthology, *Nice Jewish Girls*, in the summer of 1982 I was catapulted into a maze of strong emotion and a recognition of so many of the patterns and experiences I shared with the contributors. In her introduction, Beck had written a line that brought me right to attention. Actually it was a footnote. It said: "One wonders how anyone can wholeheartedly fight the oppression of another group when, in order to do so, she finds it necessary to denigrate and deny her own oppression."[63] In reading this I recognized much about myself.

In particular, I saw how often I had projected my ambivalence about being a Jew onto Black people. What I mean is this: in the years immediately after the Holocaust in Communist and secular Jewish circles still reeling from it, my family's Jewish identity was problematic. In the confusing, emotionally charged swirl of debates around me as a child, I absorbed these impressions. First, Jews were partially responsible for anti-Semitism because of their behavior, customs, and religious dogma. Second, Jews collaborated in their own annihilation, the more class privileged among them turning their less fortunate kin into the Nazis. Third, Jews were too divided, weak, and inept to effectively mount any significant resistance to the Nazis, with the shining exception of the Warsaw ghetto uprising. What resistance there was among the Jews was organized by Communists, and not because they were Jews but because they were Communists. I don't represent this as the actuality or totality of what was said, only that it was what I garnered, remembered, and internalized.

In contrast to this sordid, bleak, and despairing picture of the Jews, I learned about the history of Black people in resistance to slavery, lynchings, segregation, and racism. My father's writing and lectures and the company of scholars who frequented our home—men like W. E. B. Du Bois, Alphaeous Hunton, and William L. Patterson—recounted a history of relentless and inspiring struggle. I do not deny the history. But, of course, I knew Black culture only as an outsider and I experienced this resistance only in vicarious relief. It was emotionally satisfying, perhaps then, as a child even emotionally necessary, that I assign to Black people a purity, martyrdom, virtue, and self-sacrifice so wanting in my own people. I could not be Black but I could place a subordinated self at the service of this splendid and heroic race, and in this way atone for the catastrophic failures of the Jews.

My projection romanticized the Black experience, erasing the contradictions and nuance, the dailiness of equivocation and uncertainty, the violence, betrayals, and pain. I did these things even as I studied Afro-American history and literature, but erased (for myself) those parts that contradicted my illusions. Only as I assumed responsibility for my own identity as a Jew could I begin to limit if not abandon my projections. For the first time, focused outward on Afro-American people, I *felt* the suffering and the racism with a crushing force. I do not mean by this that I understood the experiences of women of color; I mean only that I had finally opened to them. With this opening I became less patronizing and paternalistic—the form in which I think my racism has most persistently expressed itself: I'll explain you (Black people) to them (white people); I'll "fix" your mistake (so no one will notice there was one); I know what to say better than you do, and so on.

This patronization was a function of my own need to continually prop up my fantasy system to make Black people into something they were not in order to serve my own needs, not theirs. In coming to grips with my internalized anti-Semitism I came to grips with at least one manifestation of my own racism. The content of this kind of internalized oppression takes many different forms, but I believe its processes operate within many individuals of diverse racial and ethnic groups, forming a centerpiece in the criss-cross pattern of racial antagonisms in the United States.

To work through this internalized anti-Semitism I began studying some of the literature, history, and culture of Jewish people. I joined organizations like New Jewish Agenda which combine a sense of Jewish identity with struggles on social issues of concern to me. I began attending synagogue services and participated in Torah study, learning something of our ceremonies and rituals, and of a biblical tradition of which I had been wholly ignorant. I grappled with the paradox of believing passionately in Israel, while abhorring the domestic and foreign policies of her right-wing governments. An essay on Lebanon, written just after the invasion of that country by Israeli troops in 1982, by the Jewish–Puerto Rican writer Aurora Morales came closest to expressing my own rage and grief.[64] I have endeavored to share all of these experiences with my students, while also acquainting them with the history of anti-Semitism (some of whom had never heard of it!) and our resistance to it.

"I need the stories of our resistance," wrote Melanie Kaye in *Nice Jewish Girls*, "laced through the horror as an amulet, inspiration and warning." She told stories of the Jewish women in the anti-Nazi resistance: in Auschwitz, in Ravensbruck (where I had stood stricken and silent when I was fifteen), in the Warsaw ghetto uprising. "Those were Jewish women," she wrote. "I come from Jewish women who fought like that."[65] For me it was the lesbian connection in a feminist context that made this understanding possible.

A NEW GENERATION of lesbians, many of whom were veterans of the civil rights and antiwar movements of the 1960s, "came out" in the 1970s. They were steeped in a healthy sense of feminist politics. Many had a sophistication in movement politics. They weren't about to be closeted or silenced. They broke with the more conservative appeals for public tolerance by their elder counterparts while honoring their persevering efforts that had salvaged the links to a lesbian heritage. Public acknowledgment of a lesbian identity brought expressions of homophobia, which is always a powerful societal undercurrent, to the surface. Defending against this homophobia in a post-1960s context, however, lesbians created a new sense of community. Indeed, what began as a defense became an affirmation and began to shape a radical understanding of both lesbian identity and what it meant to have a women-centered perspective.

As activists, lesbians joined women's organizations, including many mainstream ones like the National Organization for Women (NOW). Despite their enthusiasm, they were not always welcomed. "Dyke" was the worst epithet that many could imagine hurling at feminist proponents. A great many women shuddered at the charge, vigorously denying it. Not a few sought to purge their ranks of this influence in an atmosphere reminiscent of the Communist purges of the 1950s. It was a decade into the women's movement and after many convention floor fights before lesbian rights were firmly and broadly affirmed. Lesbian feminists responded to this homophobia in the movement and in the larger society in a variety of ways, and some of them were, I think, very funny and highly imaginative.

Appropriating the language of insult, some lesbians claimed the words and the images and infused them with new meaning. This strategy was nowhere more clearly exemplified than in the title of the perennial photographic journal called *The Blatant Image*.[66] When editors Harriet Desmoines and Catherine Nicholson of the journal *Sinister Wisdom* decided to publish on the front cover Tee Corinne's photograph of two women making love, they were sure they would be arrested on some charge of indecent exposure. They weren't. Instead, the cover was in such demand that it was made into a fund-raising poster for the journal.[67]

Groups sprang up in various parts of the country with names like: Drastik Dykes; the Lincoln Legion of Lesbians; DYKETACTICS; Amazing Amazons; Dyke Dianic Wicca Newsletter for Biophilic Hags of Magick.

In a more scholarly vein, Judy Grahn traced the probable origin of the word "dyke" in the English language to Boudica, the warrior queen of the Celtic tribes who led a fierce uprising against the Roman conquest of the British Isles in 61 C.E.[68] Mary Daly gave us the origin of the words "hag" and "haggard," among many others: "hag" meaning harpy or witch, and "haggard" meaning originally "an intractable person, especially: a woman reluctant to wooing."[69] Joyce Trebilcot, in her "Notes on the Logic of Feminism," proposed precisely the reclamation of words like dykes, bitches, and hags: "We describe ourselves in these terms with pride and pleasure. We break out of a secondary status. . . . by flipping their evaluations over, by gladly acknowledging that we are what they condemn."[70]

French feminists Monique Wittig and Sandy Zeig wrote *Lesbian Peoples: Materials for a Dictionary*, blending mythic and utopian visions into a witty discourse on the contemporary realities of our Concrete Age (as in Bronze Age, Iron Age, Steam Age, and the yet-to-come Glorious Age). Among their definitive visions were:

> HAVE: "To have," in its meaning "to possess," was formerly a key word both practically and philosophically. The companion lovers decided that they would not use this word anymore, except as an auxiliary which would permit speaking about the past.

> IDLENESS: A pleasant state of leisure practiced in excess and systematically by nearly all lesbian peoples.

> LIGHT: . . . during their most pleasant and shining moments, two companion lovers unite through rays, sparks, beating glows, strokes of lightning, mists of more or less intense light.

> WOMAN: Obsolete since the beginnings of the Glorious Age. . . . This word once applied to beings fallen into an absolute state of servitude. Its meaning was "one who belongs to another."[71]

What had begun as a fanciful act of defiance, a play on words, became more and more an invention of words, a making of new systems of meaning, the self-conscious pursuit of "the dream of a common language," as Adrienne Rich titled a volume of poetry, with which to adequately describe lesbian experience:

> . . . *I am the lover and the loved,*
> *home and wanderer, she who splits*
> *firewood and she who knocks, a stranger*
> *in the storm,* two women, eye to eye
> measuring each other's spirit, each other's
> limitless desire,
>   a whole new poetry beginning here.[72]

Until modern times few women-loving women could ever hope to have the economic means or societal grace to live together, but some might, as Lillian Faderman observed, hope to die together:

> Women who were romantic friends were everything to each other. They thought of each other constantly. They made each other deliriously happy or horribly miserable by the increase or abatement of their proffered love. . . . They vowed that if it were at all possible they would someday live together, or at least die together, and they declared that both eventualities would be their greatest happiness.[73]

A contemporary poet writes a lesbian self-portrait. The last verse of her poem records this image:

> Today the cold bites through the sunshine
> and the wind stiffens what it blows against.
> This morning I work at my desk
> and she across the hall at hers
> like children coloring, like nuns praying
> like white-haired women knowing
> that though we may die alone
> we will live together
> the hair falling down the sides of our faces
> as we bend over our work.[74]

Progress is measured in words such as these, in the contrast of meanings between one century and another.

Lesbian and lesbian-feminist journals, newsletters, and newspapers have proliferated, and publications like *The Lesbian Tide, Azalea, Feminary, Sinister Wisdom, Quest, Conditions, Chrysalis, Common Lives/Les-*

bian Lives (among many others) have portrayed the lesbian experience in stories, plays, testimonies, and poems, self-portraits, graphics, and photographs. Taken as a whole these record an enduring struggle for wholeness, humanity, justice, and identity. Many different women are represented in these pages including those who are of the middle and working classes, women of color, disabled women, and elders. Each is given voice consciously, each takes it purposefully to contribute a piece toward the whole.

Adopting a lesbian-feminist motif as their philosophical core some of these writers have explored universal themes of identity (racial, religious, class, and sexual), of healing and death, of persecution and politics. The temper of these writings reflects a significant shift in the assertion of lesbian identity. In contrast to earlier genres of "inversion," pathos, and pulp, these women, most of them grown to maturity in the sixties, are mapping the details of racism and colonialism, of working-class experience and Jew hating, of homophobia and women lovingness, of butch-femme relationships in the 1950s, in a cartography of everyday life. Many of their stories retain the unpretentious freshness and clarity of childhood memory; many blend precisely the analysis of the "simultaneity of oppression." These writings exemplify the use of storytelling as documentary, creating a record as diverse as it is layered, and rooted in a shared determination to never again permit the erasure of lesbian existence.

Some lesbian-feminist novels and plays have also displayed a less sober and more frolicking temperament, using fantasy—as in the fantastic—to ignite a specifically lesbian imagination. June Arnold's *Sister Gin* (New York: Daughters, 1975) envisioned a rip-roaring ensemble of lesbian elders, one of whose more memorable accomplishments was the capture of a rapist whom they left naked and securely bound in the center of town. Sheila Ortiz Taylor's *Faultline* (Tallahassee, Fla.: Naiad Press, 1982) heralded three hundred rapidly multiplying rabbits in a lesbian household with six kids and their beloved child-care worker, Wilson Topaz, who was Black, gay, and six foot three in his stocking feet. Rita Mae Brown's *Rubyfruit Jungle* (New York: Daughters, 1973; Bantam, 1977) recounted the growing-up story of the endearing, rambunctious, thoroughly daring dyke from the wrong side of the tracks named Molly Bolt. Terry Baum and Carolyn Myers wrote "Dos Lesbos: A Play By, For, and About Perverts," which opened at Ollie's Bar in Oakland, California, in 1981, and contains one of the funniest "coming out" to parents fantasies I have ever read. Here's part of it:

(The scene opens with Peg cleaning up the kitchen and Gracie loung-
ing in an armchair, deep in thought)

GRACIE: Maybe I should write my parents and tell them I'm a
lesbian.
PEG: That's a good idea.
GRACIE: Maybe I shouldn't write my parents and tell them I'm a
lesbian.
PEG: That's a better idea.
GRACIE: What do you think I should do?
PEG: I think it's up to you.

GRACIE: (Sitting down at the typewriter) Now, how does this
sound? Dear M and D . . .
PEG: M & D? It sounds like a tampon.
GRACIE: I really call them Mommy and Daddy. But I'm too old to
say Mommy and Daddy anymore. So to get around it, I say M
and D.
PEG: Get back to the letter.
GRACIE: Dear M and D, I have some good news and some bad
news. (Types). The good news is . . . I have finally found the
person I want to spend the rest of my life with (Types). The bad
news is . . . (Pause) she's not Jewish!⁷⁵

Reading *Lesbian Etiquette,* with humorous essays by Gail Sausser
and cartoons by Alice Muhlback (Trumansburg, N.Y.: The Crossing
Press, 1986) is a déjà vu experience for many a lesbian. Some of the brief
vignettes in this delightful book include: "Classified Ads Can Lead to the
Real Thing"; "Lesbian Potlucks through History," with an accompanying
cartoon captioned, "Tofushu: The Goddess of Lesbian Potlucks" (at least
on the West Coast, I thought); "Personality by Pet"; "Gays Need Better
P.R."; and "De-Dyking the Apartment" (for parental visits, of course). But
not all is spoof: "The strictest code we live by," write the authors on page
one, "is not to expose anyone else's sexual identity to the straight world."
Other lesbian writers who were not connected to the movement of
the sixties, and many of them published for the first time, have also shared
their stories. *Common Lives/Lesbian Lives,* a journal published out of
Iowa City, Iowa, has particularly given voice to these women. The stories

are not always edited for spelling or grammar, the level of literacy itself an essential piece of evidence, a statement of condition. Pieces are erotic and tender, the sexual energy palpable and delicious. Some stories are funny, often hysterically so. Some are raging: testimonies of rape, incest, battery, rejection, alcoholism, harassment, concealment. The writers happen to be lesbians, but the experiences are shared by a wide range of women. Some stories lack coherence and are a narrative strung together, hanging in disconnection. And some cannot be described. They must simply be read as moments attesting to the poignant beauty of the human spirit.

Lesbian separatism as an organized political movement also emerged in this period of activism and affirmation. Perhaps its most public beginning was with the formation of a group called the Furies, in Washington, D.C., in 1971. The origin of this separatist politics was located in the homophobia lesbians experienced working within the women's movement, even within its most radical sections. As many lesbians acknowledged their identity in women's organizations, they found themselves engaged in a continual and painful defense of their right to love women. Charlotte Bunch, one of the founders of the Furies, explained her decision to leave the women's movement in the early 1970s and form a separate lesbian-feminist alliance:

> When we began to proclaim our love for one another in ways that went beyond the boundaries of "familial love," most of us did not realize how savagely we would be disinherited by our "sisters." . . .
>
> Separation was the only way we saw to create lesbian-feminist politics and build a community of our own in the hostile environment of the early seventies.[76]

Bunch continued her discussion of her decision, emphasizing the crucial point that the separatist strategy allowed lesbians "to build our own pride, strength, and unity as a people, to develop an analysis of our particular oppression, and to create a political ideology and strategy that would both force the movement's recognition of us and lead to the end of male supremacy."[77]

From this separation, a lesbian-feminist politics was defined. At the center of this woman-loving politics was an indictment of heterosexuality itself, as it was institutionalized, as an instrument of male domination. Bunch expressed the point this way: "The heart of . . . all lesbian-feminist politics is the recognition that, *in a male supremacist society* [emphasis added], heterosexuality goes hand in hand with the sexist assumption that each woman exists for a man—her body, her children, and her services are his property."[78]

Although some nonlesbian women interpreted this politic as an attack on their personal choice, the analysis contributed to a much deeper understanding of women's oppression. Adrienne Rich, whose renown as a poet gave her access to publishers and a large reading public, played an important role in developing these ideas and in bringing them to a wide audience. Both in her essay on "compulsory heterosexuality" and in her critique of motherhood "as institution and experience," the institutionalization of women's subordination to men was explored in historical and experiential detail.

While separatist politics provided the intellectual space in which to articulate a more profound understanding of the lesbian connection to women's liberation, it also led to the burgeoning of physical space for women-only gatherings. In this sense separatism as a political strategy meaning separate from men was established. Women who created separate space for themselves and their loved ones in which to live—often on the land in rural areas—described its beauty and peace and the absence of strife in daily life. What was not often discussed as openly, however, were the personal difficulties and political tensions that arose between women. Bookstores, coffee houses, resorts, music festivals, and spiritual retreats nurtured thousands of women regardless of their sexual preference. Again, however, these women-only spaces served to reveal the strength of women's differences, especially those of race and class. What became clear was that one might physically separate from men, but that the process of changing internalized beliefs rooted in the social order was much more difficult. The separatist impulse also sustained publications like *Sinister Wisdom, Conditions,* and *Common Lives* in which a collective, woman-loving self-portraiture could be framed. Nevertheless, and despite these obvious benefits, many in the women's movement, including lesbians, reacted with hostility to separatist strategies when they perceived them as a form of "reverse sexism" in which all men were categorically condemned as a group. And, in racially oppressed communities, many argued that lesbian separatism was inherently racist because it separated women from men in an already embattled people.

Still, the separatist strategy employed by lesbian feminists has paralleled strategies traditionally used by many other oppressed groups. Racially and colonially oppressed peoples have a long history of using these strategies, and for precisely the same reasons. The need for pride and dignity, the need for the development of a collective self-identity freed from the constraints and prescriptions of the normative, white culture, the need for analysis unfettered by the boundaries of the white world, and the need to direct energy positively into the community rather than out, against the oppressor, have informed all such movements.

Lesbian feminists who have participated in developing what could be categorized as separatist analysis have by no means all agreed to identify themselves as "separatists," nor do they define their politics as "separatism." For example, Adrienne Rich's ideas are very complex and layered, and her writings hold tension and ambiguity. Rich does not see herself as a separatist and has repeatedly contested the grounds of such a politic.

As a lesbian-separatist politics persisted past the moments of tactical invention, a debate emerged in the lesbian community in the 1980s over the viability of separatism as a continuing political strategy. The practical, daily realities of many women's lives and issues of how to change those realities have informed this opposition to separatism as a long-term political strategy. For example, women are the mothers of sons, the daughters of fathers, and sisters to brothers. Women have male friends, coworkers, and colleagues. The insistence on a kind of "pure" separatism resulted in many confrontations and hurt feelings as women were forced to leave lesbian households because of these associations. Further, many have argued that the compelling perils of war, colonial intervention, and racial strife require oppositional coalitions with men. And the unfathomable loss of thousands who have died in the AIDS epidemic—many of them gay men—forced many to rethink the viability of separatism as a politic.

Nevertheless, lesbian activist Sarah Lucia Hoagland, in an essay exploring the importance of separatism as a continuing empowering reality, argued that such a strategy remains essential precisely because of its focus on women and because of the ways in which that focus shapes our understanding of the world and of our political engagements:

> the most important aspect of separatism for me [is] its focus on lesbians (or wimmin) and a creation of lesbian meaning, lesbian reality. Perceiving is a process of creation. As we choose what we will pay attention to we determine what is significant and what is not. I am not interested in focusing on men, whether exceptional or nor-

mal. . . . By focusing on ourselves and pursuing what we find valuable, we create lesbian meaning.[79]

The formation of a lesbian (and gay) identity, divested of Freudian origin, is in process. Feminist analysis has provided significant tools for its construction. This fortuitous combination promises a re-visioning of ourselves as women, regardless of sexual identification. This re-visioning has already begun. In relationship to and with each other, women have begun, cautiously, tentatively, and with many contradictions, to change the balance of power relative to men in each other's everyday lives: employing, evaluating, provisioning, nurturing, supporting, networking, reconnoitering, protecting each other. The crucial elements in a lesbian-feminist view propose that this kind of priority be given to women every day in small, consistent, practical, loving ways. We are still learning how to act in these ways; how to cross racial, ethnic, religious, and class boundaries; how to overcome contradiction and avoid co-optation. Through this learning we redefine both ourselves and our understanding of the world.

The elements of this lesbian-feminist view are at the heart of Adrienne Rich's essay "Women and Honor," in which she re-visions honor to mean not chastity and faithfulness to a man, but the absence of lying among women.[80] They are at the heart of Judy Grahn's poem "A Woman is Talking to Death," when her interrogator asks: "Have you ever committed indecent acts with women?" and Grahn reinterprets the meaning of indecent, not as a sexual act, and says: "I am guilty of not loving her who needed me. . . ."[81] They are at the heart of Sarah Lucia Hoagland's essay on "vulnerability and power," in which she confronts us with the fact that to be vulnerable means, literally, to be wounded. Vulnerability as a tool of connection does not lead to intimacy but to wounding; she redefines intimacy to mean strength and wholeness rather than pain and dependence.[82] These elements are at the heart of Audre Lorde's *Cancer Journals* written in the aftermath of a radical mastectomy. Lorde sees mortality as both weapon and power: "I am talking here about the need for every woman to live a considered life."[83]

The lesbian connection in its feminist dimensions is an invitation into a female-centered world, a standpoint from which to take up women's experience and with it weave a different cloth. That is, rather than always seeing women in relationship to men, as adjuncts to the political, cultural, and social movements organized and led by men, it is possible to treat women as independent human beings who have formed, and in turn, been informed by all social relations. We see women as they have acted, individually, in concert with each other, and with men, to change those relations and the social conditions of their lives. The lesbian connection is a philosophical standpoint; it is a way of seeing. It is a way of imagining ourselves as women divested of our colonized and servile status, in imagination and in life.

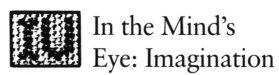 In the Mind's
Eye: Imagination
as Survival

We do not want
to rock the boat,
you say, mistaking
our new poise
for something safe.

We smile secretly
at each other,
sharing the reality
that for some time
we have not been
in the boat . . .
—Alla Renée Bozarth, "Water Women"

When my father was gone, Mama would sit down with us and tell stories. She had a special way of talking, her own wisdom. We never knew this about our mama when father was there. "Children," she'd say, "you see this apple? This apple is the same one from which Eve gave to Adam a bite to eat." "Mama," we'd shout, "how can you say this? You know how long ago this was? You think this really happened?" "Don't tell me," she'd answer. "Just listen. In every weed is growing the garden of Eden. You only should have the eyes to look."
—Kim Chernin, "The Second Story My Mother Tells (1914–1920)"

A sight, an emotion, creates this wave in the mind, long before it makes words to fit it; and in writing . . . one has to recapture this, and set this working (which has nothing apparently to do with words) and then, as it breaks and tumbles in the mind, it makes words to fit it. . . .
—Virginia Woolf, Letter to Vita Sackville-West, March 16, 1926

The key is in remembering, in what is chosen for the dream.
In the silence of recovery we hold
the rituals of the dawn
now as then.
—Paula Gunn Allen, "The Trick is Consciousness"

OOKING back. I was skinny and boney with braids and crooked arms. I wore jeans and T-shirts and played baseball with the boys in the empty lot in front of the apartment building where we lived on Washington Avenue. The lot was adjacent to the subway tracks for the Franklin Avenue shuttle train which shattered even the Brooklyn noise every few minutes, and especially during rush hour. I retrieved our baseball when it went onto the tracks, gingerly picking my way over the live electrified third rail, the unspoken condition by which the boys allowed me the privilege of joining in their sport.

I had a favorite aunt who took me to the circus every year—Ringling Brothers and Barnum & Bailey, at the old Madison Square Garden before it was renovated in the 1960s. One year we went and there was a man standing alone at the main gate with a picket sign announcing a strike. Thousands rushed past him to cross a picket line. I hesitated. My aunt took my hand reassuringly. "Come on," she said cheerfully. "It's only one. Let's go and have a good time." We went in, but still I worried about it. When I got home I told my mother about the man with the picket sign. I said I thought maybe we shouldn't have gone in after all. "Yes," she said patiently, and not really angry with me. "It's wrong to cross any picket line, even when there is only one person on it." That's when I first remember thinking that something called a principle was not a number.

I was a malleable child, obedient and quiet, especially in the presence of adults. I tried very hard to be a good girl, to please my parents, to do exactly as they wished. I grew up in the 1950s. My parents were Communists; my father was prominently identified. He was even on television— when he was subpoenaed to testify before the Senate committee headed by Joseph McCarthy. I was taught never to say any names or anything important on the telephone because it was tapped by the FBI. Many of my parents' friends were in jail or had lost their jobs. And I knew that the parents of my best friend were afraid to let me play at their house after school. My mother worked and supported the family. My father worked but made very little income. He lectured widely and wrote books. Everyone worked very hard. My work was to be good. However, I believed that I failed in my job to be good because of the fantasies that played in my head. I was ashamed of them, and kept them hidden. I was ashamed because I thought there was something wrong with me to wander off in this way into whole other worlds. And I was ashamed because I imagined myself as characters wholly out of keeping with the goodness, propriety, and perfection of the projected image I thought my parents expected of my child self. Also, I thought I was the only child in the world to have them.

My characters emerged from walls and closets, from stuffed animals and dolls, from windows, potted plants, trees, animals, birds. . . . The dolls were especially evocative because mine were no ordinary, run-of-the-mill bride dolls of the fifties. Mine were replicas of people from other cultures swathed in blazing colors, brought to me by my mother as presents upon her return from the various tours she led as a travel agent. As my collection grew more elaborate, visitors to our home, often dignitaries from various socialist countries, added to my collection. In my fantasy life I was most attracted to the male replicas adorned in capes and sashes, with dashing feathered hats and swords (or what I imagined to be swords if they weren't).

Interwoven with plots extrapolated from "The Lone Ranger" and "Rin Tin Tin," the programs I habitually watched on our television set, and the Nancy Drew and Hardy Boys mysteries I read, I became the avenging hero thwarting bandits, rescuing women and children, and otherwise displaying awesome powers. My fantasies were enacted alone, in elaborate detail. As I grew older they continued, with more complex characters and plots, complete with costume and makeup when I could manage it. I smoked my first cigarettes at thirteen to effect a more satisfying character in one of my fantasies, and I took to drinking small quantities of alcohol for the same reason a year or two later. By the time I entered university I had a substantial repertoire of characters including an ace baseball pitcher, a concert pianist, a brilliant intellectual who frequented outdoor cafés, a revolutionary guerrilla leader, and a Humphrey Bogart–type character, among many others. At times, especially when I participated in the leadership of various political movements, I enacted my roles in life. The real and the fantastic coexisted in a challenging harmony as distinct but simultaneous streams of consciousness, the one public and projected, the other private and intensely amusing yet dangerous to their audience of one.

Unbeknownst to him, my husband married this entire company, and they lived with us as my essential companions for the duration of our marriage. There were many days when I waited with passionate anxiety for the house to empty so that I could engage one of my characters. These ritual enactments required substantial physical exertion as I charged through rooms, thrashed pillows, or mimed a personage from my imaginary entourage. These actions flooded me with enormous psychological relief, after which I could go on with my day which often involved intense intellectual, administrative, political, and emotional work, sometimes extending late into the night. The need for playing out my fantasies ended when I was divorced.

About a year into my relationship with Kate, I confessed my bizarre mental life to her. She listened with that acute attention so particular to her. She laughed a few times, asked a couple of questions of detail, and then hugged me with one of those wonderful, all-encompassing bear hugs reserved for special occasions. "You had all of that repressed anger," she said to me, "all of those contradictions in your life, all the roles you were playing and had always played which had nothing to do with the interior reality of who you were, or wanted to be." I nodded, dimly recalling what felt now like the fleeting memory of a past life I could hardly imagine having lived. "It makes perfect sense," she concluded. "I don't know where you got it from, or how you thought of it, but you invented a form of *gestalt* therapy for yourself, to preserve your sanity." I had heard the term *gestalt,* but had never really understood what it meant, so Kate explained the elements of therapeutic role-playing to me. I was, she announced, psychologically sound, even sturdy. This was a new idea to me because as far back as I could remember I had always thought of myself as essentially peculiar. I could see for the first time that this feeling of peculiarity had come from the disjuncture between my exterior roles and internal being, and also between my lived and fantasy worlds. I felt greatly relieved, amazed, and more than a little clever.

One evening a few weeks later, while Kate and my daughter, Jenny, were finishing up the dinner dishes, I crept out of the kitchen and into the bedroom. I donned my Bogart-type costume and, furnished with a few props, I slipped back into the kitchen. Jenny, who was then about five, turned from the sink, and stopped dead in her tracks, in shock. She blinked hard, looked again, and started to giggle. She had recognized me. Kate turned also, and while the two of them looked on, doubled over with laughter, "Bogart" gave his last rollicking performance. He had always been my favorite character. Now, as I begin writing this chapter on imagination, I think of him as my "woman warrior" in drag.

It was, I see also, a measure of my oppression as a woman that my warriors could only be imagined in a male form, although as a child I knew of warrior women like Harriet Tubman and Joan of Arc. Also I had seen pictures of the partisan bands who fought the Nazis in occupied Europe, the faces of nameless women among them. However, essential to my fantasy life was a release from the female form in which I felt trapped. Only in the male form could I imagine myself acting with the daring, skill, competence, and compassion of the characters I invented.

When I read Maxine Hong Kingston's memoir, *The Woman Warrior*, it struck me with particular force because of the warrior fantasies I had had in my childhood. Then I found other stories about women warriors from many different cultural traditions. In this weaving of our imaginative warriors I understood more about the mechanisms of our survival as women. Maintaining our sanity has had a lot to do with our capacity to invent the possibility of change. And this invention has had much to do with our ability to imagine ourselves in powerful and commanding ways. Women seek to control their experience by imagining it on their own terms, by giving it form, by making of it a felt presence. It is another dimension of the private realm that constitutes a part of women's reality: not the domestic life but the inner life of the imagination that is also real. Kingston sought to legitimize this imaginative realm, although she knew that the truth of the imagination is often in conflict with the truth of society. Kingston also knew that this fantasy world can easily tip over into insanity. At the heart of her drama is the tension between fantasy and insanity, balanced with exquisite skill.

The Woman Warrior is Maxine Hong Kingston's personal and family story. It begins in China and ends in America. On one level, it is the story of Kingston's childhood as she struggles to mature divided between two cultures so vastly different as to make one a ghost to the other. Chinese are real, Americans are ghosts. The Chinese have ghosts also, but they are of a different order. The structure of the story is crucial to its telling. It is not linear, it is rather a spiral of events, metaphor, myth, and lesson. It is a Chinese "talk-story" on an epic scale. Each of its first four parts tells the story of a woman connected to Kingston in an essential way. The fifth, "A Song for a Barbarian Reed Pipe," is her own story woven from and through the others. She transcends cultural difference, violence, and despair, penetrating finally to the core of human memory. Wholeness and beauty are sustained in paradox and sounded in the music of a reed pipe, "a high note . . . found at last and held—an icicle in the desert."[1]

Kingston opens with the story of "No Name Woman": " 'You must not tell anyone,' my mother said, 'what I am about to tell you. In China your father had a sister who killed herself. She jumped into the family well. We say that your father has all brothers because it is as if she had never been born'" (p. 3).

The aunt is pregnant. Her husband of one night, married to her by proxy, is off in America. The husband could not be the father of the child. He has been gone too long. Kingston imagines the parts of the story her mother has not told. She imagines the village man who had sex with her aunt, whom she would have had to obey whoever he was, however she encountered him. He would not have been a stranger because there were no strangers in the village. The mother goes on. As the aunt is about to give birth the villagers attack the family home, to revenge their shame, this woman's crime. The livestock are slaughtered, supplies are smashed, everything is shattered, torn, destroyed, splattered with blood. Kingston thinks: the father of the child organized this raid: " 'Your aunt gave birth in the pigsty that night,' " Kingston's mother says. " 'The next morning when I went for water, I found her and the baby plugging up the family well'" (p. 5).

This is the story her mother tells when Kingston begins to menstruate. This is her rite of passage into womanhood: " 'What happened to her could happen to you,' " the mother says. " 'Don't humiliate us. You wouldn't like to be forgotten as if you had never been born. The villagers are watchful.' " Kingston writes: "Whenever she had to warn us about life, my mother told stories that ran like this one, a story to grow up on. She tested our strength to establish realities" (p. 5).

And she sang legends to her daughter, of a woman warrior named Fa Mu Lan, the girl who took her father's place in battle. The story of Fa Mu Lan, called "White Tigers," is the second chapter in Kingston's memoir. She sets the story of Fa Mu Lan in the context of her childhood memory:

> I remember that . . . I followed my mother about the house, the two of us singing about how Fa Mu Lan fought gloriously and returned alive from war to settle in the village. I had forgotten this chant that once was mine, given me by my mother, who may not have known its power to remind. She said I would grow up a wife and a slave, but she taught me the song of the woman warrior, Fa Mu Lan. I would have to grow up a woman warrior. (P. 24)

Kingston tells the story in the first person. This is crucial, for as she explains: "There is a Chinese word for the female I—which is 'slave.'

Break the women with their own tongues" (p. 56). The story of Fa Mu Lan is shared with us in great detail. Fa Mu Lan: a child who leaves her family and her village, who journeys into the sky, who meets an old woman and an old man with whom she lives for years, who are her teachers. Fa Mu Lan learns how to listen, how to move, how to observe, how to fight, how to "make my mind large as the universe is large, so that there is room for paradoxes" (p. 35), how to make what is in the mind's eye manifest in the material world. Armed with these varied and intricate skills, made whole by the Taoist vision, understanding, and discipline, the woman warrior sets forth to avenge her family, her village, her people who have been plagued by bandits and the soldiers of warring dynasties. Fa Mu Lan raises an army, invincible and righteous, of warriors who fight but do not plunder and rape. She marries, becomes pregnant, conceals her swelling belly in her armor, bears a son, and continues in her crusade until she has met her most formidable enemy and defeated him in battle. Only then does she return to her village and her family. The barons and the lords who have stolen from the people are tried and executed. Their wives, many of whom had been children stolen from the villagers, who are now crippled because their feet are bound, are freed by Fa Mu Lan. Each is given a bag of rice:

> They rolled the bags to the road. They wandered away like ghosts. Later, it would be said, they turned into the band of swordswomen who were a mercenary army. They did not wear men's clothes like me, but rode as women in black and red dresses. They bought up girl babies so that many poor families welcomed their visitations. When slave girls and daughters-in-law ran away these people would say they joined these witch amazons. They killed men and boys. I myself never encountered such women and could not vouch for their reality. (P. 53)

The cycle of resistance is restored to a legend within the legend. Her public duties fulfilled, the woman warrior returns to village life and joins her husband's family as a proper Chinese wife: " 'I will stay with you, doing farmwork and housework and giving you more sons,'" she says. And because of her deeds, her honor, strength, and devotion, " 'the villagers would make a legend about my perfect filiality'" (p. 54).

With this tale of the woman warrior firmly placed, Kingston moves on to tell us of her mother. She is called Brave Orchid. Hers is the story of the "Shaman," the healer, the one with special visions, resources, and power, who studied medicine in China and worked with her husband in a steam laundry in America: the warrior and wife, survivor and innovator. She is also the traditionalist binding her daughter's mind, mother and daughter cornered in contradictions—of cultures, of generations, of women. Kingston writes: "To make my life American-normal, I turn on the lights before anything untoward makes an appearance. I push the deformed into my dreams, which are in Chinese, the language of impossible stories. Before we can leave our parents, they stuff our heads like suitcases which they jam pack with homemade underwear" (p. 54).

We move on to Kingston's fourth story. It is about Moon Orchid, her mother's sister, Second Aunt, who is brought from China to claim her husband. It has been twenty years since he left her. Moon Orchid does not want to find him, but Brave Orchid insists. They go finally to Los Angeles. Second Aunt's husband is now a prominent surgeon, he is remarried, with a new American family. Moon Orchid is crushed with shame at this place of the "Western Palace." She returns home with Brave Orchid. Slowly she descends into madness: "Brave Orchid saw that all variety had gone from her sister. She was indeed mad. 'The difference between mad people and sane people,' Brave Orchid explained to the children, 'is that sane people have variety when they talk-story. Mad people have only one story that they talk over and over'" (p. 184). Every morning Moon Orchid said the same thing, imagined that each person who left the house would never return, would be turned to ashes. She crawled the floors looking for those who were trying to get her, she hid in the darkness to escape from them, she could not sleep at night. Brave Orchid tried everything she could think of to save her sister, to rescue her spirit, to calm her fears. Nothing worked. Finally, she had her committed. In the sanitorium Moon Orchid felt better. And then she died, quietly, one night, in her sleep.

Between the stories of Brave Orchid's survival and Moon Orchid's death lies the power of the woman warrior: the legend, even only partially internalized in the visions of the mother providing resources, allowing for the transcendence of a life that might be endured in ways Second Aunt could not even begin to imagine; the warrior myth chanted to the daughter who becomes a different "I" breaking the linguistic code of the female/slave; the woman warrior soothing an interior space of pride and sustenance, harboring fragments of an emancipatory vision, an ember of esteem.

Every once in a while the warrior emerges from memory into life, as in the case of Ch'iu Chin (1875–1907), a revolutionary, poet, and educator who unbound her feet, published China's first feminist newspaper, *The Chinese Women's Journal* (having enough money for only two issues), and led an uprising against the Japanese invaders for which she was arrested, tortured, tried for treason, and executed at the age of thirty-two. The poet-warrior Ch'iu Chin, writing to her friend Tzu-ying, mourning their impending separation, understands the power of connection between women which is at the center of her life:

We have drunk wine and discussed literature.
Our hearts have beat together
With the same emotions
Softly we sing together the old song
'The Sunlight in the Pass.'
The sorrow of parting will follow our horses' feet.
The melancholy of farewell
Surrounds the city like a river.
Iron strokes, silver curves, your couplets
Are limitless in their meanings.
Take care of yourself. We can have no confidence
that one day we will see each other again.
We stand on the bridge, hand in hand.
The river and the evening clouds stretch away for a thousand
        miles.[2]

The legend of a woman warrior is told again and again throughout the world. There are many versions, cultural variances, historical nuances, continuities to be traced through migrations and settlements. The warrior is not the goddess in her many forms; she is not a spiritual manifestation so much as an imaginative incitement, an instrument of survival, sometimes an avenger wrought from injustice, from the imbalance in the arrangement of human affairs, from women's fury and the passionate need for redress. At times she is manifested in life, then enveloped in legend, refueling the imaginative spiral.

In Korea, for example, she appears as Princess Pari, who performs unparalleled feats of bravery and endurance and displays extraordinary filial devotion. She journeys with Buddha's help to the Heavenly Kingdom of the Western Sky to secure medicinal water to save the lives of her dying parents.[3] Among the Nootka people of British Columbia, legend says that there is a secret society of warrior women who were able to recognize the face of the enemy as he invaded the North American continent and to keep alive the teachings of the women elders. The society of warrior women remembers all the elements of balance and harmony of the Old Way. They were entrusted to recruit among the younger women who could be taught the secrets of resistance.[4]

The Greeks of antiquity greatly feared the Amazon warriors reputed to live by the banks of the river Thermodon, "a mighty army of mounted warriors bearing ivy-shaped shields and double-bladed axes," and the Spanish conquistadores several centuries later "thought they saw in the exotic newly discovered American continent a glimpse of these mythical female warriors among some of the native Indian tribes: thus the largest river in Brazil—the Amazon—inherited its name from these mighty women. . . ."[5] From Mexico come the *soldaderas*, the women warriors, who fought in the wars for independence from Spain (1810–1821): Doña Josefa Ortiz de Domínguez, Doña Leona Vicario, Doña Teodosea Rodríguez (La Generala), María Manuela Molina (La Capitana); and, in the 1910 revolution and its aftermath: Carmen Serdán, La Coronela Carmen Amelia Robles, La Coronela Carmen Pavia Alaniz, La Coronela Pepita Neri, and La General Jovita Vadovinos.[6] A historical record authenticates their names and deeds, and a popular movement records their stories and those of many others in the *Corrido*, the Mexican ballad.

In her study of gay culture, *Another Mother Tongue*, Judy Grahn envisions the women warriors in the lesbian tradition from antiquity to the persecution of lesbians in the U.S. armed forces since World War II. Grahn begins her odyssey of the lesbian warrior with the Celtic queen Boudica. Grahn disclosed details of the Amazon peoples on the European and African continents, who lived circa 3000 B.C.E. The oldest of these peoples were Libyan in northwest Africa who "were known not only as warriors but as founders of cities," most of which were named after their female generals, such as Myrine, Mytilene, Elaia, Anaia, Gryneia, Kyme. "At the city of Ephesus the Amazons established a shrine and magnificent statue to the Goddess Artemis." Included in this section of Grahn's book is a description of one of the many horrific witch-hunts of lesbians in the U.S. army in modern times. This ended in Grahn's discharge in 1960. "Military authority," she writes, "rules by the breaking of pride and dignity as much as by any threat of bodily harm. Nor can anyone humiliate you as deeply as your own." Describing this period in her life, Grahn continues: "Discharged into a poor area of Washington, D.C., with $80 and utter demoralization . . . I found that despair has no bottom; it can multiply itself indefinitely, inside the mind and outside. . . . I thrashed about at the bottom of the well of degradation among the more demoralized of America's people. . . . But I had to put the pieces of my life back together somehow." Grahn emerged from this time "fighting, studying, making notes on my own about Gay people I knew," embodying the warrior legacy she was soon to uncover in her search and make available to us.[7]

From Jamaica, Michelle Cliff tells us the story of Nanny, the sorceress, the *obeah*-woman:

> who could catch a bullet between her buttocks and render the bullet harmless, [she] was from the empire of the Ashanti, and carried the secrets of her magic into slavery. She prepared amulets and oaths for her armies. Her Nanny Town, hidden in the crevices of the Blue Mountains, was the headquarters of the Windward Maroons—who held out against the forces of the white men longer than any rebel troops. They waged war from 1655–1740. Nanny was the magician of this revolution—she used her skill to unite her people and to consecrate their battles.
>
> There is absolutely no doubt that she actually existed. And the ruins of Nanny Town remain difficult to reach.[8]

In resistance to slavery many thousands fled, and in Jamaica as elsewhere in the Americas, including the southern United States, escaped slaves established maroon societies from which they waged guerrilla warfare on the slaveholders.[9] In Jamaica, maroons fought the British for eighty-five years and were never defeated. Nanny led many of these battles. She was descendant of a long memory of African queens; her contemporary, Queen Zhinga of Matamba in West Africa, is renown for having united her peoples and holding the Portuguese colonialists at bay for years, even after they had defeated her allied armies of the Mani-Congo and the Ngola.[10]

Today in countless Afro-American churches there are women, church mothers, who are called queens and honored for their devotion, sacrifice, wisdom, and leadership. It is perhaps significant in this regard that my first childhood memory of the name Moses came from hearing Paul Robeson singing of him, in the unmistakable deep bass that was his voice alone:

Go down Moses
Way down in Egypt land
Tell ol' Pharaoh
To let my people go

I am a Jew, but I was not raised in the tradition of the Torah. To me Egypt meant Mississippi, and Pharaoh was the slave master, and Moses was Black (as he surely was in any event), and in my mind "he" was always Harriet Tubman, the African queen-warrior, I see now, extended into North America.[11]

I made many of these connections after hearing a paper entitled, "Black Women in Resistance: A Cross-Cultural Perspective," by historian Rosalyn Terborg-Penn, in which she charted the lineage of the African queen in the diaspora.[12] Unfortunately, among some of the white male Africanists present, her paper was not well received. They disputed its historical accuracy, by which they meant that the historical evidence tended to show that the real African queens, including Queen Zhinga, never actually wielded the power attributed to them. I thought they missed the point. First, European and Euro-American colonialism fundamentally altered the historical record with conquest and fundamentally distorted or misunderstood the cultures of the peoples whom they conquered. Paula Gunn Allen, Native American poet and scholar, explored the point this way, emphasizing the philosophical implications of the historical disjuncture:

the wars of imperial conquest have not been solely or even mostly waged over the land and its resources, but they have been fought within the bodies, minds, and hearts of the people of the earth for dominion over them. I think this is the reason traditionals say we must remember our origins, our cultures, our histories, our mothers and grandmothers, for without that memory, *which implies continuance rather than nostalgia*, we are doomed to engulfment by a paradigm that is fundamentally inimical to the vitality, autonomy, and self-empowerment essential for satisfying, high-quality life. (Emphasis added)[13]

Second, the Africanists missed the point psychologically. For an op-pressed people, for women, the story *is* true, whether or not it is histor-ically verified. It exists in the mind as a vision, potent and empowering, a source of pride and self-esteem, an incitement to emulation and action. In this way it acts as a historical force whether or not it is "true."

In an analogous way, consider the story in Paule Marshall's novel *Praisesong for the Widow,* about the day the Ibo walked on water to escape from slavery.[14] This story is the inspirational thread empowering the widow, Avey Johnson. The point is not whether this, any more than the biblical parting of the Red Sea, actually happened. The point is that this story, and so many others like it, provide ancestral connection, and inspire comfort and confidence in the struggles ahead.

The story of the liberation was told to Avey by her great-aunt whom she visited every summer as a child on Tatem Island, just across from Beaufort, on the South Carolina tidewater. Avey would walk with her great-aunt to a place called The Landing. They stood there together, and Great Aunt would tell the story of how a group of Ibo were brought by ship from Africa to be slaves. "It was here that they brought 'em out of the boats right here where we's standing. Nobody remembers how many of 'em it was but they was a good few 'cording to my gran' who was a little girl no bigger than you when it happened" (p. 37).

The Ibo looked around studying the place and the land and the white folks. And, "'Cause those pure-bred Africans was peoples my gran' said could see in more ways than one, [and could] tell you 'bout things hap-pened long before they was born and things to come after they's dead . . ." (pp. 37–38), they decided it was best to leave. Great Aunt explained how they could see the slavery time and the war and the emancipation and the hard times following it, and so they decided to leave right then and there:

" . . . They just turned, my gran' said, all of 'em . . . and walked on back down to the end of the river. . . . Every las' man, woman and chile. And they wasn't taking they time no more. They had seen what they had seen and those Ibos was stepping! . . . They just kept walk-ing right on out over the river. Now you wouldna thought they'd of got very far seeing as it was water they was walking on. Besides they had all that iron on 'em. . . . 'Nuff iron to sink an army. . . . But chains didn't stop those Ibos none. . . . They feets was gonna taken 'em wherever they was going that day. And they was singing by then, so my gran' said. When they realized there wasn't nothing between them and home but some water and that wasn't giving 'em no trouble they got so tickled they started in to singing. You could hear 'em clear across Tatem 'cording to her." (Pp. 38–39)

And, Great Aunt concluded, her grandmother said they were having such a good time that " 'she just picked herself up and took off after 'em. In her mind. Her body she always usta say might be in Tatem but her mind, her mind was long gone with the Ibos . . . ' " (p. 39).

It is this vision that allows Avey Johnson to free herself from a different bondage, claiming her heritage and her life. She becomes a warrior-queen sent to alert a new generation of striving young professionals among her race of the perils and pitfalls of the "American Way":

She would haunt the entranceways of the skyscrapers. And whenever she spotted one of them amid the crowd, those young, bright, fiercely articulate token few for whom her generation had worked two and three jobs, she would stop them. . . . As they rushed blindly in and out of the glacier buildings, unaware, unprotected, lacking memory and a necessary distance of the mind she would stop them and before they could pull out of her grasp . . . quote them the line from her namesake. . . . (P. 255)

and tell them about her great-aunt's grandmother, "long gone with the Ibos."

As devastating as any overt form of physical oppression is its internalized counterpart that subjugates the life of the mind. I think of the fairy tales upon which we, in Euro-American culture at least, have been steeped since we were toddlers: Little Red Riding Hood, Cinderella, Sleeping Beauty, Snow White. There are no women warriors in these tales, only foolish, weak, wicked, competitive, and/or innocent women to be raped if they have wandered from home unprotected, or inaugurated into womanly divinity if rescued by their prince.[15] I think of my childhood fantasies, of how I always wanted to be the prince, the actor, the rescuer, the hero, not yet understanding the price to be exacted for this imbalance. This is colonization.

For women adopting the structures and values, perceptions and experiences of the oppressor, even the belief in an alternative vision may be finally erased or crushed into an almost unrecognizable form. The process of colonization is not only one of limiting access, of subjugation, of political domination, of racial superiority, of a poverty of material resources. It also involves an internal corrosion, a loss of esteem, a loss of confidence in one's knowledge, an inability to give expression to experience. To understand the colonization of women is to understand its interior dimensions, its psychological consequences, its hold on the imagination, and the enormity of effort, individual and collective, which is required to break its cycle. At the heart of the colonization is a belief in the superiority of men; in the superiority of male judgment and authority; and in the absolute priority given to achieving male approval and validation.

I see this every day in my women's studies classes. Women entering university, eighteen or nineteen years old, wrapped in relationships, crippled by drugs and alcohol either as users or as codependents, overwrought about diets and weight, energy focused on thighs, buttocks, breasts, hips, stomachs, hair, skin, shape. The women are mostly heterosexual, mostly middle class, mostly white. Many are career oriented. At Santa Cruz this means they are studying the biological or computer sciences, psychology or sociology. Some of them will go on to graduate schools, to law school, to medical school. There are some variations in these patterns attributable to race and to class and to age. Women of color are coping with racism, culture shocked in a bleached landscape. The credibility accorded white opinion, male or female, because it is white, depends upon the degree of internalized racism. But the focus on men, especially within each race, is the same.

I have taught at community colleges and the state university. There are more working-class women in these places, more older women returning to school, raising children, struggling through divorces and financial losses, working as waitresses, secretaries, retail clerks, with an eye toward the professions and a way up and out. They have more experiences with men, they are wiser, almost always more cynical and astute than their younger counterparts. But their focus on men is the same.

Women who are professionally competent and/or financially secure manifest a comparable attention on men. Sometimes, in fact, it is worse than among their less secure sisters; these women are coping as the token representatives of "equality" in major institutions. These are professional women trying to be "one of the boys," as I was for years, just as sharp as the men, just as competent, just as equipped, just as willing to put (other) women down. Among lesbians, many affect the mannerisms of adolescent

males in body image, in dress, in movement. Many don't believe themselves to be physically attractive and/or have internalized the Freudian
designations of invert, pervert, misfit. This is the wreckage, the carnage,
the debris after thousands of years of subjugation. It is not the total
picture. It is one way of looking. It is important to see, to not romanticize
or underestimate the difficulty of the liberatory effort. Whatever else
happens in women's studies, or in the women's movement, whatever else
is studied in history, literature, psychology, or art, whatever else is accom-
plished in stripping away the barriers of sex discrimination, it is unlearning this process of colonization that is at the heart of our work for
ourselves and for those whom we teach.

I teach a class called "Women's Culture." Each meeting we begin with
someone presenting a centerpiece: quilts, lace, needlework, knitting, poetry, paintings, books, flowers, candles, photographs, food—artifacts of
women's daily lives brought by students to illustrate their women's culture. An "elder-in-residence" at the University of California, Santa Cruz,
was in this class. She had been a court clerk in San Francisco County for
many, many years. Now she was retired and had returned to school. She is
a Chinese American. This elder's mother, born in China, was a pioneer
woman who helped to settle the American West. She worked a farm near
Stockton, California, for much of her life. She raised nine children. This
elder said she never once heard her mother complain. Included in this
woman's centerpiece were her mother's shoes, which she had kept. They
are very, very tiny shoes, to fit a doll's feet perhaps. They are exquisitely
embroidered in gorgeous colors, with intricately worked design. This
embroidery was done by the elder's mother to make beautiful her shoes, to
be worn on her bound feet. For the "Introduction to Feminism" class the
quarter before, this student had done a paper on the history of Chinese
foot binding. Now she explained the practice again: how the toes of the
female child were forced back under the ball of the foot; how the foot was
then tightly bound with cloth, breaking the bones in the toes; how the foot
bled and became infected; how for the rest of her life, this woman's feet
would be bound; how her mother's feet were bound like this because an
emperor in China, centuries earlier, had liked the effects of bound feet on a
dancer in his court, on the way she moved her hips. He had found it erotic
and pleasing. For a thousand years millions of Chinese women experienced this process and survived it; the mothers binding their daughters'
feet, to protect their daughters so that they would have sufficient status to

marry well. Without marriage the daughters would probably be sold or forced into prostitution, or would not survive at all. This elder's mother had bound feet but she did not bind her daughters' feet in America. These were her shoes, passed now among us ever so carefully, the colors of her embroidery blazing in the room.

I think: nothing about our oppression as women is simple. The elder student has stopped talking. She has not told the whole story. Because the whole story, or more of it at least, would mean explaining how some Chinese women came to believe in foot binding; accepting the men's judgment about its appealing and erotic effects; performing the binding on themselves and on their children. Some women even resisted men with revolutionary ideas who tried to stop the practice. This is colonization. And I see that something else has happened in our classroom which has silenced my elder student.

There is a racist bias, used now as a tool to divert attention from the real meaning of the elder's story. There is horror, of course, among the students, at the practice of foot binding. Most of them have heard of it but have never met someone whose mother had bound feet. Then after the horror, there is pity. Not solidarity, not outrage, not compassion, but pity, and an unspoken but palpable, patronizing indictment: those poor "China women"! They were so backward! So undeveloped! Couldn't they see how they were crippling themselves? How could they do that to their children? How could they be so stupid? Outrage turned on its head; twisted into anger at the women; the tiny shoes restored to their place in the center, a museum piece, remote, impersonal.

I think: nothing about our oppression as women is simple. In Intro to Feminism I show pictures of whale-bone corsets that upper-class women in nineteenth-century America wore to pull in their stomachs and accentuate their hips and bust, because men found this attractive. I tell them about women who had ribs surgically removed to more effectively wear this corset, about women who were asphyxiated in the process. We talk about cosmetic surgery—eyelifts and breast inflation (or reduction), about tummy tucks and face lifts. We talk about liposuction, a form of surgery for weight reduction. All of these surgical procedures are practiced in the United States today. They are often extremely painful, require weeks and sometimes months for recovery, and may not be successful. They may also result in permanent disfigurement.[16] The students laugh harshly at the absurdity of the procedure or they hiss knowingly to show their disapproval. I show them pictures from today's latest catalogs of spiked heels, and explain what these shoes will do to women's arches, how they cripple the feet. The more "politically correct" among the students hiss their disapproval of spiked heels, hurling unspoken indictments against their sisters in the room who still wear them, cowered now into silence, too ashamed to acknowledge that they will go on wearing them because they are attractive, because men like them and their effects on the hips and ass when you walk in them. This is colonization. Women hissing at each other; women shredding their bodies, assaulting their systems, shaving, vomiting, starving themselves, even to death. Millions of women in this country are drugged by doctors. They are on tranquilizers, antidepressants, barbiturates, and the like. Maimed by the conditions of their lives, they are "treated," numbed into compliance, while remaining "serviceable" and functional, the miracles of modern medicine. Taking women off these drugs will be like unbinding the feet of the women in China. The students had made the elder's mother "the Other," but there is no "Other."

I think: nothing about our oppression as women is simple. I remember a portion of a poem by Adrienne Rich:

In Colcha embroidery, I learn
women use ravelled yarn from old wool blankets
to trace out scenes on homespun woollen sacks—
our ancient art of making out of nothing—
or is it making the old life serve the new?
The impact of Christian culture, it is written,
and other influences, have changed the patterns

. . . .
Example: here we have a scene of flagellants
each whip is accurately self-directed.
To understand colonization is taking me years. . . .
What rivets me to history is seeing
arts of survival turned
to rituals of self-hatred. This
is colonization.[17]

One might say here, in the context of our time and the Chinese mother's embroidered shoes:

what rivets me to history is seeing
rituals of hatred (and self-mutilation) turned
into art. This
is colonization . . .

the paradox turned on its head. Both ends of it true. At the same time.

Sometimes I read aloud to my students. I do this to share stories with them that can take us into other kinds of realities, to allow them to feel what it might be like if we lived in a society in which women were not subordinated to men, in which women were respected. Tribal stories often provide such ways of seeing. For example, I read aloud accounts of Spider Woman as Creator. These are stories known among the Pueblo people of the Southwest. I read the story of Changing Woman, Creator of the Navajo people: "It is to Changing Woman that we look as we search for the wisdom of life. . . . Those who understand the ways of Changing Woman, forever walk the Trail of Beauty." I read the story of Tem Eyos Ki, a woman known among the Nootka people of what is now British Columbia. This story tells of a time when the women had stopped concerning themselves with politics and were only interested in spiritual matters. As a result, the men began to control more and more of society; they dominated many areas of life because the women were not paying attention. This society began to look like our own in which men give orders and expect women to serve them. Then a woman named Tem Eyos Ki experienced a powerful spiritual transformation which touched the lives of all the people in the village. The women were able to see how they felt about their lives and to express those feelings to the men. The men were able to listen after the intervention of Qolus, a female figure and the father of the four sons who fathered all ordinary people. More of a balance was restored in the relations between people in the village. Tem Eyos Ki gave the women a vision of empowerment, of beauty, and of song.[18]

These stories provide evidence of other realities. There is always absolute silence while they are being read. The silence hangs there at the end. The power of the words in the stories is like the power of the high note sounded at the end of Maxine Hong Kingston's "Song for a Barbarian Reed Pipe." It is also, I think, like the power of feeling that often swells in a woman when she is pregnant and begins to cry for no apparent reason. It is the sound of mourning for which there is no apparent memory or language.

Judy Grahn writes of the Queen of Wands, a retelling of Helen of Troy, worked from a translation of an ancient Babylonian text called "A Tablet of Lamentation." It tells of a queen stolen from her temple and carried away on a ship. Grahn says: "The theme of a queen who has been stolen, of cities and temples ravaged by soldiers, of people cudgled in the streets, of lamentation for a female power gone, is . . . repeated," again and again. In this collection of poems Grahn seeks to reempower, to celebrate, to engrave another tablet, to give Helen, in all her varied forms, voice:

They say she is veiled
and a mystery. That is
one way of looking.
Another
is that she is where
she always has been,
exactly in place,
and it is we,
we who are mystified,
we who are veiled
and without faces.[19]

Another poet, Michele Murray, Grahn's contemporary whose years of formative aspiration were in the 1950s and who died of cancer at the age of forty-one, wrote in her journal, June 10, 1967: "I wanted to *become somebody,* an artist entire, beginning with nothing at all—no roots, no money, no parental help, no culture, no father—to create myself from scratch through language only, to see my face without a mirror. And I have failed, naturally."[20] Murray failed, of course, because language itself is a function of culture, the symbolic codification of perception. The male experience is already embedded in the language. It is in the conceptual formulation of thought itself, as in Maxine Hong Kingston's struggle with the Chinese ideogram for the female "I" meaning slave: "Even now," Kingston wrote, "China wraps double binds around my feet."[21] Women's meanings are walled up, muted, expelled in frustration, incoherence, anger, absorbed in despair. Or the meaning emerges in a dance, a painting, a quilt, a garden, a song with melody and no words such as my mother used to sing in a soprano voice clear as morning dew. A year earlier in the same journal, Michele Murray had written: "How different a woman's perceptions would have to be, just based on her experience! How can I give adherence to an idea when I see how ideas retreat before the very small bits of reality that make up a day?"[22]

To give expression to their creative selves women have had to overcome many obstacles. Just finding the space and time in which to work has often been a great challenge. Women have also had to contend with the fears and/or consequences of insanity when they have perceived in ways so different from those of the established order of things. Moreover, finding a language or form in which to express their experiences has often been very difficult. When Tillie Olsen began to write again in the 1950s after a twenty-year hiatus, as Elinor Langer remarked, "it was not as a woman who had lived her life as an artist, but an artist who had lived her life as a woman."[23] Alice Walker, situated in her mother's garden, shares her revelation about women's insanity: "For these grandmothers and mothers of ours were not Saints, but Artists; driven to numb and bleeding madness by the springs of creativity for which there was no release."[24] The playwright Honor Moore explains to us that "Martha Graham, perhaps the most important woman dramatist who has ever lived [in Western culture] is not a playwright but a choreographer. She invented a language—modern dance—and . . . spent her long life . . . choreographing more than a hundred and fifty pieces that express her woman-centered vision."[25]

Twenty years after Michele Murray's wish "to create myself from scratch," Suzette Elgin, a woman with a Ph.D. in linguistics who was writing science fiction within the context of a women's liberation movement Murray did not live to see, imagines the invention of a language she calls Láadan, based solely on women's perceptions of reality. The "native tongue" is so compelling in its authenticity and so radical in its effects that it changes reality itself, liberating the women who speak it. A woman named Nazareth is one of the primary encoders of this new language. She and her colinguists are the women warriors of a new generation.[26]

Many contemporary women writers and artists have attempted to work with new images drawn from an explicitly feminist consciousness or from a female sensibility pulled from the experiences of daily life and made explicit in the context of the women's liberation movement.[27] The struggle to do this requires both the break-up of the interior colonization and the actualization of a women-centered reality. Erica Jong described this process in her own work as she came of age as a writer in the 1970s:

I spent my whole bookish life identifying with writers and nearly all the writers who mattered were men. Even though there were women writers and even though I read them and loved them, they did not seem to matter. If they were good, they were good *in spite* of being women. If they were bad, it was because they were women. I had, in short, internalized all the dominant cultural stereotypes, and the result was that I could scarcely even imagine a woman as an author.

Once Jong could name the problem, however, and see herself as a writer, the content of her work changed: "I stopped writing about ruins and nightingales. I was able to make poetry out of the everyday activities of my life: peeling onions, a trip to the gynecologist, a student demonstration, my own midnight terrors and dreams—all things I would have previously dismissed as trivial."[28]

Reflecting on the same problem, adding another dimension of race and culture, Chicana poet Jennie Montoya described her Anglo-centered, male-centered high school education in New Mexico in an interview in the late 1970s. She loved literature, she explained, and wanted to become an English teacher, "and come back and teach Shakespeare to my Chicanos. I didn't know there was Don Quixote. Nobody told me that Chicanos had written classics. Nobody told me that Gabriela Mistral had won a Nobel Prize. So I assumed that the only language in the world for creating classics was in English." Montoya was bilingual, but it had never occurred to her that she could write her own poetry in Spanish. She discovered this at university. She said, "That first semester I went insane!" She started writing in Spanish: "My first poem was a feminist poem talking about how women shouldn't pretend to become liberated by liberating themselves from things like housework, but we should go on to create new ideas."[29]

Reverend Renita Weems, spiritualist and critic, reflecting on the literary tradition of Afro-American women stressed the problem of "artists without art-forms," echoing Alice Walker's insight and paralleling the problem of language experienced by Murray, Jong, and Montoya. The problem of form, Weems suggested, is a theme in Black women's novels. Analyzing Toni Morrison's novel *Sula*, Weems pointed out that the problem of form impinges upon the process of creation because the Black woman's experience is neither white nor male, and is, therefore, unconventional by definition. She wrote: "Over the years the black woman novelist has not been taken seriously. 'Shallow,' 'emotional,' 'unstructured,' 'reactionary,' and 'just too painful,' are some of the criticisms against her work. That she is a woman makes her work marginal. That she is black makes it minor. That she is both makes it alien."[30]

Sounding a similar theme during an interview in 1980, novelist and screenwriter Toni Cade Bambara commented:

> there have been a lot of things in . . . the Black experience for which there are no terms, certainly not in English at this moment. There are a lot of aspects of consciousness for which there is no vocabulary, no structure in the English language which would allow people to validate that experience through language. I'm trying to find a way to do that. . . .
>
> . . . I'm trying to break open and get at the bones, deal with symbols as though they were atoms. I'm trying to find out not only how a word gains meaning, but how a word gains power.[31]

The creation of new forms, the attention to race pride and cultural integrity, the focus on the dailiness of women's lives, the projection of images out of this daily experience have all been central to the women's cultural renaissance of the 1970s. Art critic Lucy Lippard expressed the roots of this renaissance succinctly: "the overwhelming fact remains that a woman's experience in this society—social and biological—is simply not like that of a man. If art comes from inside, as it must, then the art of men and women must be different too. And if this factor does not show up in women's work, only repression can be to blame."[32]

Coming out of this repression as a traditionally trained artist in the 1940s and 1950s was Miriam Schapiro, one of the cofounders of the Woman's Building in Los Angeles. She explained how her involvement in the women's movement transformed her art:

> I wanted to explore and express a part of my life which I had always dismissed—my homemaking, my nesting. I wanted to validate the traditional activities of women, to connect myself to the unknown women artists who made quilts, who had done the invisible "woman's work" of civilization, . . . The collagists who came before me were men, who . . . often roamed the streets at night scavenging, collecting material, their junk, from urban spaces. My world, my mother's and grandmother's world, was a different one. . . . My

"junk," my fabrics, allude to a particular universe, which I wished to make real, to represent.[33]

Schapiro, Judy Chicago, and other artists embarked upon the creation of *Womanhouse* in 1971–72, precisely to give expression to this distinct female experience. Drawn from the collective experiences of the participant creators, the women provisioned a series of rooms with the everyday artifacts of their lives. Each was also a highly imaginative commentary on the politics of domesticity, menstruation, body image, and so on. The kitchen, for example, was spotless and shining, its walls, cabinets, and ceiling covered with three dimensional fried eggs, which were simultaneously images of women's breasts; a bathroom, among its other complements, was wreathed in tampax. The conventional art world shuddered, the critics condemning at once the overtly political character of *Womanhouse* and the triviality of its contents.[34] Again, they missed the point. The break-up of women's colonization requires precisely a rebuilding of consciousness based upon a validation of women's experiences and feelings, a valuing of women's work and ways of seeing, a collective imaging of what has persisted in the mind's eye of so many individual women. To do this women project themselves onto page and canvas as the subject of their own experience. In seeing themselves for the first time, the imaginative impulse incites the possibility of change that is at once personal and political. Artists have played a crucial role in this incitement.

Afro-American artist Betye Saar generated "some of the most poignant and pointed visual statements of black feminist protest" to come out of the early seventies using precisely the ideas explained by Miriam Schapiro and displayed in the Woman's Building.[35] Saar's images, however, are drawn from the specificity of Black women's history and rooted, especially in the later work, in ancestral African motifs. Saar invented her own forms of expression by combining printmaking and collage. Collecting small objects and boxes, women's apparel, and urban artifacts of all shapes and sizes she began recycling them in her work. "The Liberation of Aunt Jemima" is the best known of her protest art of the 1970s. Saar used the boxes of the pancake mix sporting their offensive "mammy" image; in her imagination Aunt Jemima was transformed into an imposing figure, indeed, she was transformed into a woman warrior. Aunt Jemima is looming in the foreground holding a rifle in one hand, a white baby in the other, while a clenched Black fist—the symbol of solidarity in the civil rights movement—explodes in front of her. The interiority of Black women's rage is given expression in this work as the artifacts of racist and misogynist culture are recycled and appropriated in relentless judgment.

As Saar's artistic vision evolved, fabric became increasingly central to her work, and in the context of the women's liberation movement of the mid-seventies this experimentation was supported and validated. Saar explained her fascination with fabric this way: "My mother was a seamstress and we always had scraps of fabric around to play with. We made doll's clothes, puppets, and costumes. Fabric, pattern and texture have been with me ever since."[36] Working with fabric Saar moved into an exploration of her own family heritage, then to a representation "of her private interior space," and finally to the use of occult and metaphysical imagery. Hers was a search for expression away from Euro-American and male-centered images of the dominant culture. In an interview in the *Feminist Art Journal* Saar spoke of these new directions: "from my involvement with the black movement I move into a concern with black history going back to Africa and other darker civilizations such as Egypt and Oceania. I was interested in the kinds of mystical things that are part of non-European religion and culture."[37] Works such as *Africa* (1968), *View from the Sorcerer's Window* (1966), and *Wizard* (1972) experiment with the mysticism drawing especially upon North African and Muslim iconography.

Saar's images are often collages and constructions, and sometimes an interior space—a room—into which one walks, not unlike the form of interiority expressed in *Womanhouse*. Works such as *Black Girls Window, Nine Mojo, Secrets, Grandma's Garden,* and *Miz Ann's Charm* in the 1970s and, in the early 1980s, such explicitly female-centered works as *A Scattering of Fantasies, Reckless Romance, Uncommon Dreams,* and *Misplaced Memories* affirm the importance of the personal relationships women form with family and friends in their everyday lives, while at the same time evoking a spiritual connection to African images. The interior vision Saar produces is intensely personal, speaking to the meaning women give to their everyday lives and activities, and to the bonds of survival women form with one another.

One of Saar's works that stands out particularly in my memory was entitled *In My Solitude*. I saw it when it was exhibited at the Smith Gallery on the University of California's Santa Cruz campus in 1983. It was an interior space, a room into which one walked. An old-fashioned straight-back wooden chair was in the center, its seat facing the far corner of the room. On the floor around it was a thick carpet of pink rose petals forming a soft circle. An antique dress, tinged pink, its neckline and long sleeves adorned in lace, hung near one corner on a hanger suspended from the ceiling by a thin wire. Along the bottom of two walls hinged by the entrance were photographs of shoes. The pictures were mounted, each a collage. Some of these images were very funny because of the juxtaposition of costume, and taken together they produced the effect of being in a closet. The lighting cast shadows across the room producing an astonishing feeling of reverence. There were a few other items in the room: a hat, gloves, lace. The room was very female, very old, very southern, and distinctly mystical. There were many other things to see in the exhibit, but I kept returning to this room. I was drawn to it like a magnet. It was a still life and, finally, a sanctuary where a woman might be caressed with memory.

Resurrection, a series of installations which Saar conceived between 1977 and 1987, represented on a most literal level the resurrection of Black women climbing up and out of the cycles of oppression and poverty. A more transcendent reading also suggested the magic—the "mojo"—worked by Black women in their everyday lives to achieve this resurrection. This idea of magic was further explored in a 1987 exhibit by Saar at the Massachusetts Institute of Technology, which she titled *Mojo Tech*. In the exhibit catalog, Saar explained her process:

> A *mojo* is an amulet or charm used in some voodoo-based beliefs (religions). Its power is somewhat ambiguous, as it depends on both the user's strength of belief and his or her motive.
>
> As a shaman gleans the environment for special ingredients and objects to fabricate the *mojo,* I glean the flea markets, estate sales, and thrift shops around my home in Los Angeles or places I visit such as Alaska, Maine, and Texas. Marketplaces in Africa, Brazil, Crete, Mexico have also divulged special materials for my work.
>
> My intuition works like radar in accumulating materials. The found objects and discards are then altered, manipulated and transformed in assemblages, collages and installations.

I have thought of Saar's art as a conjuring in the tradition of African women. She is a root worker, excavating and connecting African, Afro-Caribbean and southern Black women's cultures, recycling the artifacts of women's everyday lives—boxes, bottles, bones (from cooking, for example), feathers, fabrics, scarves, photographs, gloves, hats, lace—forming interior spaces, masks, prisms, webs of connection and meaning we have not seen before. In doing this she has taken women into the shelter of their own experiences as women, this shelter providing the feeling of sanctuary in the still life I had entered. The sanctuary is precisely a safe place where things from women's everyday lives provide the comfort of recognition, which is, after all, one crucial aspect of the women's cultural renaissance.

Particularly prominent in this cultural renaissance has been the work of artist Judy Chicago. Her work reveals the potent role of the imagination in creating alternative, women-centered ways of seeing. Technically trained in the fine arts, energetic, and ambitious, Chicago has worked with large conception and has executed her work with the assistance of hundreds of potters, painters, quilters, and needleworkers. Her two most important projects have been *The Dinner Party* and *The Birth Project*, each of which took five years to complete.

Attending to every detail of dining etiquette and combining the fine arts of sculpture and ceramics with the historically female arts of china-painting, needlework, and textiles, in its very making *The Dinner Party* memorialized women's domestic labors. There were thirty-nine place settings, each containing a hand-painted china plate. Each setting was intended to pay homage to a woman of outstanding achievement in Western civilization. Each china plate rested on a hand-woven needlepoint runner that represented the actual needlepoint of the period in which the woman lived. On the runner was also narrated the significance of that woman's life and work. A table in the form of an equilateral triangle was the basis for the setting, the triangle being an ancient symbol of the feminine. The table rested on a "Heritage Floor" of twenty-three hundred hand-painted porcelain tiles on which were inscribed the names of 999 women. The names appeared and disappeared as one walked the periphery of the exhibit, illustrating the erasure and recovery of women's history.[38]

The most striking aspect of *The Dinner Party* was its china plates displaying endless variations on a butterfly motif in brilliant colors. Chicago chose the butterfly, she said, as a symbol of transition and change. Most viewers, however, looked at the butterflies and saw vaginas. Intentionally or not, the exhibit took on a whole other aspect. Here was (many felt) the female genitalia, shrouded in centuries of defilement, open, inviting, radiating colors, and sometimes even giving the illusion of a wet and sumptuous warmth.

While under the supervision and artistic direction of Judy Chicago, *The Dinner Party* could not have been arranged without the sometimes extraordinary innovations of specialized teams of artistic workers. For example, it took more than a year to perfect the technique for making the ceramic plates so that they would not crack as they were fired and refired in the kilns. It took three years to make all of them, and there were no duplicates. Upon its completion, Chicago commented that creating *The Dinner Party* was "like building a cathedral, with each person giving a brick."[39] Ninety thousand people, 75 percent of whom were women, stood in line for as long as five hours to see the exhibit during its twelve-week run at the Museum of Modern Art in San Francisco where it opened in March 1979. It was the largest crowd in the museum's history. Despite its popular reception, however, it was condemned by the established critics of the art world, one referring to it indignantly as an excursion into "vaginal politics." Museums which had originally booked the exhibit cancelled their showings after the San Francisco opening. Chicago reported, however, that people all over the country, incensed by this official censure, "got together, raised money, pressured museums, or set-up alternative spaces to exhibit the work."[40]

The images of *The Dinner Party* were indeed rounded rather than phallic, and the exhibit's purposes were political rather than benign. *The Dinner Party* crossed all the traditional boundaries set to establish the "fine arts." It combined myth and history, craft and art; it used both symbolic and narrative forms to tell its stories. It was individually conceived but collectively executed in ways that decisively affected its original conception. It was about women's history in a formal sense but utopian in design and purpose. These innovations were emblematic of its unabashedly female centeredness. The china plates were at its center. In the ceramic process the plates had to be fired and refired in the kilns so that the colors and glazes could penetrate each other in successive layers. This physical process was analogous to the images reproduced: folded and layered, the vagina (or butterfly) was penetrated (or transformed) by the female artist. In the last plates the images rose up from their surface pushing out to birth themselves.

Before *The Dinner Party* was completed, Chicago began to experiment with birth images. From *The Dinner Party* experience, she discovered that she had an affinity for working in fibers and textiles, and this led to a significant shift in her self-image as an artist. She explained: "needlework was not considered art in any of the art schools I attended. In fact, in the sixties, working in fibers virtually guaranteed that you would not be considered a serious artist." She pursued both the images and the medium, and a new major work, *The Birth Project,* was the result. Completed after five years of experimentation, it involved the participation of scores of needleworkers and weavers working in their own homes all over the United States, as well as in Canada and New Zealand. Of it Chicago wrote:

> "The Birth Project" is not one single work of art, but is, instead, a large series of works intended to be exhibited in small groupings. All the images are mine, and all of them are executed in or embellished with needle or textile techniques. All the art is accompanied by written and photographic documentation, which includes information about the personal testimony from the needleworkers. . . .[41]

Typical of comments from needleworkers was this one from Maggie Eoyang, of Berkeley, California: "For me, this piece brings beauty and meaning into the world; I hope She will touch men and women's lives deeply, remind them of the force of life, the power of beginnings, the awe of the bringer and the brought." Another commentary came from Jane Gaddie Thompson, of Houston, Texas, in which she related her own birth experience to the needlepoint which she executed, "Birth Tear":

> It was a Sunday—the football game was on. After twelve hours with no medication, the doctor came in and said, "I think we're going to have to do a C-section." But he waited until after the football game; I was really teed off. I was completely dilated but she was too big to move down. There was a lot more pain than I expected. That's why this piece, "Birth Tear," meant so much to me when I first saw it; I felt that Judy's representation of birth was perfectly realistic.[42]

Witnessing birth for the first time, interviewing women about their experiences giving birth, researching the history of childbirth, and studying the creation myths of peoples in cross-cultural perspective, Chicago composed a series of drawings depicting the birth process. In announcing the project, Chicago observed how few images of birth there were in Western European and Euro-American art. There were many images of mothers and children, often sentimentalized, but of the actuality and drama of birth there was no representation.[43] The interior representation of women's experience which Chicago had begun in *The Dinner Party* was continued in *The Birth Project*.

In Chicago's images the female body, splayed open in childbirth, is a monument of enormous strength and beauty—radiant, centered, central to creation. It is also a body gripped with pain, with the agony of creation that is in no way passive, innocent, or weak. In the depiction of "The Crowning," that extraordinary moment when the head bursts through the dilated cervix, the female form sinks and rises into earth and sky, blending, connecting, soaring, into a blaze of strength. These images are deliberately and consciously drawn from the creation myths of many non-Western and sometimes tribal cultures in which the female principle is honored, and ideas of balance, harmony, and interconnection inform their spiritual roots. For many of these peoples, the birth experience and the nurturing of small children are at the center of the concept of a female principle. This principle embodies strength, power, endurance, and creativity. In these cultures also, the female principle is often in balance with the male principle, each containing the attributes in abstraction of "femaleness" and "maleness" assigned by the culture. One is not less valued than the other. The Navajo, for example, speak of Mother Earth and Father Sky. Among the peoples of the southwestern United States, a steady but gentle rain is a "female" rain and a forceful downpour in which there is considerable run-off is a "male" rain. The female rain is particularly valued in agricultural-based societies. By focusing on the birth experience in relationship to non-Western creation myths, Chicago's images diverge dramatically from traditional Western European views of women as passive and infantile subjects and of childbirth as a medical emergency. Executed in tapestries, quilts, and needlepoint, in colors at once subtle and intense, Chicago's images are repeated in a seemingly endless series of variations.

As in the ceramic process in *The Dinner Party,* the translation of Chicago's images from painting to fiber transformed them, in this case producing a sense of motion and life that could not be otherwise achieved. One particularly dramatic example of this transformation was effected by needleworker Chrissie Clapp of Red Bluff, California, who executed one of the more unique versions of "The Crowning." Clapp used a crocheting technique that she developed herself, which was very difficult. As she worked, she had to prevent the crochet from pulling in on itself or the image would have been greatly distorted. But in the translation of color from painting to needlework Clapp's piece took on an undulating quality, "lifting" the image in ways that greatly enhanced its effects. The quality of interconnection central to Chicago's motif was "given life" in Clapp's version of it.[44]

Judy Chicago's projects sought to convey the interiority of women's experiences in both image and form. Given the power in this work, it is when it fails that we most clearly see its essential purpose. Being white in a racist culture, it is not surprising that it is in Chicago's encounter with race that her work loses its interiority. Alice Walker, reviewing *The Dinner Party* from the distinct perspective of a Black woman, wrote:

> I was gratified . . . to learn that in the "Dinner Party" there was a place "set," as it were, for black women. The illumination came when I stood in front of it.
>
> All the other plates are creatively imagined vaginas. . . . The Sojourner Truth plate is the only one in the collection that shows—instead of a vagina—a face. In fact, *three* faces. One weeping (a truly cliché tear), which "personifies" the black woman's "oppression," and the other screaming (a no less cliché scream) with little ugly pointed teeth, "her heroism," and a third, in gimcracky "African design," smiling. . . .
>
> It occurred to me that perhaps white women feminists, no less than white women generally, cannot imagine black women have vaginas.
>
> However, to think of black women as women is impossible if you cannot imagine them with vaginas. Sojourner Truth certainly had a vagina, as note her lament about her children, born of her body, but sold into slavery. Note her comment . . . that when she cried out with a mother's grief, none but Jesus heard her. Surely a vagina has to be acknowledged when one reads these words. (A vagina the color of raspberries and blackberries—or scuppernongs and muscadines—and of that strong, silvery sweetness, with, as well, a sharp flavor of salt.)
>
> And through that vagina, Children.[45]

Walker, of course, is right, and the truth of her criticism hits hard and sure. It is also contextualized by Walker who comments that overall, "I loved Chicago's art and audacity." What struck me most about her criticism was the fact that the face is, literally, external, and the vagina is internal (and external). It would be very difficult for Chicago, as a white woman, to know the interiorized experience of Afro-American women. Unless Chicago worked with Afro-American artists in the creation of the imagery, her depiction was likely to be an externalized vision, and one that objectified the subject, in much the same way that male artists objectify women in their paintings. That is, these (male) images are projections of the male artist's ideas of how women are (or how he wants them to be). They cannot be representations of women's interior, experiential reality. The repetition of these projections, distorted by and reinforcing a sexist lens contributes centrally to women's colonization. Insofar as white women replicate this process they participate, however unwittingly, in the colonization of women of color.

The stunning achievement of *The Dinner Party* was in transforming Euro-American women into the subject. Insofar as aspects of womanness are universal, the project penetrated beyond its specific representation. However, in and through its specific settings, *The Dinner Party* claimed a more sweeping historical vision. Chicago responded to Walker's criticism with both defensiveness and pain, and in the making of *The Birth Project* she shied away from the race issue, but, of course, it remained an issue.

Three years into the making of *The Birth Project*, Chicago thought about executing a series of images she called "Father Africa" to balance the work then in progress called "Mother India." Chicago's African research, however, focused on the practice of what is euphemistically called "female circumcision," and what is actually a painful practice of clitoridectomy. Chicago correctly identified this as a form of genital mutilation performed in certain countries. Claiming problems of staff overload and time constraints in addition, Chicago explained her decision to abandon the African sequence:

> I was really daunted by the question of visually representing genital mutilation—I frankly didn't know how I could present the African birth experience without confronting it. [Also] I had been severely trashed, both in person and in print, for my representation of the black feminist and abolitionist Sojourner Truth in the "Dinner Party," and I was somewhat afraid to deal with an issue that was so fraught with political ramifications.[46]

The Birth Project images of "The Crowning" and the "Creation Myths," among many others, work because they come from an interior,

experiential space, transcending both time and culture. One can see immediately, however, that in the Indian and (projected) African imagery, the
externalized objectification of women of color exhibited in *The Dinner
Party* presents itself again. These cultures are beyond Chicago's experience. Also, she is not sensitive to the feelings of peoples subjected to
centuries of colonial rule and cultural imperialism. In *The Birth Project*
Mother India appears repeatedly as the victim of her own oppression; the
strength and agony of the earlier images dissolved (literally) in tears.
Moreover, to focus on genital mutilation in Africa is to reassert the
thematic primacy of victimization in two ways. First, Chicago does not
know the interior reality of the women's experience of the mutilation or
the cultures which they have invented to accommodate and/or resist it
(and if she knew this it would undoubtedly have helped her to solve the
problem of representation and would make these images congruent with
the rest of the exhibit). Second, the focus on mutilation distorts the
African birth experience because it does not represent the diversity, antiquity, and beauty of African cultures of which, again, Chicago seemed
clearly uninformed.[47]

Within the community of feminist artists, Chicago has also been
controversial around issues of process. Seeing herself in charge, she has
not worked collectively with the potters, painters, sewers, and needleworkers she has employed. Their labor was unpaid, and they had very
little, if any, opportunity to create their own stitches, patterns, and art
work. The process then, replicated a hierarchy between "fine art" and
"craft" found in the mainstream art world, which has traditionally reinforced the subordinated status of women. Yet the content of Chicago's
work validates the beauty, strength, and anguish of women's experiences,
on their own terms.

The power of Judy Chicago's work comes from her ability to take
women's ordinary life experiences and make us think about them in new
ways. Dinner parties are female orchestrated events. They are rituals of
continuity and connection to family, friends, community, religion, history,
culture. They mark rites of passage and commemorate significant events.
They provide children with the stories and ceremonies upon which to
build their sense of cultural, racial, religious, and/or class identity. They
may not always be called dinner parties, and they may not always be
marked by the formality and etiquette of the upper-class ambience evident

in Chicago's work, but the communal process of sharing food, prepared and arranged by women, is apparent everywhere. In these ways, dinner parties have intrinsic purpose and meaning. These are made visible in *The Dinner Party*. At the same time, Chicago invites us to attend a new arrangement. Here is a dinner party, a ritual of connection and ceremony, in which women are not only the instruments of its perfection but also the subject of its festivities.

Likewise, in *The Birth Project* Chicago's images diverge dramatically from traditional Western European views of women as passive, incompetent, and/or fragile subjects. Tribal consciousness sees the conception, pregnancy, and birth cycle as the quintessential metaphor of the human experience, and in this way honors the female principle as the source of all life. In both her depiction of women's strength and in her invocation of tribal consciousness, Chicago imagined women in empowering and self-affirming ways. These ideas about women, birth, and Creation are not simply (or inevitably) a reformulation of the "woman is to Nature as man is to Culture" paradigm that pervades Western ideology. This paradigm sees men as the inventors of "culture," and women as the personification of "nature." It has been used by men to justify (and explain) their domination of women and nature; and it has been reappropriated by some feminists as a celebration of Woman, blurring the difference between the female principle, which is a spiritual and philosophical abstraction, and women as they are lodged in the real social conditions of their lives. Central to Chicago's achievement in *The Birth Project* is her success in riding the tension between the spiritual and the actual. The female principle as a spiritual manifestation and women as they exist in the material world are both represented in distinct and definable ways, visually and in the accompanying texts.

Chicago "gets inside" the birth experience to a degree that has been rarely, if ever, achieved in Western European and Euro-American art. As in *The Dinner Party*, Chicago takes women's ordinary life experience, in this case giving birth, and endows it with new meaning, restoring the specialness of each birth. Penetrating to the core of the miracle, with all the muck of oppression momentarily cleared away, women are seen as intelligent and courageous actors in the birth process. Women's strength and endurance are made visible and honored. Chicago, and the needlework artists who contributed so centrally to the *Project*, help to restore women's sense of Self—not as the abject subject of patriarchal medical practitioners but as bearers of life in a world of sometimes monstrous brutality which each has, at that moment, survived and transcended.

The struggle to transform woman into the subject of her own experience has been pivotal in the work of women artists haunted, as Chicago has been, by the problems of confidence and independence in the male-dominated world of the fine arts. These artists have traveled a largely uncharted course littered with the debris of centuries of material and emotional privation. Through their struggles, however, one can see the ways in which the imaginative impulse has been used as an instrument of survival for the artists and for the women viewing their work.

The work of the Japanese-born artist Mayumi Oda provides us with another example of innovation and transcendent illumination. Mayumi Oda was born in Tokyo in 1941, six months before the Japanese bombed Pearl Harbor, and her early life was fiercely marked by the chaos of war. Despite dislocation and physical suffering brought on by the war's destruction, Oda had a relatively secure and loving childhood. Her father was a teacher of Buddhist history at the Imperial Army Academy; her mother had been the youngest of seven daughters in a cultured and artistic family. Oda was named after her paternal grandmother. In an autobiographical prelude to a book of her prints, she writes:

> My name, MAYUMI, is Buddhist; it means "sandalwood," a hard, fragrant wood used to make Buddhist rosary beads and incense. My grandfather chose a Buddhist name for me in memory of his wife Ai, a devout Nichiren Buddhist and a passionate Socialist. Long before I was born, Ai had taken her own life, possibly because she was ill with incurable tuberculosis and possibly because of her despair with the political oppression of the times. Although the family never spoke about her death, it was clear to me even as a child that everyone had admired her as a woman of great compassion.[48]

Oda's early interest in art was evident, and she was encouraged by her family, especially by her mother, to pursue her studies. Having completed high school, she worked diligently to perfect the technical skills necessary for entrance into Japan's prestigious National Academy of Art. On her third entrance examination she was admitted. However, Oda was soon disappointed because of the academy's academic approach to art. She felt trapped, her artistic impulses stifled. In her freshman year she met a young

American named John Nathan. He had just graduated from Harvard, was fluent in Japanese, and was in Tokyo to study Japanese literature. They fell in love. Her parents consented to the marriage on condition that she finish her four years in the art academy. They were married in 1962 and Oda was graduated from the academy in 1966. Then she and Nathan moved to New York City. It was an enormous and very difficult shift for the young artist and soon-to-be mother. By 1970 Oda had two sons and was living in Cambridge, Massachusetts. Her art studio was in the dark basement of her Victorian home. "When I could steal time from housework and caring for two small boys," she writes, "I would rush downstairs to work. . . . It was in that dim basement beneath the deep Boston snow that I began to silk-screen prints of women in exorbitant color. Working there in the basement, I felt that I had reclaimed myself" (p. 11).

Oda's return to an artistic self-expression coincided with the first stirrings of the women's liberation movement. Caught up in the sweep of its energies, Oda felt renewed and invigorated, but she also felt that its emphasis on women as victims of male oppression did not coincide with her own experience. In giving birth, in carving out her own space as an artist, she recognized her strength and the potential power of all women. While acknowledging oppression and anger Oda struck out on her own, giving expression to women's strength.

Drawn back to her own cultural and spiritual roots, Oda rediscovered the writings of one of modern Japan's first feminists, Raicho Hiratsuka. In 1911, in the first edition of the magazine SEITO (which means Blue Stockings, from the English feminist movement) Hiratsuka had written:

In primeval times, women were one with
the sun and truth of all-being.

Now we are like pale faced moons who
depend on others and reflect their light.

Women, please let your own sun, your
concentrated energy, your own submerged
authentic vital power shine out from you.

. . . .
Woman, when you paint your own
portrait, do not forget to put the golden
dome at the top of your head. (P. 12)

Inspired by Hiratsuka's "golden dome" and by her own womanist re-visioning of the Bodhisattvas in the Buddhist pantheon of compassion and wisdom whom she had known as a child, Oda worked with vigor and purpose. She transformed the (almost all) male Bodhisattvas into female figures—some playful, others powerful, all radiant and irreverent to tradition. Large silkscreen prints, two to three feet in height, in wonderful colors, many blazing with humor, depicted Oda's world of goddesses. Plump, buxom, bare breasted, nipples and cheeks tinged with color, Oda's goddesses soar, swim, and swirl, wielding symbols of power and vision. Speaking of her work, Oda said that for her "art is not illustration; it is embodiment."[49] Oda explained that for her, living in a domestic world of wifely and motherly duties in the early 1970s, her goddesses became the lifeline to her sanity and survival. Endowed with talent and passion, the work poured from her, a veritable flood of consciousness revealing again the power of imagination in staking the claim to Self. Thus came, for example, *Sea Goddess* evoked by a novel called *The Wheel of Life,* written by the early twentieth-century novelist Kanoko Okamoto, who, Oda explained, was born on the banks of the Tama River:

> In her novel . . . a woman named Choko (child of butterfly) aban-doned her home and her lover and became a beggar drifting down the river, until finally she is swept into a vast sea called Life. For Kanoko Okamoto, both the river and the Sea represented the vast power of womanhood. She wrote:
>
>> The river is bountiful, as though nourished by an inexhaustible breast; the River empties into a vast Sea enfolding everything, never ending. (P. 18)

In another print called *Treasure Ship on the River of Our Mind* which is part of a *Treasure Ship* series, we find the goddess seated on her dragon-crested ship, sailing the river, strumming her lute. Oda's caption noted that "traditionally, there are seven happy deities aboard the Treasure Ship. Six of these are male, including the Gods of Wealth, Fortune, and Longevity. The sole female is Benten, Goddess of Art and music. Benten is the Muse of the East" (p. 30). There are six prints in this series, and in each a different goddess represents another aspect of kindness and beauty, sailing on the waters of Life. One of the most beautiful in this series is *Goddess of Flowers,* of which Oda wrote:

My grandmother was a wonderful seamstress. All the day long, sitting in a sunny corner of our family room, she sewed kimonos and quilted vests for her family. Toward the end of her life she was nearly blind, but she continued sewing until the day she died. When she finished something she would hold it up to me and say, squinting to see the cloth, "What a lovely design for you, Mayumi." We both loved flowered patterns, especially chrysanthemums, peonies, and wisteria. (P. 32)

These flowers bedeck the ship of Oda's goddess on her *Treasure Ship,* memorializing her grandmother's work and vision. In *Goddess of Snow,* we find another goddess, her ship bedecked with green, the bountiful spread of life and renewal, while around her the wintry signs of snow fall. She is playing a flute. Of her, Oda wrote this playful explanation: "Ai Huang is a Tai-chi master and a wonderful self-taught flutist. His ancient bamboo flute came to him through many many people's hands. This flute had an amber color and was almost transparent. One day he played it for me and I painted him as the Goddess. I hope he doesn't mind" (p. 38). In this *Treasure Ship* series, Oda transformed the male gods representing material well-being into goddesses celebrating the beauty of the natural world as symbolized by the female principle. Likewise, women's industry and peaceful visions of life are imagined in quiet, pleasant ways.

In contrast are Mayumi Oda's representations of *Thunder Goddess* and *Wind Goddess.* Here are revealed women's power to create and transform life in which, "our maternity comes out of a universal womb" (p. 42). Both prints convey intense motion, the goddesses generating great swirls of energy. While neither image is frightening or cast in anger, both suggest that theirs is a force to be reckoned with. The power to create life is inexorably linked to the power to end it, in a seasonal cycle of renewal, death, renewal.

Among the most beloved of the Bodhisattvas is Avalokiteshvara, the embodiment of compassion. This Bodhisattva appears in female form in Japanese culture, the only one in the Buddhist pantheon to do so. Her name is Kannon Bosatsu. Mayumi Oda offers us two depictions of this wonderful source of unconditional love. In each print she sits aloft a giant, red-crowned crane, one of the most beautiful of birds. In each print Kannon's legs are crossed in the traditional lotus position for meditation.

But there is no sense of stillness in Oda's vision. Kannon is an energy field alive with purpose, and in one of the prints, the flute of the Tai-chi master reappears. *Goddess Hears People's Needs and Comes* is the title of one, depicting "a person who *sees* the *sounds* of the world and perceives the cries of people in distress" (p. 26). *Goddess Coming to You: Can You Come to Her?* is the title of the second, conveying the active claiming of Self and compassion as one process: "Repeating the name of Kannon Bosatsu . . . hundreds and thousands of times, people eventually get in touch with their own source of power energy and compassionate self. This is the simplest, probably the most powerful Buddhist practice. Kannon Bodhisattva is liberating universal energy, and your belief in her makes you a Kannon goddess" (p. 68).

Perhaps the most humorous and intentionally subversive of Mayumi Oda's goddesses is the female impersonation of Manjusuri, "the perfect wisdom Bodhisattva, usually depicted with a sword." Oda's Manjusuri is female and "carries a sutra as a symbol of clarity" (p. 14). Traditionally, the male Manjusuri is astride a huge lion. In Oda's version, the female Manjusuri is self-propelled on a bicycle, the lion dashing alongside, with a comical, green-colored mane flowing wildly behind him. The bicycle is an old Victorian model, with its front wheel hugely enlarged, dwarfing its rear anchor-wheel. A naked Manjusuri pedals full-steam ahead, the sutra held aloft, the unbound scroll trailing outstretched in the wind. In a further explanation of this print, Oda said that when she got her first bicycle as a little girl in Japan, she loved to ride it. It provided her with her first sense of freedom. Endowing Manjusuri with self-propulsion and proclaiming the sacred text of the sutra as emblematic of female wisdom, the radical message of Oda's vision is confirmed. In the reassertion of female beauty and power Oda draws inspiration from the ideas of Raicho Hiratsuka and Kanoko Okamoto, both of whom were Buddhist practitioners. They "discovered through their . . . practice," Oda explains, "a source of vital power within themselves which they identified as a long-forgotten female vitality and strength—the creative power of primeval Woman" (p. 11).

Mayumi Oda's work is inherently subversive of the Buddhist tradition insofar as that tradition has been institutionalized in a male-dominated pavilion. Her work draws upon what she sees as a vital female energy. She restores the balance between female and male principles as mutually essential symbols of compassion. In this way her work penetrates to the enlightened core of Buddhist teachings stripped of their surrounding cultural constructs that privileged men and subjugated women. Oda's work is an imaginative incitement to female power reminiscent of the woman warrior in all her many forms. Oda's goddesses were instruments of her own survival. They also serve as a transcendent representation of female beauty and wisdom. While drawn from a very different cultural, aesthetic, and spiritual tradition they are reminiscent of the transcendent qualities of female energy represented by Judy Chicago in *The Birth Project*.

Mayumi Oda's images devolve from a spiritual quest and designate the female principle as divine. In a world in which religious dogma codifies woman's spiritual profanity and sanctions her subjugation, Oda's work is particularly significant; for women are seen as a representation of spiritual uplift and sustenance, a source of divination and wisdom. Other contemporary artists in the United States have also invoked representations of the goddess, albeit from diverse cultural traditions. For example, Karen (K) Lee Robins divines wonderful goddesses such as *Juno, Amazon Lady Gaia,* and *Ishtar.* Soft rounded bellies and breasts are shaped from the wood she sculpts. Mary Beth Edelson uses the goddess extensively in multimedia presentations that include installations, sculptures, drawings, paintings, and ritual enactments. As with Robins, Edelson celebrates mainly the goddesses of Old Europe and the Near East drawn from Neolithic times exuding "celebrations of free contemporary women."[50] The Cuban-American artist Ana Mendieta drew upon African, Cuban, Mexican, and indigenous traditions to produce powerful goddess imagery in her performance art. Her *Silueta* series in the late 1970s and early 1980s used both her silhouette and a natural outdoor environment to create a reflection in which women see themselves as the goddess and the goddess in themselves.[51] Chelo González Amézcua from Del Rio, Texas, uses multicolored ball-point pens on paper or cardboard "to represent in highly intricate linear patterns, Aztec poets, rulers, muses, and other regal personages, which in themselves evoke a certain mystical or magical quality." She calls her paintings " 'Filigree Art, a new Texas culture' because they are so much like the intricate metal work in the earrings and bracelets she loves to wear." Her work is highly stylized, emphasizing her Indian and Mexican heritage.[52]

While Judy Chicago and Mayumi Oda, each in their respective ways, designate an imaginative abstract of "woman power," the contemporary Afro-American artist Elizabeth Catlett projects a social realism drawn precisely from the material and the mundane. Pieced from the dailiness of Black women's lives, and influenced by the civil rights and women's liberation movements, Catlett's images of women affirm the daily experience of struggle and survival in North America.[53]

Born in Washington, D.C., in 1917, and supported through her early training in art school by her mother's labors as a domestic worker, Catlett was the first Black person graduated with a master's degree in fine arts from the University of Iowa. That was in 1941. She traveled to Mexico City a few years later in order to further her studies and elected to remain in that country, preferring residence in a Third World culture where she would be less fettered by the daily pressures of racism. She married fellow artist Francisco Mora, a part Tarascan Indian from the state of Michoacan. Together they helped staff the Taller de Gráfica in Mexico City and became friends with Frida Kahlo and Diego Rivera, among others, sharing a commitment to revolutionary politics and art. The Moras had three sons born in rapid succession in the late forties and early fifties, and Catlett, inundated with child-rearing responsibilities and financial hardship, had little time to pursue the sculpture that was at the heart of her creative expression. Persecuted by the U.S. government because of her radical views and affiliations, Catlett found it very difficult to return to the United States. In 1963 she gave up her American citizenship and became a citizen of Mexico. Public protests in the late sixties forced the U.S. government to allow her entry into the country to lecture and exhibit her work. She has also traveled widely to China and Africa and throughout Europe.

Catlett's work is rooted in the heritage of African-American, Mexican, and Indian peoples. Engaging a blend of technique and vision commensurate with the intimate range of her multicultural experiences, the portraiture of African-American womanhood resides at the core of all her work, the images strong and dignified and the residue of women's labors visually abundant. Catlett's cultural context provides her mature work with an internationalist perspective.

Among Catlett's earliest sculptures are three dating from the thirties and forties when she lived in the United States. Each is the portrait of a Black woman. The first, *Reclining Figure* (plaster, 1938) depicts a female form lying back, upper torso resting on her elbows, her head bent forward, her face smoothed and without features. An evocative work, poised between the realist and abstractionist schools, the tension of form produces an intense pathos. The second, *Mother and Child* (limestone, 1940), was her master's thesis and is thoroughly realist in expression. The mother is seated, a child crouched in her lap and enwrapped in her arms. The portrait balances strength and tenderness, protection and serenity. The third, *Tired* (1946), worked in terra cotta, depicts a Black woman barefoot, seated, her enormous hands clasped in her lap, her large feet planted firmly in the ground. She is a powerful figure, her head jutting forward and to the side, fatigue marking the contours of a beautiful face, her breasts in a full and sweeping curvature.

Four linocuts dating from 1946–47 depicting overtly political themes place Black women at the center of the resistance to slavery and racism. In each, Catlett's figures are large powerful women with immediately identifiable, working-class origins, cut from the knowledge of everyday life. *I'm Harriet Tubman: I Helped Hundreds to Freedom* is reminiscent of lithographs by the German artist Käthe Kollwitz depicting the uprising of German peasants in the nineteenth century. In Catlett's work, Tubman looms in the foreground, upright and fearless, pointing the way. *I Have Given the World My Songs* is a blues singer, a big-boned woman, in the ordinary clothes of everyday life, seated, strumming a guitar. Behind her are the shadows of a lynching, the artist's representation of Billie Holiday's "Strange Fruit." *I Have Special Reservations* is the portrait of ordinary Black women riding a segregated southern bus, their section marked "Colored Only," the scowling, tired, angry faces foretelling the defiance of the Montgomery bus boycott ten years later. *I Have Studied in Ever-Increasing Numbers* shows the struggle of Black women for education, a group of four studying, books opened, their faces marked by fatigue, and yet still animated, attending to their lessons.

Catlett has reworked these early portraitures over the years, using various techniques, forms, and postures, creating a gallery of life rooted in the dailiness of Afro-American women's experiences. Later, she integrated Mexican women into her work, reflecting experiences in her adopted country. Writing about her vision as an artist Catlett affirmed how central women have been in her process of creation:

I don't have anything against men but since I am a woman, I know more about women, and I know how they feel. Many artists are always doing men. I think that somebody ought to do women. Artists do work with women, with the beauty of their bodies and the refinement of middle-class women, but I think there is a need to express something about the working-class black woman, and that's what I do. I am interested in women's liberation for the fulfillment of women; not just for jobs and equality with men and so on, but for what they can contribute to enrich the world, humanity.[54]

Rejoicing in this process of self-affirmation, Catlett has observed that while technique and formal training are essential, a representation of one's core experience is the most important artistic element. She explained: "I learned from Diego [Rivera] that the more you know about anything, the greater an artist you are. So I think the depth of what you know about everything—and especially about yourself, where you come from, what you're doing—is much more important than knowing what's going on in the galleries of Paris" (p. 148).

Catlett has been influenced by West and central African art forms as well. She has, as one critic succinctly put it, "used the spirit—and frequently the form—of African art to express universal ideas. Use of masks, and a simplicity of form mark this influence in Catlett's work." Commenting on her formal technique, Catlett observed: "When I carve, I am guided by the beauty and by the configuration of the material. When I use wood, for example, I might exaggerate the form to bring out a little more of the grain of the wood. I like to finish a sculpture to the maximum beauty attainable from the material from which it is created" (p. 90).

Viewing Catlett's work, I am particularly partial to those carved in wood where the African influence and female curvature are most pronounced. Examples of these works include: *Mother and Child* (pecan, 1972); *Magic Mask* (polychromed mahogany, 1971); *Pensive Figure* (cedar, 1968); *Two Heads* (mahogany, 1982); *Pregnancy* (walnut, 1970); *Mujer* (mahogany, 1964); *Figure* (apricot wood, 1974); and *Homage to My Young Black Sisters* (cedar, 1968).

The last three works, and two others—*Mother and Child* (terra cotta, 1978) and *Rebozo # 3* (limestone, 1968)—are reminiscent of imagery from figures of the ancient goddess. In *Homage to My Young Black Sisters* this is particularly striking, as the tall abstract figure, with her upraised fist, is hollowed out in the center. In antiquity this circled, empty space in a carved figure (this is prominent, for example, in the totems of the Northwestern peoples in British Columbia) is believed to have suggested the female principle as represented by birth: the ceaseless generation from infinite space. The imagery of regeneration seems an appropriate tribute to the Black women warriors of the southern civil rights movement. Perhaps the most beautiful of Catlett's works is the bronze head of the Black woman simply titled *Glory* (1981). Its poignant detail creates an energy that reminded me of how I envisioned Avey Johnson in Paule Marshall's novel *Praisesong for the Widow*.

Poised on the hinge between realism and abstract art, Catlett has been acutely aware of the tension in her work. She always wanted, she said, to be an abstract artist, but she believed that modern art was inaccessible to the masses of people whose experiences she sought to represent. Of this tension Catlett wrote: "Combining realism and abstract art is very interesting to me. People are always trying to separate them out and say that you are either abstract or you are realistic; either you are abstract or you are figurative. And I don't believe it. I think any good figurative artist relies strongly on abstraction" (p. 85). It may be that as in any "theoretical" form, the accessibility of abstract art is not so much a function of its level of abstraction as it is a question of its points of reference. If it bears no relationship to people's everyday lives and feelings and experience, it is not accessible. Catlett endeavored to resolve the tension between abstraction and realism by synthesizing the formal attributes of African and Mexican art. The African is more abstract, the Mexican is more realist, and each bears an affinity to African-American culture that European models lacked. To claim African-American women as the subject Catlett struggled to shed the crippling restraints of both masculinist and European (Euro-American) models.

The struggle of African-American women artists to transform themselves from object into the subject, as Michelle Cliff has observed, has been particularly difficult because of the historical legacy of enslavement.[55] Black people have been objects of sale in slave auctions and objects of a so-called scientific discourse proving race inferiority in nineteenth- and early twentieth-century academies. Artists have been confronted with a compelling urgency to establish the humanity of Black people in a white world of furious indictment. For the Black woman artist this struggle has often also been a double bind: to establish the specificity of *her* humanity as well as her man's, and to represent an interior landscape of authentic feeling that often and inexorably indicted his male supremacy, while loving him fiercely. Placed in this historical context, Catlett's work represents an important example in the struggle for a collective self-portraiture because her work is centered on women, and on the dailiness of life. Catlett's women reveal strength, endurance, intelligence, and often great beauty. They are also grounded in a sturdy realism revealing strife, and fatigue, and the toll of incessant poverty.

Saar, Chicago, Oda, and Catlett are representative of contemporary artists whose works are "womanist" in inspiration and form and whose imaginative impulses have been drawn from an interior knowledge of women's experiences, feelings, and labors. Their works originate in distinct cultural traditions, yet they share a process of struggle toward a gathering of women on their own ground. Artists and writers have been crucial to this struggle to find our ground because they have been among those gifted to transform the sight of the mind's eye into a concrete manifestation. The woman warrior, rescued from imaginative seclusion, is publicized and displayed. Beauty is envisioned not as an object of male projection and consumption but as the subject of female self-affirmation and love. Women's work becomes visible, acknowledged on its own terms and made important in the scheme of things. Women's fantasies, which so often have been used for individual survival, now also provide artists and writers with new forms of expression and new ways of looking at culture.

We are witness to and participate in the painstaking reconstruction of another way of seeing reality, lodged for centuries in the mind's eye, a memory for which there often has been no language. There has been feeling, however, because no colonization is ever complete, because women are human beings who have labored, and birthed, and perceived. They have given expression to this reality before in flares of inspiration, in what Michelle Cliff has called "the resonance of interruption":

> If we multiply one woman's silence of self across space and over time, we may see that the cultural history of women takes the form of an interrupted sequence of silences: outright silence, the inability to speak; or silence about the self, the inability to reveal. The interruptions in the silences occur when the voices of one or two women rise to speak the truth in an expression of the self; and we cannot doubt the courage of these few. . . . [56]

And women have also handed on the evidence of their reality in the course of their everyday lives in small ways that have accumulated nonetheless, as things do, this gleam of light in the mind's eye, now given expression with growing momentum, continuity of thought, and collective strength.

"Get Over This Hurdle Because There's Another One Coming": Women's Resistance & Everyday Life

We must hear what they were saying
before us
We must live inside their houses
inside their bones
where they remember
everything
  —Susan Dambroff, "Skeletons without Country"

I knew my mother as a Church woman, and a Club woman—and there was
something special about when she said "Sister," and when all those other
women said "Sister." They meant that in a very, very fundamental way. . . .
They seemed to me the most extraordinary people in the world. . . . we lived
within 23 blocks—which they could not break.
  —Toni Morrison, "Intimate Things in Place"

haha ga ima yo-koto
sono uchi ni
wakatte kuru

What your Mother tells you now
in time
you will come to know.
  —Mitsuye Yamada, *Camp Notes*

People who are the *targets* of any particular form of oppression have *resisted
and attempted to resist* their oppression in any way they could. The fact that
their resistance is not generally recognized is itself a feature of the oppression.
  —Ricky Sherover-Marcuse, "Liberation Theory: Axioms and Working Assumptions
  about the Perpetuation of Social Oppression"

HE WORD "resistance" is freighted with historical interpretation and nuance. We bring many assumptions to this word because of the way in which it has been defined in general (by men) in society. When we look at it from the point of view of women's lives, however, the meaning of the word changes. The purpose of this chapter is to propose a different concept of resistance as it has been generated by women out of their daily lives. This resistance is evidenced in many women's oral histories, narratives, stories, and poems. It is about creating the conditions necessary for life, and it is about women expanding the limits of the restrictions imposed upon them by misogynist, homophobic, racist, religious, and class boundaries.

This chapter focuses on the resistance strategies employed by women in their everyday lives and on how those strategies inform women's participation in those struggles traditionally recognized as resistance movements. Women's actions, cast as forms of resistance distinct from those usually engaged in by men, imply the existence of a women's history connected to, but also distinct from History as it has been recorded and told by those in power. There is here, as it were, a women's memory—in the words of the poet, a "memory in bone," to be excavated, studied, and put to everyday use.[1]

To a child growing up in the 1950s in a Communist family of Jewish heritage in New York City, the word "Resistance" could have only one meaning. It was always spelled with a capital "R" and it referred to the anti-Nazi underground in Occupied Europe during World War II. Women, of course, were part of this movement. For instance, Madame Marie Madeline-Fourcade led an underground network based in France. Her code name was "Hedgehog" and the rescue operation she headed was known as "Noah's Ark." Jewish women like Hannah Senesh in Hungary, Marianne Cohn Baum, Alice Hirsch, and Edith Fraenkel in Germany, and Zivia Lubetkin in Poland had been antifascist fighters.[2] But in my childhood it was understood—and I certainly understood—that the Resistance had been organized and led by men. They were the heroes whose stories filled my childhood.

As I grew older my world expanded and so did my understanding of the word. Phrases like "resistance to slavery," "resistance to oppression" were part of the Marxist vocabulary, but men were still the heroes. In the late 1960s, the young men of my generation, refusing to participate in fighting the Vietnam War, referred to themselves as draft resisters, and adopted the slogan "From Protest to Resistance." The "R" was again capitalized, emblematic of the many parallels expounded in that movement between Germany in the 1930s and the United States in the 1960s. As a participant in the student, civil rights, and antiwar movements of the sixties and seventies I had always thought of myself as a part of a resistance effort and as an inheritor of and contributor to the traditions of resistance upon which I had been raised.

In my experience, resistance had always been defined in terms of "opposition" and "power." That is, I had always understood that resistance to injustice required oppositional politics and a struggle for power against those responsible for maintaining social injustices. Embedded in this were three crucial assumptions. First *social* injustice was distinguished from the *private* injustice suffered by individuals. Second, resistance was counterposed to ideas about accommodation and collaboration. Third, social change was defined in terms of movements for political power. Examining these assumptions is important because it enables us to contrast them with those that inform women's everyday experiences and realities. Indeed, women's resistance as defined by the social conditions of women's lives exists, but it casts a very different glow back across the historical landscape.

Our ideas about resistance in the conventional sense have been tied to our ideas about progress. When we think of resistance we think about the ways in which progressive social changes will be gained, and most often we measure the success of a resistance movement by the sweep of the changes it effects. Even when a resistance movement fails—as in the case of the Warsaw ghetto uprising, for example—we memorialize its symbolic meaning in relation to its progressive and humanitarian aims. Progress is conventionally defined in terms of modernity, referring to the industrial capacity, agricultural abundance, technological sophistication, and medical proficiency of a society. In a political sense progress also usually refers to the class, racial, and (now) gender equality of a society, its advocacy of world and domestic peace, the access of its citizens to religious freedom, representative government, civil and political rights, and the provisioning of food, education, employment, housing, health care, economic security, and so on. At the very least, we can say that this is the discourse (if not the reality) framing a more or less global governmental consensus about progress.

Likewise, in the traditional understanding of resistance, it is assumed that change is social rather than individual, political rather than personal, and that resistance implies a movement embracing large numbers of people in conscious alliance for a common goal. These assumptions are informed by various theories of social change, some of which arise from liberal ("pluralist") ideas and seek to affect the policies of those in power. Other theories arise from more radical traditions, most notably the Marxist, and seek to remove a ruling class from power. It is useful also to note here that in these theories of social change (as they have been constructed by men) women, if they have been seen at all, generally have been considered as objects of oppression: either as the victims of circumstances to be rescued, educated, and brought into productive and public life; or as the backward and misguided pawns of reactionary (or counterrevolutionary) forces to be won over to progressive and revolutionary movements. In neither case are women seen as an autonomous, purposeful, active force in history.

The women's liberation movement was, in many ways, inaugurated by the consciousness-raising groups formed by women in the late sixties and early seventies. In these groups women shared their experiences and provided support for each other. From them a theory of oppression emerged that sharply diverged from the assumptions of both liberal and radical social theory. Namely, many women felt their oppression as women to be rooted, at least in part, in what the society defined as personal conditions, e.g., family, marriage, sexuality, motherhood.[3] In designating the personal *as* political, the women's movement revealed the extent to which "private" and "public" were boundaries of masculinist invention and initiated a whole series of actions—in the streets, in the courts, and in the legislatures—to redress women's grievances and meet women's needs. For example, domestic violence, marital rape, sexual harassment, child-support payments in cases of divorce, paid maternity leave, quality and low-cost child care have become matters of political struggle, however as yet unresolved.

While contesting the boundaries of what is political, the women's liberation movement also defined resistance on essentially the same grounds as those conferred by masculinist tradition, although the priorities of women's concerns have often been radically different. That is, the assumptions about progress, social change, and social movement informed the actions of the women's liberation movement. The politics are oppositional, and the struggle is for power.

In women's studies, and specifically in the excavation and interpretation of women's history, we have followed these same patterns. Since the early 1970s a lot of work has gone into reconstructing the participation of women in resistance movements—from the peasant uprisings in feudal Europe and Japan, to the militant strikes of women workers in the United States, to the struggles for national liberation in Asia, Africa, and Latin America, to the defiance of apartheid in South Africa. Likewise, women's historians have explored specifically female-organized movements such as those for woman suffrage, or against lynching, and what has been called "female institution building" in the United States, by which is meant the creation of stable, all-women's organizations for social, political, or economic reform. All of these movements have exhibited the essential features of oppositional politics characteristic of resistance, albeit within more radical or more liberal traditions. Women's historians, including myself, have almost always also accepted the underlying assumptions about progress and social change. This has led to the creation of a compensatory history. That is, we have inserted ourselves as women into social history, as participants and supporters in movements initiated by men and as founders of our own women's movements for social and economic justice. This history has been an empowering and exhilarating source of pride for those women who have had access to it. The historical models of courage, dignity, and endurance have fundamentally changed many women's sense of themselves and their heritage.

Moreover, because the women's liberation movement in the United States emerged in the flush of activism generated by the civil rights and antiwar movements of the 1960s, and because many of us in women's studies were personally engaged in those movements, we have been most attracted to and most comfortable with the discovery of our counterparts in prior centuries. Even historical studies that are not about resistance per se, such as those reconstructing women's lives in particular communities and times, and others taking up issues of domesticity, the frontier experience, church clubs, or literary circles, retain the same assumptions about progress and often allude to the influence of these forces and events on movements for social change, or vice versa. Women's history has added whole new categories to the professional discourse, such as sexuality, violence against women, reproductive freedom, child care, and maternity. And by inserting women into old categories we have forced new ways of looking at politics, education, employment, slavery, patriotism, nationalism, and "Manifest Destiny." But beyond this there is yet another view. There is a women's resistance that is not "feminist," "socialist," "radical," or "liberal" because it does not come out of an understanding of one or another social theory, and it is not informed by experience in conventional politics. It is a resistance that exists outside the parameters of those politics and outside the purview of any of the traditional definitions of progress and social change. Women's resistance as I am defining it here is shaped by the dailiness of women's lives. It comes out of the sexual division of labor that assigns to women responsibility for sustaining the lives of their children and, in a broader sense, their families, including husbands, relatives, elders, and community. This responsibility is knowingly accepted, albeit under enormous social pressure. Women's resistance also comes out of women's subordinated status to men, institutionalized in society and lived through every day in countless personal ways. Women's resistance is not necessarily or intrinsically oppositional; it is not necessarily or intrinsically contesting for power. It does, however, have a profound impact on the fabric of social life because of its steady, cumulative effects. It is central to the making of history, and, as I will try to show, it is the bedrock of social change. Too often we have not seen this kind of resistance or appreciated its cumulative effects because we have been looking for social movements as these have been traditionally defined, and we have looked for the historical moments when these movements have reached their apex, making sweeping social changes. To see women's resistance is also to see the accumulated effects of daily, arduous, creative, sometimes ingenious labors, performed over time, sometimes over generations.

Perhaps no more dramatic illustration of this concept of cumulative change can be found than in the current rates of divorce in the United States, which have reached such high levels that Arthur Norton of the U.S. Census Bureau estimated that 59 percent of all children born in the United States in 1983 were likely to live in a single-parent family before they were eighteen; and Sandra Hofferth of the National Institute of Child Health and Human Development projected that two-thirds of all children born in wedlock in 1980 would experience their parents' divorce by age seventeen.[4] What right-wing and conservative elements fear as the break-up of the American family is due at least in part to the growing refusal of many women to remain in oppressive marriages. This is so even though the consequences of divorce mean that a woman's income will plummet an average of 73 percent, while a man's income will rise by 42 percent. In other words, what we increasingly refer to as the "feminization of poverty" is not only a consequence of a deteriorating economic situation marked by inflation and a declining standard of living in general.[5] It is also a consequence of a steady and increasing resistance by women to marriage as it has been traditionally defined by men. As growing numbers of women have entered the work force, they have gained a degree of economic independence that makes divorce possible. This is not to say that men do not divorce women. It is not to say that women have collectively agreed upon a new concept of marriage. It is to say that women have played a significant role in effecting the structural changes in the work force and in the family that are now reshaping American society.

Women's resistance is informed by the logic of survival. For women, survival has meant both physical sustenance and emotional connection for themselves and their children. Women may be driven to opposition and confrontation as in strikes, but their emphasis is often on forging connection, especially within family, church, and community. Characteristically, women's resistance is informed by values of nurturance, beauty, connection, community, family, and endurance.

Hemmed in by patriarchal, racist, and class restrictions, the overwhelming majority of ordinary women have made their existence around the cracks and crevices allowed them by this multifaceted authority. Some are impoverished as single heads of household; some remain economically dependent on a male provider's income and benefits even when they themselves are employed. There is also, as one woman put it: "a no man's land between poverty and the middle class. . . . if people can get just a little above welfare income, it can scare them to death. Like my neighbor who has six children. When she got a job at minimum wages, she said, 'I'm so scared. I don't have the medicaid card for the children's injuries, and I don't make enough to pay any hospital bills.' "[6]

Professional women and others in highly skilled crafts, e.g., electricians, carpenters, and construction workers, may be economically solvent, but they must contend with the daily harassments of male managers, colleagues, administrators, and superiors. All women workers face these harassments, some of which are a result of gender and/or race discrimination and some of which are a result of sexual intrigue and pressure. Women also cope with their internalized oppression, with their loss of confidence and self-esteem, with feelings of despair and depression, with a deep-seated passivity ingrained through years of female socialization. The form of internalized oppression depends greatly upon ethnic and cultural background, but all women experience it. This oppression often keeps women in otherwise intolerable marriages, relationships, and jobs. Women juggle the competing demands on their energies and contend with the interminable tasks of provisioning their families.

To focus on women's resistance as it exists within the parameters of their daily lives is not to celebrate the confinement or to romanticize the enormity of the damage inflicted. It is to acknowledge the meaning women invest in their daily lives, to acknowledge this work on its own merits, to acknowledge that many women are indeed activists who have participated in the shaping of history, and have "walked purposefully in and out of the front door of their lives."[7] Moreover, it allows us to see the continuity, the connection between women's participation in resistance movements as these are conventionally defined and women's resistance as it has been invented out of the rigors of daily life. That is, the traditional forms of resistance engaged in by women have inexorably widened the options for women's resistance in daily life. For instance, the winning of woman suffrage, or of reforms in the divorce laws that established women's rights to community property and to custody of their own children, or of child labor laws, collective bargaining, and civil rights and affirmative action laws, has changed the grounds of struggle in many women's daily lives.

Likewise, the strategies used by women in their daily lives have informed their actions in more traditional forms of resistance at least as much, if not more, than those provided by conventional politics. For instance, there are many examples of strikes by predominantly female workers in which family and community networks previously formed by the women were at least as important as the union during a strike and often more enduring.

These networks have played a crucial role in facilitating women's resistance both on the job and in marriages, families, and personal relationships. While family and work compete with one another for a woman's time, a kind of family networking system is adapted by many women on the job to provide a key avenue for resistance. This network, however, is not limited to the discussion or resolution of on-the-job issues only. For women, work moves along a continuum traveling the route between job and family, family and job, daily. The workplace provides women with a new location in which to process significant problems at home, and resolve others on the job. Shop floors and offices (when possible), cafeterias, bathrooms, parking lots, carpools, subways, and buses become the settings for intense conversations. Subject matter can range from working conditions, such as wages, overtime, benefits, safety and health, production rates, and supervisors, to personal and domestic issues, e.g., taxes, bargain sales, diets, the Soaps, men, sex, drugs, and children. What may appear as idle and insignificant chatter (and sometimes is!) may also, at other times, be a vital, effective, and surprisingly intimate exchange of information. This network operates every day and in innumerable ways. At its core is the protection of women's dignity.

These networks also promote unity among women workers, essential when facing the continual barrage of management incentives. For example, anthropologist Louise Lamphere, working in a New England garment factory in the late 1970s, reported that the workers created ties among themselves in the face of production and ethnic conflicts by humanizing and "familizing" the work force. The piece-rate system, where workers were paid according to how much each produced rather than by the hours worked, set the women in competition with each other. In addition, a majority of the women were Portuguese, and some were recent immigrants who spoke little English. Other workers were French Canadian, Polish, and Italian. Lamphere reported that there were anti-Portuguese sentiments, and among the Portuguese women there were conflicts between those from the Azores and those from the continent. Whatever their divisions, Lamphere reported, the workers celebrated weddings and births, retirements, birthdays, and other special occasions. When there was a death in someone's family everyone pitched in to express condolences with flowers or cards. Everyone, regardless of her piece-rate grievances or her ethnicity, contributed money for presents and participated in these life-cycle events. They were held in the shop at lunch or during breaks. Lamphere emphasized the significance of the female workers' network: "Celebrating special events and sharing family pictures 'humanized' the workplace, bringing family life into the industrial setting where the piece-rate system drove workers apart and where ethnic divisions were clear. . . . These [events] might be termed part of a strategy of worker consolidation."[8]

Anthropologist Patricia Zavella, in a case study of Chicana cannery workers in the Santa Clara Valley, California, observed a comparable networking apparatus. Conditions in the canneries are extremely demanding physically. Zavella summarized the work conditions this way:

> Canning production is geared to a continuous conveyor belt that moves raw produce through various stages as it is processed, canned, cooked, and cased for storage or shipment to market. . . . the constant motion of so much produce on the conveyor belt, the humidity from water baths, the din of crashing cans and cooking machinery, as well as the nauseating odors of rotten produce and chemicals (such as chlorine) used in processing, make the job both distasteful and demanding.[9]

At the time of Zavella's study in the mid to late seventies, the overwhelming majority of cannery workers were Chicano, and most were women. Anglo men drawn from the Italian and Portuguese populations who once dominated among cannery workers were now in supervisorial positions. The Chicanas Zavella came to know had established elaborate kin and friendship networks essential to worker survival and to women's survival. These networks often crossed the boundaries between job and home:

> Work-related networks also operated like kin networks and served as sources of exchange among members. In particular, network members were good sources of information regarding problems that arose from their work situation. Women found babysitters through their networks or learned from coworkers how to qualify for unemployment benefits or how to claim disability pay. Work friends were also sources of advice and emotional support. Women discussed work and personal problems, especially those concerning children. Marital problems were important topics, and work friends provided a crucial source of support in women's struggles with their husbands.

Zavella concluded that the women's friendships flourished, and "especially if they were *comadres*, women were fictive kin and could feel free to develop *confianza* (trust or familiarity usually reserved for kin) with coworkers."[10] In the canneries, the networks were the setting for women's resistance—on the job, in their marriages, and with the Teamsters Union of which they were extremely critical. But this resistance, as Zavella observed, was not always or intrinsically oppositional.

The oral history of Maria Garcia, transcribed and analyzed by Kate Miller in the mid-1970s, provides additional insight into women's resistance strategies and their attitudes toward family and friendship networks. Summarizing Mrs. Garcia's life experiences, Kate wrote:

> She was born in the mountains of Arizona, and spent her early years in a thoroughly rural environment. Both of her parents were born in Mexico; her mother spoke no English and avoided contact with Anglo society. Her father was a stern, solitary man who preferred living in the mountains to life in town. The values transmitted to her in her mother and father's home included Catholicism, the importance of woman's role as homemaker, and the responsibility of the female family members to carry out this role by working industriously to maintain the comfort of the household. After her marriage, Maria and her husband moved to two mining towns in Arizona; then, during World War II, the family migrated to the Los Angeles area and from there to San Jose, California.

Noting that Mrs. Garcia's experiences were typical of the majority of Chicanas of her generation, Kate also summarized the class realities that marked her life:

> Maria's life story is a graphic depiction of struggle against racism and poverty. She bore four children, only one of whom survives. She has done hard physical labor her entire life. When she was a young girl and then a housewife, she kept house without the benefit of running water, plumbing or electricity. Later, she worked in the agricultural fields and orchards and in the packing houses and canneries. She had also spent many years doing domestic work and child care for Anglo families. . . . [11]

Extended families, and the families and friends of women's *comadres* formed a wide base for female support in Mrs. Garcia's life. Women provided each other with mutual aid, worked together, and "cooperated among themselves to enrich their lives and to make it easier for them to achieve their ends. . . . There were many ways in which this . . . network operated to circumvent male orders or wishes and to provide mutual protection to its members." However, Kate thought that "most of this rebellious activity was not deliberate on the part of the women." That is, it was designed to improve the quality of daily life for themselves and their families rather than to engage in a form of oppositional politics against their husbands. "Men were not expected to inquire too closely into the mechanics of their wives' daily chores," Kate wrote, "and the women usually felt that it was not necessary to *bother* their husbands with details of their day."[12] Women could give the appearance of compliance with male authority while providing support for each other in doing things of which their husbands might not approve. Women's resistance was not self-consciously oppositional, but it was self-consciously pursued and frequently subversive of male will and authority. Although Kate's conclusions reflected upon the particular experiences of a Mexican-American woman, they are more generally applicable.

In their efforts to resist the incursions and assaults on the quality of their daily lives women have bonded together in love and friendship, filled church pews, and sung in church choirs. They have held countless bake sales to raise money for every conceivable charity and community project. They have staffed child-care centers for little or no pay, negotiated interminably with school principals, teachers, welfare officials, social workers, and court clerks (many of whom are also women). They have made and mended clothes, cared for the sick and elderly, made something from nothing. Introducing an anthology of poetry by "ordinary women" in New York City, Adrienne Rich described women's daily lives in these terms:

> It's the women who cope. . . . The women are salvaging and building what they can, refusing to go quietly, putting up a struggle to the death. Every ordinary woman is extraordinary. The grandmothers, the mothers on the street, the angry housewives, the women in the empty office buildings late at night, the women who never planned this city, never had a thing to say about its priorities, the women whose work is always being undone, whose wars are waged against leadpaint/leaking toilets/rats/roaches/arsonists . . . who still make gardens in flower pots on housing window-sills, worry about holidays, the taste of special foods, rituals for birthing and dying, cleanliness and seemliness, the powerless responsibility for the lives of children, the consequences of sex, the despair and violence of men; women whose labor to create a decent space in an indecent system is perpetually mocked. . . . Women cope.[13]

What Rich describes as coping may be interpreted as a form of resistance. The shift in language is important because "coping" connotes the more passive and accommodating qualities precisely contrary to the passion of Rich's point. Women focus on improving the quality of daily life and on strengthening the connections between people in family, at work, and in the community. In the context of a society in which the quality of daily life is continually undermined and in which connections between people are continually threatened, such strategies, which form the sinews of life, are strategies of resistance.

The strategies women employ in their daily lives are relative to their conditions. They are relative to the tools and resources women have available, including the internalized fears of being and acting themselves. By and large women have been marginalized in or excluded from the centers of power like trade unions, political parties, social movements, and the armed forces, from which men have waged their resistance. Women's strategies have pivoted from different centers and engaged different priorities. Often the choices women make about how to resist and in what ways are made outside the rules and outside the boundaries of conventional politics. They cannot be judged or their effectiveness critically assessed by the designations employed in conventional social theories about the relations of power in the society.

For instance, what appears as collaboration or accommodation in a masculinist perspective (i.e., from men's point of view) may be reinterpreted from women's standpoint as resistance. This is not a contradiction in the sense that one point of view must overturn the other. It is rather a paradox that results from the imbalance in human affairs in which men have not only set the ground rules for social existence, but have also had the power to name what is collaboration, what is accommodation, what is resistance, what is progressive, as though the only viable and correct perspective was theirs (and from whichever circle of liberal or radical politics they happened to be standing). Women's stories, related in fiction and in oral histories, provide us with the evidence of another way of seeing these issues, and of thinking about resistance.

A short story called "Harvest," which is about women's resistance in a rural setting, by the novelist and poet Meridel Le Sueur, suggests ways in which a women's standpoint allows for a different concept of progress and social change. Le Sueur's family background and experiences provide a significant context in which to consider this story. She was of radical socialist parentage and of Dutch, Irish, and Indian heritage. "I was born,"

Le Sueur wrote, "at the beginning of the swiftest and bloodiest century, at Murray, Iowa, in a white square puritan house in the corn belt."[14] She began writing in the 1920s and celebrated her eightieth birthday in the spring of 1980. From the time she began writing, Le Sueur always identified herself with the radical Left in the United States. Her writing was blacklisted for thirty years. It was rescued from oblivion during the women's renaissance of the seventies and is now being issued through small but prolific presses. One woman writer, inspired by Le Sueur's work, described her this way: "bedecked with Indian turquoise bracelets and rings, a string of ominous teeth around her neck, a bright multi-colored serape covering her body—this walking heap of archetypal images is not your idea of somebody's grandmother. A grandmother no; a wise and maybe occasionally avenging ancient goddess, yes."[15] Actually, Le Sueur has seven grandchildren and many great-grandchildren, and the two images are not necessarily as contradictory as this writer thought.

Le Sueur's stories are usually brief, immensely powerful vignettes. They are scenes drawn from the dailiness of women's lives, gaunt, repetitive, cumulative images. Consciousness of women is distilled and mapped across a stark, interior terrain structured by the dailiness of poverty, patriarchy, and the struggle for survival.

"Harvest" was written in 1929. The plot can be briefly summarized, but to get the story, as it were, is more difficult because it requires the summary of a texture, a spatial and temporal sense, a way of seeing the world different from conventional assumptions. Ruth Winji is young, married, and four-months pregnant. She has been wildly in love with her husband and he with her. They live on a farm somewhere in the Midwest. Wheat is their major harvest. Ruth also has her own garden of berries, vegetables, and beans.

The husband has decided to buy a threshing machine to harvest the wheat. Ruth is unalterably opposed to this decision. Husband and wife quarrel for weeks. It is with her dowry money that he will buy the machine, but it is not his right to the money that she disputes. Ruth is unable to explain the reasons for her opposition: "She couldn't say why she was so afraid [of the thresher], but she knew that it was against her and against him. It was a new way." We learn from the other men talking to the husband that "lots of our women folks takes it that way at first."

The husband wants her consent, her approval, wants her to like the

machine. He thinks she is being unreasonable, stubborn. Ruth is forced by
the circumstances of her survival to submit to her husband's decision. The
thresher is bought:

> She began to cry, not lifting her hands. The sight of her exasperated
> him. "What are you crying for," he said in real anger but his face
> looked guilty. "What are you crying for," he shouted, raising his
> hand. "Stop that bellowing," he swore and struck her.
>
> She recoiled, her face lifted wide to him. He saw her falling back,
> her great eyes open upon him in grief. He gave a cry and caught her
> falling arms, thrust her toward himself. Against her he stood straight
> and she began to cry from her shaking body, rent by the grief in her.
> He held her and for a moment seemed to know what she had been
> feeling but it was only for a moment.[16]

For Ruth Winji, Le Sueur explains, the wheat was like the sea in a
slight wind that crested and foamed gently and receded in heavy fruition.
The harvester mutilated the crop, "mowed the wheat in terrible broad
swaths," she thought. Taking up Ruth Winji's point of view, Le Sueur
continues: "She saw the big knives thrust back movement even in their
stillness, and then on driving power and the tiny man-seat hidden inside,
where the little living man was supposed to sit and pull the levers as her
husband had been showing her. She was revolted." The harvester would
change the relationship of her husband to the soil, to the earth, to the act
of planting and reaping the harvest. In this way, the machine would also
change him and change his relationship to her: "Now she felt she was
losing him, as if he were falling out of some soft burr, their ancient closed
fertile life, being shaken from the old world tree, in ways beyond her, that
she could not go."[17]

Ruth Winji was not opposed to change. She was opposed to change
as the men in her life (and in ours) defined it. She was opposed to
knowledge defined as "cunning." She was opposed to progress defined as
"power" and "control" and "conquest" over the land. From her visions,
and with the resources and ideas she had available to her, Ruth Winji
resisted the purchase of the thresher as the other women had resisted
before her. That she and they failed in no way detracts from the significance of their effort.

Ruth Winji had a different, if as yet only partially articulated vision of
the world, of her relationship to it, of her place within it, structured by the

dailiness of her life, of her work, of her survival. Progress could come of this vision:

> From the hour's picking of berries and beans she had leaned over in her own heat and the sun's heat driving through her until earth memory and the seed memory were in her in the hot air and she was aware of all that stood in the heat around her. . . . Root darkness. Tree darkness. Sun. Earth. Body. She thought: *And my dark body in the sun, root-alive, opening in the sun dark at its deep roots.* . . . [18]

This vision of change articulated in disjointed or abbreviated images, tied somehow to earth and growth, appears repeatedly in women's stories. It is a vision of change structured by the dailiness of women's lives, especially in child work, seeing in this the practical things, the details that make life possible, understanding its vulnerability, the fragility of its roots and branches and flowers. There is also in Le Sueur's telling the sense of connection between Ruth Winji and the earth in the heat and darkness marking her feeling of place.

This vision of change is correlated to balance, to the interconnection of all things, to the urgent, deeply felt terror of a Ruth Winji that if you separate one thing from the whole, moving swiftly forward simply because it yields to your intelligence and will, you upset the balance upon which all life depends and in ways which cannot be easily, if ever, restored. Le Sueur's vision here reflects her Native American heritage, and the understandings she gleaned from it. She speaks finally of a different kind of harvest at the end of her story—of the husband's fear as he mounts the thresher and prepares to take the controls for the first time. It is a fear born of the realization that his wife might, in fact, be right about the nature of the machine: "for a moment a kind of fear struck him through the marrow. . . . Down his soft loins went a doom of fear . . . for leaving the moistness of sleep, the old world of close dreaming . . . the space of mystery where the seed unfolds to the touch in the cool and thick and heavy sap. . . ."[19]

In focusing on women's resistance in this way Le Sueur makes us think about the ways in which change and progress have been posed by the dominant culture as mutually reinforcing values. This story is not simply about the problem of feeding vast numbers of people. As Ruth Winji knows, Le Sueur certainly knows that the adequate provisioning of food (shelter, clothing, health care) changes the quality of women's lives in dramatic and wonderful ways. At issue in this story is *how* that provisioning is to be secured. Le Sueur asks us to consider whether productivity is to be privileged over the connections between people, over the delicate balance in which life is sustained. She asks us to consider the consequences of such a choice, one posed in opposition to the other. She asks us to consider the ways of knowing embedded in the life experiences of farm women, of rural women, of agriculturalists, accumulated over centuries of labor provisioning themselves, their families, their communities. Provisioning is not merely or exclusively a technical problem. For human beings it is also a social problem connected to our consciousness of ourselves, our ways of being, our accountability as sentient beings on the planet. Technology and change can come, but in time, and with care, and with respect for the intricate and infinite balance of things.

This is another story. It teaches us about the rescue of children, about cultural roots, and about definitions of betrayal from women's standpoint. This is a piece of the oral history of Elmas Tutuian. It was first told to her granddaughter, Arlene Avakian, when she was fourteen years old. It is the story of an Armenian woman who survived the massacres of her people in 1915, who engineered the survival of her three children, and who managed finally to come with her children to the United States. The genocide against the Armenian people by the Turkish majority claimed one and a half million lives in less than three years.[20]

Mrs. Tutuian was living with her husband and her three children, one son and two daughters, one of whom was to be Arlene Avakian's mother, in the village of Kastemoni in Turkey, in 1914. They were relatively secure economically, but World War I was imminent. Turkey was soon to be engulfed in the war and was intent on building its armed forces. Mrs. Tutuian's husband was inducted into the Turkish army. She never saw or heard from him again. Many years later she learned that he had died from exposure and exhaustion. The same year her husband was inducted into the army, Turkish soldiers rounded up all the Armenian men and boys over fifteen in the village of Kastemoni, took them to the outskirts of town, and shot them. While the Turks were engaged in a nationalist struggle against the British for control of what was then the remnants of the Ottoman Empire they were also seeking to repress the national aspirations of the Armenian minority within their country. On the one hand, the Turks needed soldiers; and, on the other hand, they intended to crush the Armenian people. Some Armenian men were shot while others were inducted. Armenian women and children were systematically murdered, exiled, or forced to renounce their identity and "become" Turks.

With her husband gone, the men of the village dead, the Turkish terror swirling around them, Mrs. Tutuian knew that her own survival and that of her children depended upon her. Raised to be dependent on a male provider, socialized to defer to male judgment and authority, she was faced with an awesome challenge. She struggled through the winter of 1914–15, preparing somehow to leave Kastemoni in the spring. Avakian narrates:

> On Easter Sunday [1915], while the Armenian women and children were in church, government officials sealed and bordered their houses leaving only one room open for use. Elmas came home to find she could only get into the dining room. The family had no clothes other than what they had on and no provisions for eating or sleeping.
>
> Elmas went to the police commissioner, who had been a friend of [her husband's] to ask for help. He told her that all Armenians were going to be exiled and he advised her to become a Turk. . . . She told him, "If my husband heard I became a Turk he would go to his grave. . . . what my nationality is—I'll be the same."[21]

The police commissioner warned her that it was going to be very bad. However, Mrs. Tutuian believed that she and her children would be exempted from exile because her husband was in the Turkish army. She refused to become a Turk. Meanwhile, the police commissioner did arrange for one more room in her home to be opened. Mrs. Tutuian was wrong in her hopes of reprieve. She and her children were exiled to a remote village, along with her sister-in-law and her children. Altogether eleven people were forced to live in one room.

Turkish soldiers came to the village of exile. They came into their one room. They wanted to know how many boys were in the house. Two, they were told, Visim and Ashot. Visim was too little to interest the soldiers. But they decided to take Ashot. "They are collecting the boys," they said. Mrs. Tutuian's memory of this scene was vivid:

> "You can't," I said. "I won't give him," I screamed. "I won't give him," I screamed. "I won't give him. You can't," I said. "Who are you to take my boy," I said.
>
> He said, "He is the king's boy."[22]

Ashot was to be raised as a Turk. He was taken.

Two days later Mrs. Tutuian set out on foot for the village of Dadai where, she was informed, her son had been taken. She left the two younger children in the care of her sister-in-law. She had no provisions. A stranger showed her the way. She walked over a mountain, alone. Eventually she found Ashot. He came running to her. Mrs. Tutuian had a vivid memory again:

> "Mother, save me. You save me."
>
> "That is why I came—to save you. I am going to save you. I won't leave you in the hands of these Turks. Don't worry."

Mrs. Tutuian left Dadai. She walked from there back to the village of Kastemoni to find the police commissioner who had helped her before. She traveled by night and hid by day to avoid being detected by police and soldiers. She managed to get to Kastemoni. She found the commissioner. She begged him to help her.

> "Tell me what it is I have to do to save him. I have to save him. I have to save him." He said, "today I am going to see my superior. I will speak to him and see what can be done. . . . But don't tell anyone you are here. There are some Turk dogs, who, if you say Armenian, they will cut your throat."[23]

The police commissioner arranged for Mrs. Tutuian to legally renounce her Armenian nationality and become a Turk. She was able to do the same for her children and for all her other relatives in exile. Ashot was released. All were then allowed to return to Kastemoni. Mrs. Tutuian, her two brothers, her sister-in-law, and the three children lived in two rooms. They eked out an existence. Mrs. Tutuian did sewing for soldiers and for neighbors, peddling her wares on her back. Threatened with rape by Turkish soldiers who tried to break down the door to their rooms, faced with near starvation, they survived the war.

At the end of World War I, the Turks defeated, the British temporarily in charge, Armenian orphans were being sent to Istanbul. Mrs. Tutuian approached the British officer in charge of this operation. She wanted to go with her children. But his orders were orphans only. "She convinced him that he needed someone to care for the children on the trip to Istanbul and she would do that for him in exchange for herself and her children."[24] The officer accepted her offer.

In this way Mrs. Tutuian escaped the village with hopes that in the city she could make a better living. She had her eye clearly focused on America. Her sister and brother-in-law were already living in New York City, having emigrated before the war. After many years of poverty and struggle in Istanbul, Mrs. Tutuian located a nephew of her husband's living in Iran. Told of her plight and her desire, he put together the money needed for their passage to New York. She and the children set sail.

This is a story of resistance. With incalculable strength, endurance, wit, and courage Mrs. Tutuian rescued her son and saved as many members of her family as she could. Betrayal defined from *her* point of view would have been to abandon Ashot to his fate. Resistance defined from *her* point of view was to protect the integrity of her family and to save her children's lives. To do this was a matter not of public display but of private will. Mrs. Tutuian was Armenian. She did not believe she could change who she was no matter what she signed because to her Armenian was a matter of ancestry, of heritage, of the heart. It could not be "taken." Only when her son's life was threatened, when there was no other way to save him did she "become" a Turk. The interiority of this belief coincides with the interior reality of women's lives—certainly of this Armenian village woman. That is, Mrs. Tutuian's world was that of the home, of the family, of community networks, especially through her church.

Mrs. Tutuian passed on her Armenian heritage to her children and to her grandchildren. She also passed on to her granddaughter, Arlene Avakian, a women's heritage steeped in courage and strength. This stood in stark contrast to the "submissive compliance" that patriarchal customs embedded in Armenian culture, which Mrs. Tutuian had also internalized. Avakian recalls, for example, that her grandmother deferred to male authority in the family and consistently favored her younger brother over herself. When she first heard her grandmother's story, Avakian was a rebellious adolescent striving to be "American" and "fit-in" with her high school crowd in an urban, working-class, ethnic neighborhood. She was not interested in her grandmother's story. However, she remembered the outlines of it, and it sifted in her mind and in her heart. It was part of the reason she joined the civil rights movement in the late sixties, and it informed her understanding of the women's liberation movement a few years later. What she understood in particular was that while women were deeply oppressed, they were not passive, compliant, victims. Women acted.[25]

Mrs. Tutuian's story set in World War I reminded me of others from the Jewish ghettos of World War II. Many of these also begin in Europe and end in America. A conference was held in New York City, March 1983 titled "Women Surviving: The Holocaust." Four hundred people attended. There was a panel on the ghettos. It was chaired by Alice Eckhardt of Lehigh University. There were three panelists, each of whom told her story: Susan Cernyak-Spatz from Vienna, then Berlin, then Prague, then a ghetto, then three different concentration camps; Luba Gurdus from Bialystok, Poland; and Vladka Meed from Warsaw. Luba Gurdus said:

> I was first of all a mother. In 1937 I married my husband Jack Gurdus and in 1938 gave birth to a child. My child was one year old when the war broke out. To me, it was most important to protect my child, as well as my parents. As a woman I felt that I was above all the mother of my child, and the daughter of my parents. . . . The whole load of guardianship and the whole load of sustaining the family had fallen on the shoulders of the women.[26]

As in the Armenian experience, the Jewish men were rounded up first, many, in this case, sent to labor camps, later to concentration camps.

Susan Cernyak-Spatz was in the Theresienstadt ghetto from May 1942 until January 1943. Her experience was in some ways different from the others because of the nature of this ghetto. She said:

> Theresienstadt was structured as a sort of showplace for the Germans whenever they wanted an inspection to show how *normal* things were for the Jews and how nicely they treated them. The Theresienstadt ghetto had such an aspect of normalcy that it was almost a microcosm of the life we had left in Prague. . . . Women were very active in sustaining a level of cultural life, which was a way of pushing out the possibility that there was any finality to this situation. . . .
> . . . We lived as much as possible. Maybe we somehow supported the German efforts in sustaining this normalcy, but it had a much farther effect in that we kept our cultural and intellectual aspect very high and very intense on all levels.[27]

Vladka Meed was in the Warsaw ghetto. She fought in the Warsaw ghetto uprising of April 1943 and subsequently escaped and joined the partisans. She said:

When we talk about food it is very hard for me not to recall the times of starvation in the ghetto. . . . Starvation in the ghettos was so big that the only thought for me as a youngster was how to obtain more bread. My mother managed to keep the bread away from us by hiding it in the bed; we kids knew the hiding place, but she was always looking at it. We were afraid to take it because she knew that if we will eat it up then, there was no food later on. . . . Women played a specific role as people who were conserving and managing food. I would say my poor mother, who was taken to Treblinka, was a genius; she didn't finish high school, but she was a genius in how she managed to do this.[28]

After the panelists had made their initial presentations there was discussion from the audience. Many there were survivors too, and they had an opportunity to tell of their experiences and feelings. Several of them talked about "The Selection" in the ghetto. This was when the German soldiers would come and line up all the Jews in the center of the ghetto and "select" those who were to be deported to the concentration camps. The first selected were usually the old, the very young, the infirm, and the deformed (eye glasses were considered a deformity). Upon the women fell the task of feeding their children, camouflaging their colds and fevers and sores and sticking-out bones. The women were responsible for keeping themselves and their children, their parents, and their husbands fit enough to survive the selection. In the discussion period Gertrude Schneider spoke to this experience:

Survivors as parents are sometimes totally irrational. I remember having children and waking up in the night and being 100% sure that the next day there'll be a selection. It was America and it was crazy. That's all. And my husband the same way. . . . Now, eight weeks ago, I got a grandchild. Now I have to go through the other things again, waiting until he is big enough to go through a selection. I say to myself, "Come on, don't be an idiot. You know you are safe." But . . . you never are totally safe again. Never, ever. . . . [29]

In the juxtaposition of these stories we can see the particularity of women's labors, the ways in which women bore this terrible responsibility for feeding and clothing their families under "impossible" conditions, and the ways in which "failure" led to almost certain death. We also see the ways in which the women sought to sustain the webs of Jewish culture. We understand that there is no psychological mechanism to overcome the fears of selection, of betrayal, of annihilation, even decades after the war is over, and we understand that these fears are communicated to the next generation, and to the one after that. We also see the way in which the women, within the purview of their responsibilities and their will to survive, strove to sustain the culture and its rituals, to maintain the life cycles, to make things as normal as possible. For women the struggle for normalcy was a strategy of resistance. Vladka Meed said:

> My closing comment is about survival. We are talking of life and it is true—everybody wanted to live and to survive. But I guess we also have to emphasize what kind of life. Life which also has meaning—cultural and ethical meaning. After 40 years I still have a feeling that we people, and even those historians who are writing and teaching about the Holocaust, still don't grasp the level and the meaning of every day life in the ghetto. It was really full of humanity, full of sacrifice and full of heroism. Don't ever think that only killing, resistance with a gun is the highest point of resistance. I guess we have to think now and see the labyrinth of everyday trivial life which our Jews and the women specifically lived in the ghetto.[30]

The stories from the Jewish ghettos and the story of Elmas Tutuian may be seen as examples of women's heroism, and such heroism has always been acknowledged. While heroic in that sense, these are also the stories of ordinary women performing their everyday tasks under siege. The very dailiness of their work, carried out with a stubborn, inexorable strength, what Vladka Meed called "the labyrinth of everyday trivial life," made *visible* under siege, was the bedrock that gave meaning to life and served as the underpinning that made all else possible.

The experiences of Japanese-American women, interned in concentration camps during World War II, reveal similar patterns of resistance built from daily life. These stories, however, also reveal the contradictions women face when forced to balance conflicting loyalties. These words were spoken by the Japanese-American artist Miné Okubo. They give us a sense of the shock of evacuation:

> We were suddenly uprooted—lost everything and treated like a prisoner with soldier guard, dumped behind barbed wire fence. We were

in shock. You'd be in shock. You'd be bewildered. You'd be humiliated. You can't believe this is happening to you. To think this could happen in the United States. We were citizens. We did nothing. It was only because of our race. They did nothing to the Italians and Germans. It was something that didn't have to happen. Imagine mass evacuating little children, mothers, and old people![31]

These words were written by sociologist Valerie Matsumoto in her study "Japanese American Women during World War II":

Shikata ga nai. "it can't be helped," the implication being that the situation must be endured. The phrase lingered on many lips when the Issei, Nisei, and the young Sansei (third-generation) children prepared for the move—which was completed by November 1942—to the ten permanent relocation camps organized by the War Relocation Authority: Topaz, Utah; Poston and Gila River, Arizona; Amache, Colorado; Manzanar and Tule Lake, California; Heart Mountain, Wyoming; Minidoka, Idaho; Denson and Rohwer, Arkansas.[32]

"They called it a relocation camp, but it was a concentration camp. There was barbed wire. They told us the machine guns were to protect us, but the machine guns were pointing toward us."[33] These words were spoken by the Japanese-American artist Hiro Mizushima.

Miné Okubo also said:

After being uprooted, everything seemed ridiculous, insane, and stupid. There we were in an unfinished camp, with snow and cold. The evacuees helped sheetrock the walls for warmth and built the barbed wire fence to fence themselves in. We had to sing "God Bless America" many times with a flag. Guards all around with shot guns, you're not going to walk out. I mean . . . what could you do? So many crazy things happened in the camp.[34]

Two months and twelve days after the bombing of Pearl Harbor in December 1941, President Franklin D. Roosevelt issued Executive Order 9066 which authorized the removal of 110,000 Japanese people from the western half of the Pacific Coastal states and the southern third of Arizona. By the spring of 1942 the forced removal of the Japanese community was in full gear. Families were given a week's notice in which to "wind up their affairs, store or sell their possessions, close up their businesses and homes, and show up at an assembly point for transportation to an assembly center." Each person was only allowed to bring that which s/he could physically carry—which meant not more than one or two suitcases.[35]

Lili Sasaki said: "We sold all our things within two weeks. Put everything out front, sold my wedding presents and furniture for fifteen cents, twenty-five cents, and went into camp. Now of course, when they told us we had to get rid of everything in two weeks, every house had to make a bonfire to burn off their junk. Then they'd say, 'They're burning off all the evidence.'"[36]

Historians Timothy Lukes and Gary Okihiro give some sense of what this relocation meant in economic terms in their study of the Japanese-American community in the Santa Clara Valley of California where agriculture was the principal form of livelihood. Of the 1,152 Japanese Americans in the valley in 1940, 882 were employed in agriculture, 120 in personal service, 75 in the wholesale and retail business, and 18 in manufacturing. The rest were in miscellaneous categories. Many of those employed in agriculture leased or owned the land they worked, and many of those employed in businesses and manufacturing were small shop-owners. Forced to sell out at once and liquidate their assets, homes, and personal possessions, fantastic profits were made by the primarily Anglo buyers. These sales wiped out years and sometimes generations of labor by their Japanese owners.

"The Farm Security Administration," Okihiro showed, "reported on April 17 [1942] that all but 190 of the 580 Japanese farms registered with that agency [in Santa Clara County] . . . had been taken over by non-Japanese operators," and the remainder were disposed of either by the farm administration or by private arrangements between Japanese farmers and their Anglo and Mexican-American neighbors in the hope that something could be salvaged at the end of the war.[37] Fanned by the war hysteria and nearly a century of anti-Asian racism and fueled by greed which allowed for sale or confiscation of millions of dollars in private property all through the western region, the U.S. citizenry permitted internment to be carried out with virtually no protest.

Japanese men, women, and children were ordered to report to assembly points, forced into detention centers, searched, tagged, and herded onto buses and trains for transport to the concentration camps. They were delivered to camps that were virtually uninhabitable. Construction was completed with the help of the prisoners themselves. Spartan barracks, ill-

equipped latrines, poor food, and remote desert were the standard conditions. Valerie Matsumoto described the impact of internment based upon
her extensive interviews with the women:

> The conditions of camp life profoundly altered family relations and
> affected women of all ages and backgrounds. Family unity deterio-
> rated in the crude communal facilities and cramped barracks. The
> unceasing battle with the elements, the poor food, the shortages of
> toilet tissue, milk, coupled with wartime profiteering and misman-
> agement, and the sense of injustice and frustration took their toll on a
> people uprooted, far from home.[38]

The lack of privacy, especially in the latrines and in the sleeping arrangements, and large communal mess halls which encouraged family disunity
were especially difficult to bear. Moreover, while everyone was encouraged to work within the camps, the wages were only sixteen to nineteen
dollars per week, regardless of one's skill or proficiency, which made for a
highly exploited work force.

For the women, camp life presented an astonishing array of contradiction and irony, and women's resistance strategies and consciousness
reflected this. Women set about making life bearable. Blankets, for example, were used to erect "partitions" in the barracks, creating at least a
modicum of private space. Scraps of lumber and metal used in the construction of the camps were salvaged to make shelves, chairs, tables, and
other amenities of a home. "Victory gardens and flower patches appeared," Matsumoto reported, and women tried to keep up with the latest
American fashions and hairstyles through the Montgomery Ward and
Sears Roebuck catalogs and fashion magazines. Day passes, which allowed visits to nearby towns, were coveted. When they could afford it,
women shopped from the catalogs or on such visits when they were
allowed. In this context, the fashions and gardens and home improve-
ments were part of women's struggle for normalcy. They were part of a
struggle to provision their families and protect their children from the
worst and most degrading features of internment. Moreover, as Matsumoto observed, the women's concerns with fashion reflected their "efforts to remain in touch with the world outside the barbed wire fences;
they reflect as well women's attempt to maintain morale in a drab depress-
ing environment."[39] From women's standpoint, resistance was marked by
the struggle to improve the quality of daily life. The irony, of course, was

that the struggle for normalcy—meaning American normal—inexorably pressed toward assimilation and eroded cultural and family bonds. Under these conditions the generational conflict between the older Issei mothers and their Nisei daughters was greatly exacerbated.

Camp life accelerated the erosion of Japanese cultural norms which had begun before the war. The exploitation of Japanese labor within the camps, the pressure toward American patriotism, and the imposition of American cultural values changed the conditions for women in complex ways. For example, women's employment under the pay equity between men and women enforced by the American authorities gave Japanese women a greater, if paradoxical, equality with men, and a greater latitude in employment opportunities. Educational opportunities also became available, especially late in the war when evacuees could get permission to relocate in midwestern and eastern cities. One Nisei woman, interviewed by Matsumoto, recalled her decision to leave the camps to attend college: "[Father] became more broad-minded in the relocation center. He was more mellow in his ways. . . . At first he didn't want me to relocate, but he gave in. . . . I said I wanted to go to Chicago with my friend, so he helped me pack. He didn't say I could go . . . but he helped me pack, so I thought, 'Well, he didn't say no.' "[40]

The communal living arrangements and mess-hall meals, while terribly painful for the Japanese women, also, ironically freed them from the work load normally carried by the mothers of each family. Women not only had more time to work for wages but also to engage in a wide variety of leisure activities. The most important of these was learning new arts and crafts for the beautification of their barrack homes. Finally, romances flourished under the confinement of camp life and the uncertainties of war. The tradition of arranged marriages was increasingly replaced by notions of individual choice and romantic love. Women found themselves in an intensely complex situation. In many ways camp life improved their status as women and their economic independence from men. They attempted then to balance the need for cultural cohesion and family bond against the loosening of patriarchal conventions. Loyalty for the women was a triple-edged sword: to the Japanese culture, to the American normal, to themselves as women. Concluding her study focused especially on the second-generation Nisei women, Valerie Matsumoto wrote: "Nisei women drew not only upon the disciplined strength inculcated by their

Issei parents but also upon firmly rooted support networks and the greater measure of self-reliance and independence that they developed during the crucible of the war years."[41]

Although their cultures of origin were widely different, and the conditions of war and racial persecution differed in very significant ways, the stories of Mrs. Tutuian, the Jewish women in the European ghettos, and the Japanese women in the American concentration camps bear strikingly similar patterns. In each the women strove to protect their children, to strengthen family and cultural connection, and to improve the quality of daily life. And in each case they were caught in unfathomable contradictions imposed by the collision of racist violence, global war, and misogynist assumption. In the maelstrom of this collision women negotiated an almost impossible terrain simply to survive.

As the women struggled to improve the quality of daily life and strengthen interpersonal connections by extending cultural bonds, they undermined their own autonomy as women because their cultures assumed patriarchal relations. Conversely, if they rocked the safety of the family and cultural boat to enhance their position as women, they undermined the traditional bonds of racial and cultural security in a world of precarious existence. Balancing these kinds of contradictions is an integral part of many women's strategies in everyday life in the United States, and especially for those women from racial, ethnic, or religious minorities. We are made acutely conscious of it in these stories because of the extreme conditions imposed upon the Armenian, Jewish, and Japanese women.

From a woman's standpoint, what is progressive and what is counter to progress, loyalty to whom and betrayal of what must be viewed from her point of view as well as the predominant masculinist one. The moment this is done—the moment *she* is accorded equality with him in the assessment of human affairs—the conventional definitions of resistance must be reexamined and expanded to encompass the vastly complex lives of women.

This is another story. It introduces the way in which class position affects women's lives. It illustrates how women must balance their personal relations within the limits of their class options. This story comes from a novel by Isabel Miller called *The Love of Good Women*.[42] This story teaches us about the struggle for women's independence. Informed by a lesbian sensibility and a strong class consciousness, Book 1 of the novel focuses on the internalized oppression of a white, lower-class woman. Gertrude Sunup married "up" at a young and precarious age, into a family whose fortunes were declining.

To Gertrude, her husband Earl Sunup appeared to be very intelligent because he was college educated. He also appeared to be understanding, patient (especially in light of her ignorance, she thought), hard working, and a good father. Earl may not have loved her, but he dutifully provided. She saw his marriage to her as a sacrifice he had made for inexplicable but noble reasons. Gertrude's self-image, already impoverished by feelings of class inferiority, was further eroded as Earl cast his continually critical eye over her looks and her labors. Burdened with numerous children and still grieving the loss of those infants who died at birth, Gertrude struggled on in pathetic spurts of innovations to please and self-deceptions about her marriage. Gertrude's one ally was her sister-in-law, Milly, married to Earl's brother. But Milly was also a lesbian, feared and disliked by Earl, and Gertrude was too oppressed to recognize Milly's love and potential support.

Gertrude's consciousness began to change when she went to work in a munitions factory during World War II. Earl approved of this venture as long as Gertrude continued to do all the household chores and gave him her paycheck at the end of the week. She set out for work the first day exhilarated to be out of the house and filled with fear and self-doubt about her ability to work successfully in the factory.

Gertrude was set to work on the "zygoline," inspecting, greasing, and sorting valves. Alert to her new conditions she tried to fit in as best she could with her coworkers. Shocked at first by their bawdy speech, outlandish hairstyles, makeup, and coveralls, she soon began to listen and to learn. Their network provided Gertrude with her first essential lessons, and they were all about men. Conversations whirled around her as the valves zipped along their line, and Gertrude's marriage was soon cast in a very different light, first by the women and then finally by herself. Much of what Gertrude had seen as "her fault" and "Earl's patience" began to look like her fortitude and Earl's negligence, her strength and Earl's weakness, her patience and Earl's temper. The network on this assemblyline in the 1940s worked as effectively as any consciousness-raising group in the 1970s. By the third week on the job Gertrude had figured out just where "Sonny" was spending his nights and their money. The name, used by a coworker to describe a frequent customer at two sporty nightclubs in town, clicked into place as Gertrude pieced her puzzle together. When Earl reached for her paycheck that Friday as he had done every week before, Gertrude turned on him. Invoking his "club" name and threatening to gather the support of her sister-in-law, Gertrude said:

> "Sonny, I've decided that if you take my money again I'm going to tell Milly."
>
> "Keep your damn pin money," Earl said.[43]

This was Gertrude's first act of resistance. Her coworkers had given her a new way of thinking about her marriage, and her paycheck had given her the independence to act on it.

Gertrude is not alone in pondering the problem of who gets the paycheck. Indeed, coworker Crystal turns her paycheck over to her husband every week. She explains her thinking to Gertrude:

> "Well, it's what you have to do. I guess it don't matter. It kills them, you know to think you make any money. So you got to give it to them like you don't notice what you're doing. And once they get it cashed, they forget where it come from. I know hundreds of girls that do the same things. . . .
>
> "It's their pride," Crystal said. "You just have to handle their pride with kid gloves or uh oh! I don't know what's supposed to happen to *our* pride. I guess we ain't suppose to have none."[44]

The struggle for independence and copartnership in marriage must be balanced against the tensions that may finally break it up. When there are children involved the balancing is harder. Gertrude's resistance at this point is overt and stated; Crystal's is not. Crystal is aware of the unfairness, and her strategy here is to accommodate herself to her husband's wishes. For Crystal, in weighing the balance of things, this seems the best strategy for maintaining the quality of her daily life, at the present time. For Gertrude, weighing the balance of things, the break-up of her marriage will improve the quality of her daily life. Women weigh choices such as these every day. Weighed individually and in contrast to the greater power exercised by men in general in the society, the woman's choices are more limited. When they can be weighed collectively, with women assisting each other, thus shifting the balance of power, more options are available. The point of resistance is not contained in the act of opposition or compliance, but in the consciousness of the woman (or women), and in the estimate of what is necessary to sustain or improve the quality of life. It is *this* estimate, repeated over time and circumstance and collectively enforced by women, that eventually changes the grounds of choice from which women in future generations will negotiate the complex balance of their lives and those of their children. What is apparent in this story as well is that employment provides only the beginning potential for women's independence. A husband's (or father's) access to women's wages was codified into law for much of the nineteenth century in the United States. As late as 1974 a woman in Socorro, New Mexico, was forced to file suit in order to compel a hospital administration to make her paycheck out in her own name rather than in her husband's. The ACLU took the case and won it. The need for emotional connection, the genuine feelings of affection, the socially ingrained and deeply felt responsibility for the success of a marriage (or relationship), women's internalized oppression, especially the feeling that one is being selfish or trivial or unreasonable, fears of impoverishment, especially as a head of household on women's wages, of loneliness, of the burdens of childrearing, of failing to provide children with a "normal" family life, all weigh heavily in the balancing of these choices. Who controls the paycheck is emblematic of a whole range of issues all or most of which hinge on the woman's assertion of her independence, her autonomy, her claim to personhood.

The oral histories of working-class women replay Gertrude's and Crystal's stories in myriad ways. These oral histories also illustrate the cumulative effects of women's labors seen as a collective force, stretched out over the seasons and across the generations. They give us a new way of thinking about the mechanisms for social change. The following are taken from a collection relating life stories of southern mill workers recorded in the early 1980s. Clara Thrift is a white woman, a mill worker from Thomasville, North Carolina.[45] She was born in the early 1930s. Her first job was as a waitress in the T-ville Diner on Main Street. She began working there when she was fourteen and stayed four years, which saw her through the birth of her first child. She sometimes took the baby to work with her because she didn't have a babysitter: "She'd sit there by the screen door next to the juke box in a highchair. I'd keep her supplied with creamed potatoes with stew gravy and she'd be just as happy sitting there smearing them potatoes all over herself and the juke box" (p. 110). Mrs. Thrift went on, describing the way events shaped her life: "I had always wanted to be a school teacher, but I quit school in 1949 in the tenth grade when I got pregnant. Neither one of my parents could read or write a word. Daddy worked at the Thomasville Furniture Factory. Mama has worked in the Amazon Cottonmill since she was ten years old. She's seventy-five now and she still works six nights a week" (p. 113).

In 1950 when her child was a year old, Mrs. Thrift also went to work in the mills. She got a job at the Carolina Underwear Company with the help of her sister-in-law who was already working there. She could make as much as eight or ten dollars a day, which was a lot more, she said, than she had made as a waitress. But, "back then," she explained, "minimum wage was lower for a woman than it was for a man." She could make the maximum pay if she made the production quota for the day. If you made more than the quota you got paid for it. If you made over the production quota too often, however, management sent a quality control man around to see how you were doing it. Then everyone was taught your method and the production quota was increased.

The father of Clara Thrift's first child was the son of the Methodist minister in town. She was very much in love with him. When she told him she was pregnant, "he just said that he had to finish getting his education and that he'd see me around. In other words, he didn't care what I planned to do." She went to live with an older sister in Greensboro, and she was supposed to give the baby up for adoption. But she couldn't do it. She kept the baby, went to work in the diner, and eventually in the mills. Seven years later she married, had a second child, and went to work as a sewer in Archdale Lingerie. Her husband was a fireman. He felt he was superior to her, she said, because he came from a family of independent farmers who also owned some real estate that turned over a profit when the land was developed. Of her ten-year marriage Clara Thrift reported:

> I worked there [Archdale Lingerie] the whole time I lived with my husband, except when I was in the hospital from him beating me up. My husband wanted me to work and bring the check home. He also thought that I should do all the housework, take care of the children, and take care of him. I'd work all day, come home and put out a wash, fix dinner, clean up the kitchen, get the kids' things ready for school the next day, get them to bed, and then sometimes I'd be up to three or four in the morning mopping floors and ironing. All he did was go to work, come home, and booze it up. . . . I ask God forgiveness every day for what I put my children through during those years.

He would get mad anytime I showed any independence. . . . I did it
[stayed with him] because I thought if my kids had a home and if my
daughter had a last name like the rest of the family, we could be
happy. . . . I was thinking about appearances, the way things looked
to everybody else. He resented my daughter and called her ugly and
names like bastard. He had even less respect for me and called me
whore and linthead. . . . I didn't think I deserved better. He took my
paycheck and mistreated me and my daughter too. I took that shit for
ten years before I finally woke up. (Pp. 112–13)

She left her husband when she was thirty-three years old.

In order to support herself and her two daughters Clara Thrift
worked two jobs. "I wasn't getting any child support from my ex-husband, and of course I never got a penny from my older daughter's father."
She worked at Burlington Industries from three P.M. to eleven P.M., and
at the Amazon Cotton Mill from midnight to eight A.M. When she got off
work she'd pick up the children and take them to school. Then she'd come
home and sleep from ten A.M. to two P.M. and go back to work. She
worked through the lint, the grease, the heat, the dirt, the noise, the speed-
ups, and the sexual harassment of the floor boss. She worked both these
jobs for six years. She quit the job at Amazon finally because she couldn't
take it any more. Of the sexism in the plant she said: "The men had jobs
like strawbosses, overseers, supervisors, and the high executive jobs. . . .
They never gave a boss man's job to a woman. I resented that, I know that
I was smarter than a lot of them I worked for. The supervisors watched
every move you made" (p. 119).

When she told her supervisor she was quitting he tried to get her to
stay. He said if she'd stay he'd give her a better position by using her to
replace another woman. Clara Thrift refused:

[This woman] was in her fifties and she had been working there much
longer than me. I was in my thirties then so I said, "Yeah, and when I
get in my fifties, you'll take my frames and give them to somebody
thirty. No thanks." This woman was real nice and she worked as hard
as I did. I thought since she had been there for all these years she
deserved to keep her frames. I wanted to make as much money as her
but I didn't want to take money away from somebody else. (P. 119)

Eventually Clara Thrift left the mills altogether. It was a great relief.
She still worked two jobs to keep up with all the bills. She went back to

waitressing and she got a job at Control Data collating computer cards. Then she suffered an accident on the job when her arm caught in a machine. She wasn't able to work after that. About a year after the accident she remarried. Her new husband was a man she had known since childhood. He had been recently widowed. After her children were out on their own, she and her husband moved to St. Petersburg Beach, Florida. She said of her life now: "I walk miles and miles on the beach every day." Of her long years working in the mills, Clara Thrift said:

> The cotton and the lint would blow everywhere and you would perspire something terrible, but you'd just go on, your hair would be wet and everything, and you'd just go on working like that. That was just a way of life, so I didn't think much about it. I just thought about making money to get me a house and to raise my kids so they would never have to do the things I've done. I was just trying to make a better life for them. All the women felt the same way. (Pp. 116–17)

The collection of life stories of southern mill workers from which this oral history is taken was transcribed, edited, and compiled by Victoria Byerly. The book is called *Hard Times Cotton Mill Girls* and is a collection of "personal histories of womanhood and poverty in the South." Byerly supplies brief introductions to each section of the book to provide a historical context for the stories. There are twenty oral histories, and about half of the stories are told by white women and half the stories are told by Black women. Black women weren't hired into the mills until 1962 because of race discrimination. They often worked as day servants for white mill-worker families earning a dollar a day. They also worked in the cotton and tobacco fields, and as cooks, dishwashers, and in steam laundries. When Black women were finally hired into the mills they were very clear that it wasn't going to be in a janitorial capacity. Corine Lytle Cannon was the first Black woman hired at Cannon Mills. It was 1962, and she was forty-three years old. She recalled: "I had planned to tell them that I was going to work a production job. I told them I wasn't going to lift a broom. I told them that when I signed up. I said, 'Y'all can get all the janitorial jobs that you want, but I'm not a servant and I'm not going to lift a broom'" (p. 150). Mrs. Cannon went to work in production and so did the three other Black women hired with her.

However, the mill was segregated. Black women worked virtually alone, had a separate outside toilet, and a "colored only" water fountain.

They were paid less also. It was some years before these arrangements began to change, first with the impact of the civil rights movement and then in the early 1970s with the renewed struggle for unionization when the workers themselves broke through the racial barriers in order to organize. Crystal Lee Sutton, whose story as a union organizer at J. P. Stevens ends Byerly's book, recalled her first union meeting:

> I never will forget it. Liz and I pulled up at this church—it was a black church—and I had never seen so many blacks in all my life. Liz said, "You sure you want to do this?" and I said, "Well, we're here. We might as well go in." So we went in and there were maybe four or five white people in there. We went down and sat on the front row 'cause I didn't want to miss out on nothing. After the meeting, I agreed to go into the mill wearing a union button. . . . We were real strong with the blacks, but we were weak with the whites. So I knew a lot of people I was going to talk with. (P. 206)

Although race defined significant differences among the women workers whose stories are recorded by Victoria Byerly, poverty is an overwhelming equalizer in the ways of class. Clara Thrift's story is not unusual. Not everyone, of course, was battered. Many of the women experienced less traumatic and, occasionally, decent marriages; many others did not. But in virtually all cases there were very early pregnancies, early marriages, limited educational opportunities (although some of the Black women had a better education than their white counterparts), care and respect and love for elders, and hard, hard, hard, exhausting work. Clara Thrift's story is unusual in that she had only two children. Most of the women had between five and eight children. Several said that had they not been ignorant of their bodies and had access to birth control they would have used it. Many times, however, they reported that their husbands objected to birth control even when they knew about it and could get it. Aliene Walser, a white mill worker also from Thomasville, like Clara Thrift, said:

> I was fifteen when I had my first baby and thirty-two when I had my eighth. I raised seven of them. No, I didn't know how *not* to have babies. If I had known, I don't think I would have had eight. No, I never heard tell of birth control pills. Lord mercy, honey, them things

come out since I quit having kids. I wish I had had them back then. Maybe I wouldn't have been so tired. (P. 81)

Orphaned at six, Aliene Walser spent her childhood in a variety of relatives' homes. Her aunt, with whom she lived for the first five years after her parents' death, was very cruel to her. Having one more mouth to feed and one more child to clothe in an already over-burdened household was at least part of the reason. When she was fourteen Aliene went to live with her older brother and his wife. Of the onset of menses, and her entrance into womanhood, Mrs. Walser said:

> The first time I ever started my period I was going to the spring to get a bucket of water. . . . All at once I looked and blood was going down my leg and it scared me to death. I didn't know what to do. I ran in the house and told my brother's wife and she told me what to do. . . . She told me that it would happen again. I said, "What for?" She never did explain nothing like that to me. Didn't nobody. (P. 81)

But with her own children Aliene Walser was very open about marriage, sex, and childbirth so that they wouldn't have to go through the things she did:

> I tried to raise my girls differently than how I had been raised. I tried to tell them when they first started wanting to date that I didn't want them to start dating early, which they didn't. They said, "But, Mama, you did." I said, "I got married when I was a child. You need to get a little more out of life than just getting married, having children, and working in that mill." I explained to my girls about going with boys and things like that, and having babies and things like that. We just talked about it like there wasn't nothing to it. (P. 85)

Billie Parks Douglas, a Black mill worker from Kannapolis, North Carolina, had a similar experience with motherhood. She said:

> I had my first child when I was sixteen and my tenth when I was twenty-nine. Some of them are the same age for a few months, so I had some of them less than a year apart. . . .
>
> I didn't want to have ten children. No-o-o God. I tried birth control, but what I used hurt me. And when I would try to do something, my husband would object. See we were about pleasing these

men. We just thought that was what we was. Oh, would I change things. . . . My attitude on that has changed. See, 'cause I look back over my life and I'm not bitter, but I resent the fact that I done everything that I could. I gave up everything and I done without everything, but in the end he left. (Pp. 97, 109)

Many times, Mrs. Douglas said, she just felt like leaving Kannapolis, especially after she and her husband were separated, but it could not be done: "Probably if it had not been for my children, I would have left. I would have gone, but I didn't have that much time to feel like leaving, 'cause I was too busy. Before you know it, one day was gone, and before you know it, it was another year and you was pregnant again. I mean, if you getting pregnant every year, how you gonna think about leaving?" (p. 102). Mrs. Douglas had wanted to be a missionary and go to Africa. "Oh, I thought I could do great things, but it didn't work out that way." Her first pregnancies interrupted her schooling, but Mrs. Douglas went back twice, and she finished the eleventh grade at the top of her class.

Unlike Aliene Walser's experience, Mrs. Douglas had a very good childhood. She recalled: "I had a good mother and father. And we young-uns didn't know that we was poor until they told us on television. We really didn't. My mother and daddy never made us feel like we was poor" (p. 96).

Of her mother, Anne L. Parks, Mrs. Douglas spoke with great pride and respect:

My mother was a teacher long time ago when it was unusual for a black woman to be a teacher. My mother was a smart woman. She would give these phenomenal addresses, speeches like, to me nobody could give. I didn't have the privilege of hearing her much, but when I did, she would go in all the churches, white and black, where she would deliver these messages, and they would be fantastic. (P. 96)

When Anne Parks's children were expected to walk three miles to school and the white kids were bussed, she protested. It was in the late 1930s, Mrs. Douglas recalled: "My mama said you won't walk a step, not a day. You will not walk a step to school. And my father would say, 'Annie, well now, you know you can't buck society.' And my mother said, 'They will not walk a step'" (p. 98). They didn't. Negotiating with the school officials in an adjacent county, Mrs. Parks arranged to have her children enrolled there and a bus picked them up every morning.

Inspired by her mother's example and by her own dreams, Mrs. Douglas developed a local missionary program through the church to "encourage women," she said: "Mostly my ministry is to women. Things like Women's Day and Mother's Day. Those are usually the kind of occasions that I speak on. . . . I hope, like for black women in the South, the message I give is an encouraging message, that we don't have to roll over and lay down and die" (p. 96).

When her mother became ill, Mrs. Douglas organized her care with the help of her sisters and brothers and all of their children. Mrs. Parks was not only physically very sick, she also was often mentally disoriented. It was clear to everyone that it was very important to her to remain in her own home. Her home was run-down, and she wasn't able to take care of herself or it. For these reasons she had been staying at the home of one of her daughters. But every day she would get up and try to walk home. Mrs. Douglas explained what they did:

> So I said to my brother, "You know we got to get Mama back home." So he said, "What's your plan?" I said a friend of my husband's said he would fix the house for nothing if you could get the material they needed. That was like at about twelve o'clock and at two o'clock he laid the money in my lap. When we fixed the house, the children went down there and enjoyed it so much that the grownups never did have to go. Course I was in and out constantly. I did the cooking for her. She had a big wood stove and I'd go down there and build a fire in the mornings. But it worked out good 'cause the kids, they would stay down there. (P. 108)

Corporate, racial, and patriarchal brutalities cut the boundaries of the women whose stories are recorded by Victoria Byerly in this remarkable book. Endurance lies at the heart of their resistance, and their resistance lies along a continuum of daily life. In educating her daughters about sex Aliene Walser was giving them a tool of resistance that she had not had. Extricating herself from a brutal marriage and working two jobs Clara Thrift was expanding the boundaries of her life to provide greater access for her children. In providing daily care for her dying mother Billie Parks Douglas was putting into practice the love for Black women that she preached. In refusing to work a janitorial job in the cotton mill Corine Lytle Cannon was resisting the racist practices that had defined her access to employment. Southern mill women have organized for better wages, better working conditions, and compensation for the deadly disease of brown lung caused by the ubiquitous mounds of lint and cotton breathed daily in the mills. They have endured the relentless incursions of poverty, racism, and the persecutions of men. Byerly is profoundly right when she concludes that: "Southern mill women's strength lies not so much in their ability to organize successfully to counter the tactics of the powerful textile industry, but in their ability to survive poverty, humiliation, and isolation from the rest of the world. There is no room for weakness in this life. One learns to carefully weigh risk and to fight only those battles where there is a chance of winning . . ." (p. 164).

Out of this resistance of endurance, social change comes. But here it comes slowly, and time is measured in generations. Changes are marked by the ages at which the children of these women will enter the mill. Aliene Walser, for example, only got through elementary school, but all seven of her children graduated from high school, a testament to her resistance. Then gradually, some of the children escape the mill. This happened to Victoria Byerly. She was born and raised in Thomasville, North Carolina. She was the first in four generations of women in her family to get away: "[My grandmother] Iola Mae never saw one day of schooling, so when I graduated from high school, the first one in all of those generations to do so, she was proud of me . . ." (p. 3). For lack of a better alternative, however, Byerly went to work in the mill the summer of her graduation. She writes: "Like many of the women in this book I was terrified my first day. Not so much because of the noise or the lint or even the heat. I was terrified that when that mill gate shut, it would never open for me again, and I would be stuck in the mill for the rest of my life . . ." (p. 4).

Then, in late July, Byerly received a letter from the scholarship committee at her high school where everyone had organized to present her and her family with a viable alternative: "they had arranged for me to attend a small Appalachian college, and had managed to find me a grant and a work-study job to cover the one thousand dollar-a-year tuition. My family was too stunned to speak, but somehow I was not surprised. Somehow I just knew that I wasn't meant for the mill" (pp. 4–5).

A few others had gone before Byerly, and more would follow; this small rupture in the cycle of poverty would be widened. The story could be read as Byerly's luck, or as her personal pay-off for her hard work in school and for her family's devoted efforts. This individual reading is true. But it is only one reading, and it misses the larger and more significant frame. In returning to Thomasville and Kannapolis and Greensboro with her tape recorder and her skills as a writer and her knowledge of history, Byerly provides us with that larger frame in which to understand her piece of this story of resistance. The individual stories she records, pieced together, tell a much larger, collective story. The dailiness of women's endurance in the southern mill towns, accumulated over four generations, becomes a story of collective resistance, the women using the tools and resources, ingenuity and courage and skills they had available to them. When Clara Thrift had said: "I just thought about making money to get me a house and to raise my kids so they would never have to do the things I've done. I was just trying to make a better life for them. All the women felt the same way," she had spoken truly of this collective will. Social change had come, but it had come slowly, and through enormous effort, made by those who stand on the very peripheral edge of political life.

The work of historians Elsa Barkley Brown and Jacqueline Jones studying the lives of Black women in the South reveals similar stories of resistance. Brown, in a pioneering essay called "To Catch the Vision of Freedom: African American Women Struggle for Peoplehood and Community," re-visions our understanding of Reconstruction and political democracy and the role of Black women in framing each.[46] Situating her study primarily in Richmond, Virginia, and using a wide range of documentary evidence, Brown is able to show the ways in which the entire African-American community participated in the political life of their city following the Civil War. They elected representatives to a Constitutional Convention in Richmond in 1866 charged with the responsibility for drafting a new state constitution based on freedom rather than slavery. However, these representatives were never left to conduct business without the overwhelming presence of their constituents. In the tradition of African tribal communities, Black women, men, and children also attended the convention en masse, leaving their work for days while they packed the convention hall and made their views known by voice and vote.

Showing the ways in which Black women asserted their own definitions of political democracy, family, and community by their mass presence, Brown concludes that the African-American definition of democracy was not based exclusively or primarily on the model of representative government characteristic of bourgeois democracies but on mass participation and an "ethos of mutuality" in which the ballot was collectively owned and used. Further, in enacting their own view of emancipation, Black women resisted the class, racial, and patriarchal assumptions of white men and enforced their equality with Black men in the affairs of family and community. "These Black women," Elsa Barkley Brown concludes, "operated out of a notion of community wherein all—men, women, and children; freeborn and formerly slave; native and migrant—automatically had rights and responsibilities requiring no higher authority than their commitment to each other."[47] Thus, Brown suggests, the sense of community (rather than citizenship and representative government) and of a collective peoplehood (rather than individuated personhood) has informed the resistance strategies of African-American women.

The study by historian Jacqueline Jones, *Labor of Love, Labor of Sorrow*, confirms the paradigm of mutuality and community defined by Elsa Barkley Brown. Jones's book shows the ways in which African-American women sustained these definitions of peoplehood and community until the end of the nineteenth century, at least. Jones's book is a study of the way in which Black women have juggled family and work from slavery times through to the modern period. In this juggling they have carved a wedge of resistance. Jones's work focuses on the dailiness of Black women's lives and weaves a crucial understanding of women's labors as a force for social change. "This study," she wrote, "seeks to offer more than a chronicle of changes in patterns of black women's work as slaves and wage-earners . . . it is also a testament to the stubbornness of a mother's love in opposition to the dehumanizing demands of the marketplace."[48]

In summary, Jones's central point was this. Since slavery times Black women have labored intensively outside of their own homes, whether it be in the cotton and tobacco fields, southern canneries, textile mills, and steam laundries, or as domestic servants in white homes. Central to Black women's resistance has been the struggle to care for and nurture their own children. To do this they had to take time away from employers who expected them to work ten to fourteen hours a day, and, in the case of live-in servants, to be on-call all day and night with perhaps a Thursday afternoon off. The crashing irony of this experience has been most apparent when Black women were employed as domestic servants for white families. They fed, clothed, and nurtured white children while their own were left unattended, or left without their mother's supervision at the very least. In this context, Jones has suggested that the will to nurture—and its attendant labors of acculturation, education, and race pride—became a form of resistance. She demonstrates the individual and community effort that went into this resistance as provisions for children were made.

One chapter of this book struck me in particular, because it cast a new and revealing perspective on an important period in Afro-American history. The chapter is called "Between the Cotton Field and the Ghetto: The Urban South, 1880–1915." This chapter illustrates Jones's point about the ways in which Black women fought to nurture their own families and developed a vital sense of community. It was a period of migration for many Black women who moved from a rural to an urban existence in the South. Often single parents because they were widowed, divorced, or separated from their husbands, the women came with their children and sought employment in whatever capacity might be available to them. Domestic employment was most common. In the struggle to nurture their own families, Jones reports:

> Domestics sabotaged the best-laid plans of white house-wives, to-bacco workers declared their own holidays whenever family or community interests dictated, and laundresses continued to engage in a traditional task-oriented form of labor carried out in their own homes apart from white supervision. . . .
>
> Domestics [who were day workers] arrived at work late, left early in the afternoon, or stayed away for days at a time to mark special holidays and events. Communal celebrations in their own neighborhoods took precedence over the needs and expectations of their employers.[49]

Obviously Black women workers could not always successfully engage these strategies. But Jones suggests that for a variety of reasons in this particular historical period in southern cities it was possible, and Black women took full advantage of the opportunity.

Jones also relates many stories of mothers who were forced to leave their children to go to work, only to find them ill-kempt, hungry, and crying when they finally got home in the evening. It is clear, however, how much individual and community effort went into sustaining the children as day-care centers, colored schools, and church-related activities were organized, as well as the neighborly "looking-after"—which the children sometimes did not appreciate because they could be counseled and scolded through an apparently endless gauntlet of maternal figures.

In Afro-American history writing, this period between 1880 and 1915 is referred to as "the nadir."[50] This is so because in these years southern segregation was set firmly into place, Black men were almost completely disenfranchised, and Black families lost almost all of what little land some of them had owned, usually through the most unscrupulous tactics of white speculators. It was also in this period that the terror of the Ku Klux Klan reached a high point as literally thousands of Black men and women were tortured and killed in public ritual lynchings.

Yet it was within this nadir that growing numbers of Black children not only completed their public school education for the first time, but also were sent onto college; that is to Black colleges in the South. The collective labors shouldered by Black women which harbored and nurtured so many generations had begun to reap their rewards. In succeeding generations more and more children would make it to college as parents, teachers, and administrators, mostly women, worked together to encourage, counsel, and raise the necessary funds to keep the doors of the Black schools open and to supply the scholarships necessary to secure so many years of education. When one considers that fully 60 percent of the Black women employed in the 1930s were still engaged in domestic labor, the accumulated effects of women's resistance summoned in the labors of daily life stagger the imagination. One knows that in addition to the tuitions, scholarships, and supplies their labors funded, it was the nurturing work of Black women—the teachers in the colored schools, the mothers, grandmothers, and neighborly consorts—that provided the children with sufficient emotional resilience, intellectual curiosity, and race pride to tackle the rigors of higher education. While Black women and men engaged in many traditional forms of resistance in this same period, for education, suffrage, and against lynching—the NAACP, for example, was founded in 1910—it was the dailiness of the labors performed by Black women that anchored the resistance. And, as in the case of the Southern mill workers in Byerly's book, social change came slowly, over time, and with the generations. But it did come, the particularity of women's resistance visible with historical hindsight.

Although the South has been consistently one of the most depressed economic regions of the United States, the stories of working-class women throughout the country are strikingly similar to those recounted by Victoria Byerly. Differences are largely in terms of the somewhat higher wage scales in other regions, and a somewhat wider selection of employment opportunities for women. Sociologist Fran Buss, in her book *Dignity: Lower Income Women Tell of Their Lives and Struggles,* provides compelling evidence of these realities. Introducing the oral histories she put together, Buss wrote: "I am deeply interested in the means by which people find meaning in life and what religious, philosophical, or ethical understandings underscore their courage, commitments, methods of confronting suffering, ideas of justice, and efforts to change themselves and the world."[51] Explaining the scope of the interviews she conducted, Buss observed:

> I couldn't just limit [them] . . . to the women's work lives, or, for example, the economic issues faced by displaced homemakers. The totality of their lives kept coming out, with work and economics only an important segment. I became deeply moved by each woman, especially by the ways she tried to find meaning in her life and how she tried, almost desperately at times, to explain that meaning to me so others would see it. (P. 1)

Dignity comprises ten oral histories combining personal life stories and work experiences. Three Black women, four white women, and a Native American, Japanese American, and Chicana woman tell their stories. The youngest of the women are in their late thirties, the oldest in their mid-sixties. Several of the women have grown up in the South and a few still live there, but the rest are scattered in different parts of the country, some urban, some rural, from Wisconsin to New Mexico, from Minnesota to Illinois to Tennessee to Alabama. Each oral history is introduced by Fran Buss to set the scene of the interview and record a few of her impressions. Speech patterns and dialects are reproduced in the text as much as possible. Each interview presents a fine, often intimate portrait.

Many of the women married young and had children during their teen-age years. To many, marriage seemed the only escape from the poverty of childhood, and many of the women felt that by leaving home as early as they could they helped their mothers to cope with the remaining younger children. Most lacked formal education beyond some years in high school. Many experienced great brutality from men, including severe beatings from husbands and lovers, and in one case, incest. Several of the men refused to allow their wives to use contraception, causing many unwanted pregnancies. All of the women labored long, long hours. Stories of resistance become visible in the tellings.

Mary Robinson, thirty-six years old at the time she was interviewed, was from Alabama. She had been working for many years at J. P. Stevens and was an organizer for the Amalgamated Clothing and Textile Workers Union. Of her years as a union organizer Mary Robinson said:

> I don't sleep much, work all night at the plant and spend most of the day organizing, so I just get patches of sleep, and then sometimes I get sad and think, "Nothing really good ever came out of my life but my kids." And I think, "Why don't I just give it up and do nothing and just lay down for a while?" . . . The main thing that has made me fight against Stevens is that I don't want my kids to have to work under the same conditions that I had to. Or anybody else. Because I know it can be better. . . . I think about the union in terms of my mother. She would have been proud of me for doing it. . . . Her life had been devastating too, and she'd been oppressed all of her life. . . . There were just too many kids and never enough to go around, and she was depressed when we couldn't be in school. She would have been very proud of me for trying to change that. (Pp. 227–28)

Mary Robinson's closest friend, a white woman named Mildred McEwen, was also in the union. Mildred had survived many years as a battered wife and finally extricated herself and her children from the violence. Explaining the reasons for her marriage, Mildred McEwen said: "I think a lot of the reason I decided to get married was just because I was so unhappy. We were both seventeen and ran away to a little town in Mississippi, which I thought was exciting. . . . It seemed thrilling, but it wasn't. It was stupid, very stupid, but I thought it was all going to be so great" (p. 233). The beatings started almost at once. But Mildred stayed, hoping that things would get better. Before she was twenty-one she had had three children. Trapped by fear, shame, and poverty, feeling she could not go home to her parents who were still raising her younger siblings, she endured. The children were everything to her: "I was close to the children, and I somehow believe that the love you have when you're very young sticks by you. As babies, they were the only things I lived for. They were beautiful children, all of them. They were my life" (p. 235).

Summoning enormous courage Mildred McEwen gathered her children with her one night and left her husband. She found temporary refuge at the home of a friend and her husband. Three weeks later, in the aftermath of a funeral and family gathering, Mildred was caught alone by her husband. He beat her almost to death. As he pulled out a gun to finally kill her, something, she said, snapped inside of her. With her remaining strength she stood up. She walked past him and out of the house. Just before her collapse in the home of a neighbor she heard the shot with which he ended his own life.

Mildred McEwen's resistance, etched in this agony of domestic violence, cemented in the abiding love she had for her children, is testament to the inner strength many women have displayed. Life now, at the time she was interviewed is still not easy, but it is infinitely better:

> I'm better off now than I ever have been in my entire life, but sometimes it seems like there is nothing in my life; it's just empty. That's especially because I work nights and sleep all day. . . . I think back to what had happened, and all I felt was that I had to survive; for what, I don't know, but I've always had a dream that someday everything would work out fine. I guess that's kept me hanging on. I haven't really given up hope. (P. 241)

Maria Elena Ortega, born and raised in Texas, was the daughter of migrant farm workers. She was the oldest of seventeen children. She finished only up to the sixth grade in school and then was working virtually full time in the fields. At the time she was interviewed she was living in Illinois and was an organizer for the United Farm Workers Union. In an effort to relieve her mother and escape the poverty that engulfed her family, Maria Elena Ortega agreed to marry a man, a neighbor whom she barely knew. She was fourteen years old. She was to have seven children, and she took care of many of her younger brothers and sisters also. She endured many terrible brutalities from an extremely abusive husband. Her mother was to provide the support that allowed her to leave her husband, despite pressures from her father and from her husband's family. Of this time, she said:

> My marriage was so bad, and, finally, when my mom came and my brothers and sisters were going to come up North to work the fields, I took my seven kids and left my husband and came with my mom. And I found out I could make it on my own, very good. . . . So that's the way it happened. It was sad but I had already made up my mind that I wasn't going back. I found out I could make it on my own. I said, "My God, we're so happy and I'm so happy now." The pressure

was gone and even though I was working very, very hard, still I felt good. I felt free. (P. 267)

It was while she was employed in a cannery that Maria Elena first made contact with the farm workers union. She was impressed with their union organizing and with their community activities and support for people in their daily lives. Describing her work in the union, she related these feelings:

> I come on pretty strong sometimes, especially with men. I know that I'm a woman and sometimes they look at me and they talk, and I hear rumors that they say that for a woman I come on very strong, very militant sometimes. There's lots of guys where it sort of hurts their pride to see that a woman would be the one to tell them how we can change things, especially in our race. The man is the boss and there is the macho image.
>
> But when I talk to them I say, "What have you got to lose by organizing? We have to sacrifice a little bit."
>
> The men say back, "Well, my job."
>
> "Your job! You're worried about losing your job? I'm worried about losing my life over this." Boy, that hits them pretty hard.
>
> I say, "I don't want a revolution but we can change things together," and that shakes them up a little bit, and then they look at me as if I was a very macho woman too and they listen. (Pp. 274–75)

Mary Tsukamoto was born and raised in California. Her parents— first her father, and later her mother—immigrated in the early part of this century. Her oral history is filled with the memories of her childhood and of the hardships endured because discrimination against Japanese people was so widespread. She talked in particular about the ways children internalize feelings of inferiority. They deny their Japanese heritage and try to hide things that might be associated with the Japanese culture. Her life has been dedicated to undoing this damage. She put herself through college at a time when it was very rare for a woman to be admitted, especially a Japanese-American woman. She graduated from the University of California at Berkeley. She taught school for many years. At the time of the interview she was officially retired but was still continuing many volunteer activities with children. She and her daughter survived internment in a concentration camp during World War II. Of her work with the children Mary Tsukamoto said:

When I was still teaching in the public schools, I had started to teach the children about the events in Hiroshima, and then I taught about them in my Japanese cultural school. Each year the children folded a thousand paper cranes and sent them to a school in Hiroshima, as a memorial to the children who died there and as a prayer for peace. . . . I felt great pain teaching about the bombings and great pain teaching about the evacuation. I tried to teach the fourth-generation Japanese American children, "You have wonderful parents and wonderful roots," but the story always has to come out that we were mistreated. We were discriminated against and despised and put into camps. . . . I learned through teaching . . . that children need the [United States] government to admit the truth. It's important for the fourth-generation children to know there is nothing to be ashamed of. (P. 107)

Lee, an Anglo woman from New Mexico, told Fran Buss her story, but asked to remain anonymous in order to protect the privacy of her family. She was extraordinarily open about the very great difficulties she has encountered, and the ways in which she has sought to heal herself and her children. Of her, Fran Buss wrote:

Lee is a heavy, sensuous Anglo woman in her early fifties, of medium height, with quiet and tolerant blue eyes and arched eyebrows. . . . During the years that I have known Lee, I have seen numerous people turn to her for help and comfort and have heard her respond with a wisdom based on her intimate understanding of the struggles of life and a belief in the renewing possibilities of hope. (P. 170; Lee's story is told on pp. 171–99)

Growing up as a tomboy and "knowing any girl that hangs around boys like I did has to be twice as capable as they are in order to con membership," Lee explained that she had a very hard time in adolescence and early adulthood adjusting to fit the definitions of "woman" as prescribed by the mainstream culture. After having two children out of wedlock, and being deserted by their father, Lee married a man named Ed, reluctantly and with considerable reservation. He had asked her to marry him repeatedly. Of her decision Lee said, "so out of sheer being worn down, I went ahead and got married to be polite, to keep from hurting his feelings."

Trying to fit into the traditional woman's role, Lee said, "I didn't argue for my rights very much, and I tried to do all the housework things. . . . I wasn't aware of anybody who had other kinds of marriages at all, equal type marriages. The only ones I ever knew about were the dominant male kind. I know I worked hard at that because I thought that is how you made a marriage work, and if you were going to be committed to a marriage, you try to make them work."

Working two jobs, mother to six children, suffering from severe postnatal depressions, surviving two self-induced abortions because she could not see the means of bringing more children into her family, Lee struggled to keep her marriage and her family together. Of this, Lee said: "I stayed with Ed as long as I did because I was so determined to make a go of that marriage that I refused to believe it wasn't possible. I just didn't want to go through marriages and divorces like my parents did."

The end of her marriage came on a Sunday afternoon when Lee's daughter Terri, who was then eight years old, told her that she and her older sister were being sexually assaulted and raped by Ed. "Of course, she didn't use those words," Lee recalled. "It was like somebody had hit me with an ax. I was just totally stunned when it dawned on me what I was hearing. I remember I was very quiet, and I wanted her to explain, so I didn't want my tone of voice to change. So I took a deep breath and asked her, "What do you mean? What has Daddy been doing?"

Thinking through as best she could the implications of everything her children disclosed, Lee took action the next evening. "When Ed got home from work that day I told him to pack up and get out. I told him why and he didn't argue about it at all. He didn't deny it; he just packed up and got out."

Lee's life was extremely difficult. She has spent years attempting to heal the wounds inflicted on her and the children by Ed. Lack of resources, both financial and emotional, continued to plague her; illness and deaths in her family have been hard, draining, and painful. Lee has moved through these times, persevering, doing the best she could to care for, protect, provision, and nurture her family, and, later, many other women who have needed the benefit of her experience and advice. Fran Buss reported that:

> Lee is now head of a program for parents with problems, primarily child abuse, and works mostly with mothers of young children. . . .

Lee works extensively with these women, taking calls at any time of the night, meeting with women individually, searching out the social services that they need, and running groups in which the members help each other. These people, in turn, respond warmly to her intense acceptance, empathy, and care. (P. 171)

Lee's story is a story of resistance. It is a story shared in various ways by many, many women in our society. Lee's choices, first to stay and then to leave her marriage, were determined by her first priority, which was to sustain and improve the quality of her daily life, to nurture and support her children. Her strategies were based upon the options she saw available. In clearly and immediately acknowledging the incest and acting on that knowledge, Lee demonstrated her love for her children and her courage. In providing services now for women in need Lee has used her cumulative experience so that they may not feel as alone as she once did, without resources, counseling, direction, and hope.

Darlene Leache, from the Appalachian Mountains of northern Tennessee, had been married at fifteen and was the mother of six children. She also, like many whose stories are told in this and other collections, married when she did in an effort to escape the poverty of her childhood family, and in an effort to relieve the pressures on her own mother. Darlene Leache had been severely beaten by an alcoholic husband. After years of abuse she extricated herself and her children from this situation. "Mostly I live for my children," she said. She also helped to organize the Mountain Women's Exchange. Explaining the work she is engaged in with the exchange Darlene Leache said:

> It's just a bunch of women who got together that thought they could come out from under just the direction of men, that they could do other things besides sit at home and have babies, that they could help themselves and other people. The main thing about Mountain Women's Exchange is helping people, helping other women with the needs they have.
>
> It is like helping battered women. Battered women always thought that you had to sit and you had to take it. . . . But there is a shelter now so there is a place where women can go with their children. . . . It's women working together to find peace of mind and to help bring other women together. (P. 144)

Almost all of the women Buss interviewed related innumerable ways in which they had acted to improve the quality of their daily lives. Many had tried to secure emotional relationships with men, most of whom were reluctant at best and abusive at worst. From these stories also, the ingrained passivity with which many of the women had to cope, especially the white women, could be seen—a passivity inculcated by the particularity of female socialization in an oppressive culture. For many women the first act of resistance is precisely *to act:* to break the cycle of passivity. From this women's standpoint we can see that what constitutes resistance is framed within the context of women's practical, material, personal, and psychological resources. These oral histories also show us that women's resistance is along a continuum in which the personal and the political are inextricably woven. Women's daily actions have a cumulative effect, and the phrase "for the sake of the children" expresses one of the most powerful motive forces for social change.

In reading these oral histories I was struck by the ways in which they corresponded to many of my lover's experiences. Forced into marriage at eighteen because she was pregnant, with only a year of college, Kate struggled through years of emotional turmoil, hard work, and poverty. For the six years of her marriage she lived in five states moving from North Dakota to Minnesota, to Utah, to South Carolina. She ended up in Los Angeles in the early 1970s with a daughter to raise alone. But she felt herself lucky to be in Los Angeles, a large metropolitan area with resources and cultural opportunities she had never before had. Kate did years of clerical work. She was helped through many a personal financial crisis by the thoughtfulness of neighbors who would come by with soup for dinner, or clothes, or presents for her daughter. For a number of years Kate's mother-in-law provided important emotional support. Kate often worked two or three different jobs trying to make ends meet. Her return to school was an act of extraordinary will. When she completed her studies with a master's degree she was able to teach. Her daughter tells many stories of Kate's ingenuity in the cheerful restoration of their various residences and in managing celebrations for birthdays and holidays, innovating festive occasions with presents and dinners which seemed to materialize from nothing. And what I realized from this was that Kate's story and those of the women I had been reading about not only had much in common but also represented the experiences common to a substantial majority of women in this country, sociological pronouncements about a vast "middle class" notwithstanding.

The ways in which women's personal and political resistance are interwoven, and how these can effect significant social movement are also reflected in the stories of lesbian survival. A book called *Long Time Passing: Lives of Older Lesbians* represents perhaps the first sustained collection of oral histories by lesbians living in the United States who are over the age of fifty. The book was compiled and edited by Marcy Adelman.

Long Time Passing contains the stories of twenty-two elder lesbians. Most of the contributors were in their sixties and seventies at the time they wrote their stories or were interviewed. They are from many different racial and ethnic backgrounds. Most were working-class women. Some of the stories were jointly written by lovers who had been together for many years. Some of the women whose stories are told had been married. There are lots of children and grandchildren in and around the lives of these women. Some had lost custody of their children because of their lesbian identity. Several of the women had been in the military; one was a member of the Communist party until she was expelled in 1948 because she was a lesbian. Some were professional women—one, for example, had had a long career as a physician. Nobody ever said anything about being gay, she reported, but gay patients were always sent to her. Some of the women tell stories of cruising the gay bars, and some were afraid to go anywhere near them. Every one of these women lived her entire adult life "in the closet." It was only with the coming of the women's liberation movement, and the Gay and Lesbian Pride actions that they felt safe enough to reveal their identities and tell their stories. Many were not "out" even to themselves for years, others were "out" to only their closest and most trusted friends. Virtually all were "passing" in the straight world. One couple who had been together for twenty years—a Black couple living in Oakland, California—described never kissing or holding hands in their own home while they were raising the children. They slept in separate bedrooms and snuck into each other's beds in the middle of the night. They did this so that their children might have as "normal" a childhood as possible. There have been great losses in these stories: the death of loved ones were especially difficult, magnified by the extent to which no one in the "straight" world comprehends the meaning of loss. Adelman writes in her introduction: "Whatever their adaptations: marriage, celibacy, the closet—most old lesbians spent a long time passing." Adelman continues: "My contact with these elders provided me with the context that I was searching for—a sense of a past and a future. . . . We shared the gift of lesbian continuity, which is reciprocal between the generations. We provided each other with a context to understand ourselves as part of a greater whole."[52]

Each woman tells her own story. Each appears as an individual, making discrete choices out of her set of personal circumstances. Compiled in this way, the personal stories map a political reality. The ways in which heterosexuality is compelled become more apparent. We see the ways in which women were forced to marry through either economic necessity or social pressure. We see the ways in which women had to remain closeted or risk the loss of employment, of housing, of the custody of their children. There is here too a collective strategy which becomes visible when the individual stories are put together. Whatever their circumstances, these women (and thousands more like them) shared an estimate of their potential survival as lesbians. Their estimate was that they could not be out and survive. They went underground. In passing since the 1920s in the United States, they lived a precarious existence, and many paid a terrible price. They internalized homophobia, lived with the fear of discovery and retribution and rejection, and with loneliness. But they survived. They lived, and loved, and worked. There is also such a sense of joy in many of these stories as these women are finally able to talk openly about their lives. For me—closeted for a long time and out now in my middle years—I knew almost every experience, every feeling of which these women wrote. I was filled with pride at our history of resistance, our heritage of survival, and their courage.

Stories about how women have maintained their cultural identity against the demands and invasions of the mainstream white society and passed this onto their children are also effective in highlighting the many diverse, courageous, and ingenious forms of women's resistance. These stories also allow us to see the "simultaneity of oppressions" and the complex arrangement by which questions of class, culture, race, and gender locate the tactics of women's resistance. The poet Mitsuye Yamada once described her mother's courage as she came to understand it reframed in the context of the women's movement:

My mother, at nineteen years of age, uprooted from her large extended family [in Japan], was brought to this country to bear and raise four children alone. . . . Stripped of the protection and support of her family, she found the responsibility of raising us alone in a strange country almost intolerable during those early years. I thought for many years that my mother did not love us because she often spoke of suicide as an easy way out of her miseries. I know now that for her to have survived "just for the sake" of her children took great strength and determination.[53]

In the context of her cultural experience in which her marriage had been arranged to a husband she did not know when she came to California, in the context of her cultural dislocation in a country of virulent racial hostility in which there were long internments on Angel's Island enforced by immigration authorities, immigration quotas, restrictions on land ownership by Asian peoples, and antimiscegenation laws prohibiting marriage between Caucasians and "negroes, Mongolians, members of the Malay race or mulattoes," this mother's survival for the sake of her children was an act of resistance.

Puerto Rican writer Nicholasa Mohr composed a short story about a woman named Amy Guzman which she called "Thanksgiving Celebration."[54] It shows the ways in which a grandmother's stories became tools of resistance. Mohr's story was probably set in the South Bronx, New York City, given the description of Mrs. Guzman's apartment and the "rows and rows of endless streets scattered with abandoned buildings. . . ." The South Bronx in the 1970s looked like London after the German blitz in World War II. Mrs. Guzman was a widow. Her husband was killed by a drunk driver on an expressway in a head-on collision. She had been promised a settlement by the insurance companies, but it has been two years since the accident and there is still no settlement and no money. She has four small children. She has survived on welfare, credit from neighborhood grocers, and the help of family and friends.

It was the day before Thanksgiving. There was no money to buy a turkey, even a small one, and still make it to the first of December. Of late Mrs. Guzman had been short tempered, snapping at the children; she was feeling overburdened and overwhelmed. The children had felt her tension and her fright. Affections strained, bonds snapped. Amy Guzman pondered Thanksgiving. She knew she needed some ritual of connection with her children. It needed to be their day together, as a family.

Abuelita, Amy Guzman's grandmother, came into her mind. She had told her so many stories about her childhood on a farm in Puerto Rico. The stories were often about animals—all varieties of animals from beetles to goats—who talked amongst themselves and to Abuelita. How could this be true, the child had challenged. From these musings and reminiscences an idea took shape in Amy Guzman's mind.

The next day the four children and Amy Guzman were seated at their own Thanksgiving dinner. Orange streamers festooned the kitchen and at each setting a name card had been elaborately printed: Michele, Lizabeth, Carlito, and Gary. On the center of the table was a platter. On the platter was a mound of bright yellow rice, flavored with a few spices and bits of fatback, and surrounding the rice were a dozen hard-boiled eggs colored bright orange. "Turkey eggs," Amy Guzman exclaimed triumphantly! "What's better than a turkey on Thanksgiving day? Her eggs, right? . . . ," she said to her wide-eyed and astonished children. "You see, it's not easy to get these eggs. They're what you call a delicacy. But I found a special store that sells them. . . ." The children, originally skeptical and cautious, dug in.

"Mommy, did you ever eat these kinds of eggs before?" Michele asked.

"Yes, when I was little," Amy Guzman answered. "My grandmother got them for me."[55]

Regaled with Abuelita's stories as told now by Amy, restored by their mother's self-confidence and joy, feelings of connection and love were rekindled. Thanksgiving is placed before us by Nicholasa Mohr as a "ritual of survival." In the context of Amy Guzman's life, of the resources, choices, and options she had available, of her will to act, of the importance of belonging and believing and loving in the lives of children this is also a story of resistance. It is a story of a woman's refusal to submit to the ravages of poverty. It is a story of a woman who drew upon the strength of Abuelita—and in this sense, drew upon the collective strength of Puerto Rican women—to pull herself up and over the crisis, making something from nothing.

This miracle of making something from nothing is described by women over and over again in countless stories about their mothers.

Bernice Johnson Reagon, writing what she called a cultural autobiography, recalled her childhood in the South in these terms:

> My father would work from sunup to sundown
> and would come home exhausted
> eat, and go to bed
> My mother would work from sunup to sundown
> would come home
> and work from sundown to sunup
> to work from sunup to sundown again
> The bottom line
> . . . .
> When a dress had to be made for a play
> if my father did not have the money to buy the material that was it
> For mama that was just the beginning
>
> She then had to figure out a way to get the cloth for the dress and
> stay up all night making it
> for this child to be in this play
>
> It's called
> making a way out of no way[56]

Enedina Casarez Vasquez described the inner life of what she called a "House of Quilts" pieced together by the six migrant worker families who shared temporary accommodations in Oconto, Wisconsin, while they picked the crop of their employer. It was 1956. She described this incident with the grower:

> He had apple trees and one day he saw the other children and me
> sitting on the fence looking at the apples and asked us if we wanted
> some of them. We jumped at the chance to get some of the apples and
> let out a loud, "Yes!" He told us to pick up only the apples that were
> on the ground and not to touch the ones that were on the trees. The
> apples on the ground were rotten. We picked them up anyway and I
> took home a basketful to my mother. She made pies, my mother
> could always make something out of nothing.[57]

In this story the making of the pie not only salvaged the apples. More important, it salvaged a piece of the children's dignity, the mother outwitting the selfish "benevolence" of the grower and producing a treat to boot.

A Jewish elder, whom we are introduced to as Basha, was interviewed by Barbara Myerhoff in her study of a Jewish neighborhood center for seniors in Venice, California. Almost everyone at the center at the time of Myerhoff's interviews had been born and raised in the *shtetels* of Eastern Europe. Basha described how she still served meals, even those she took alone in her room: "This my mother taught me to do. No matter how poor, we would eat off clean white linen, and say the prayers before touching anything to the mouth. And so I do it still. Whenever I sit down, I eat with God, my mother, and all the Jews who are doing these same things even if I can't see them."[58]

In the context of a childhood in the *shtetels*—the village ghettos of Eastern Europe—in the context of the destruction of European Jewry during World War II, in the context of the pressures toward assimilation in a *goyishe* land, in the context of the pressures of poverty and old age, of "letting down" one's standards, this ritual act of linen and prayer is an act of connection, of affirmation, and of self-esteem. In this context, to connect is to resist.

In the oral history of Maria Elena Ortega compiled by Fran Buss in *Dignity,* Mrs. Ortega related a story about her mother's work as a midwife in a Texas community. She explained how her mother had to be certified, and how the clinic was set up:

> Now my mother's been doing the midwifery for many years and she's got a certificate. She had to go to some kind of training so that she could get it. It wasn't against the law to be a midwife in my younger days, but nowadays they're very strict. My mom rents a little place, and she's got a clinic with beds and cooking facilities and everything else. So now when she delivers babies, she not only brings the babies, but for a whole week she takes care of the baby so the mother can really recuperate. She sleeps with the babies, and if she's got too many, she's got friends to take over. She really takes care of the ladies. She feeds them homemade soup and good food. (P. 279)

In the context of a society in which little or no prenatal care is available to poor working-class women and women of color, and in the context of a society in which private obstetrical care routinely costs thousands of dollars and in which public assistance in general hospitals is all too often administered with indifference to the welfare, health, and happiness of mother and infant, this clinic run by Mrs. Ortega's mother is an outpost of resistance.

Anna Lee Walters of the Pawnee/Otoe people tells another kind of resistance story. She calls it, "The Sun Is Not Merciful" and it is part of a collection of stories all of which come from her peoples' culture and history.[59] This story is about two sisters, Lydia and Bertha, survivors, elders, and of Old Man who raised them almost three quarters of a century before. Old Man built their home "in the valley between the corn and alfalfa and rows of cotton," and he told them stories of survival which swim now in and about the crevices of their minds like the fish that glide in the waters of the lake in which Lydia patiently casts her line. It is the summer, and it is very, very hot. There is no wind. The sun beats down on Lydia and Bertha. Long ago, when they were children, Old Man had told them: "Don't fight the sun girls. Let it be. It's going to whip you down if you fight it. Let it be." The sun is not merciful, he explained, but you can learn to breathe through its heat, catch a rare breeze, and survive its relentless, scorching heat.

There is an exchange, but not a direct confrontation almost every day with a man named Hollis who whips his Jeep along the dirt road stirring up clouds of dust. He parks and trudges through the dense undergrowth to the lake's edge where Lydia casts her line and Bertha sits beside her doing beadwork. Hollis is a ranger. Fishing here is prohibited. He alternates between issuing warnings, threats, and fines. The lake which now floods Old Man's Valley is part of a recreational park. New homes are soon to go up on the east shore, but these will not be for Bertha and Lydia's people. Lydia and Bertha talk pleasantly to Hollis. He is, after all, just doing his job. They are doing theirs. Old Man had explained the way that fishing and seeing the world was connected to preserving the ways of the ancestors and was at the heart of who they were. Old Man had said: " 'Girls we're fishermen from way back yonder, way back when time first began. Fact is, alla us came outta water. Happened up north, round Canada somewhere. Well, girls, we found ourselves on the shore of this wide lake. We came outta it, see? Weren't no other people then—jus us back then. And that's why we're fishermen from way back, for time even began.' "[60]

One day a small group of women and men join Lydia and Bertha at their homestead, before it was flooded. They are from the same Indian people. They explain how the government is offering the people lots of money to sell their land and their homes so the area can be drowned and a big power plant built mainly to benefit the predominant society. Most have agreed, have taken the money, and are leaving. This group of people has refused. How do Lydia and Bertha feel about it, they want to know. No, Lydia and Bertha agree, they will not sell.

Lydia is very ill, the infirmities of age and of poverty. In the hospital her leg must be amputated. The amputation of Lydia's right leg is a symbol for something lost, the drowned homestead and earth. But Lydia and Bertha were not taken down in the water because they understand it. In another time, it was a place of people's birth. And this is why Lydia and Bertha were not drowned by it.

Lydia can't help returning to the lake's shore. She is carried there now by her children because with only one leg she cannot walk. She sits on her rock. She casts her line into the water. Bertha beads. This is what they do to survive. Hollis returns. He is furious. He whips out his book. Today it is going to be a fine.

> "What's your full name Miss Lydia," he asks.
>
> Lydia says, "Lydia Mae Wind."
>
> He writes that down, pressing his pencil hard on the tablet.
>
> "Address?" he asks, as Lydia looks up at the trees to find the best shade.
>
> "Route 2," Lydia says. "You welcome to visit us Hollis, whenever you can."
>
> "Age?" he asks. Lydia answers, "Be seventy in the fall."

When Hollis is finished interrogating Lydia, Bertha puts her needle down and says: " 'Now it's my turn. My name is Bertha Old Soldier. Ah'm sixty-seven, be sixty-eight in a few months. Ah was born here,' she said, 'beneath this old lake, the reck-re-ashun area, What else you wanna know?' She is looking up at Hollis in a frown. Her braids rest on her lap beneath the scarf with beads. The sun shines directly into her glistening face."[61] It is then that Hollis sees that Lydia has only one leg. He has not seen this before, as many times as he has spoken with her. He is appalled. She shouldn't be out here in this heat, he says. Lydia talks to him. She is gentle, even kind: " 'We fisher people, Hollis. Fished since time began. We came up outta water, Hollis. . . . My heart is in the water, Hollis. Can't be drowned, Hollis. We bound to keep coming back, Hollis. Have to, there's no other way.'"[62]

Hollis takes back the slip of paper he has given Lydia. He tears up the fine he has issued. He pulls on his hat and walks away. And "the two women hang over the edge of the lake . . . waiting for the sun to cool. . . . a connection to all beings."

This is a story of women's resistance. It has been repeated hundreds and thousands of time by tribal peoples everywhere, and by women of other peoples too, as variations on a theme of cultural integrity, a protection of Mother Earth, a devotion to sacred land, a stubborn will cleaving to the ways of the heart.

Irene Mack Pyawasit is of the Menominee people. She lives in Wisconsin. Her oral history is recorded by Fran Buss in *Dignity*. At the time of the interview she was in her late sixties. She told the same story as Anna Lee Walters in a slightly different way. This is how Irene Pyawasit described her grandmother:

> My grandmother was a tough, little old woman. . . . first thing she taught me was not to be afraid of the white man. She said, "God gave you a big mouth, and I'm going to teach you how to use it." . . .
>
> She died in 1929 when she was ninety-six years old. My grandmother was a good hunter, a good fisherman, a good gatherer. And she did the most exquisite needlework that you ever saw in your life. . . .
>
> My grandmother knew they were going to white wash us [at the mission school]. She knew the methods they employ and she knew that we were going to have to learn to speak nothing but English because they were not going to let us speak our own language, and they would try to take our religion away. She said, "You have to keep your religion inside you, in your heart." . . . to the government employees, we were just a bunch of pagans, uncivilized savages. So I had to keep within me all that I had learned from her. (Pp. 147, 152, 153)

Irene Mack Pyawasit survived the mission schools in large measure because of her grandmother's strength and teachings. After she was married and had children, she supported herself and them as a circus performer, "a snake charmer" she was called in the western, Anglo circus. In more recent years she has been a teacher, social worker, community leader, and traditional Indian healer. She has worked especially with the Indian children in the inner cities, passing on the language, the culture, and the community her grandmother had instilled in her.

Irene Mack Pyawasit's work is the work of resistance. In her story, and in so many others told by women of many different racial, class, religious, and ethnic backgrounds, cultural heritage is an instrument for holding family and community together—a task that is often seen as women's work. From women's standpoint the forging of cultural heritage is often a weapon of resistance against the racism, ethnocentrism, and anti-Semitism of the dominant culture that seeks to degrade, punish, and dominate those it decrees as different and "other." By the standards of masculinist privilege this form of resistance can sometimes seem to be conservative, traditional, narrow, clinging to old ways. Sometimes it is. Sometimes it produces in women an inability to focus anywhere but on their own house, their own culture, their own problems in ways that divide women from each other. Yet the dream of connection, the need for ritual and beauty, the drive to nurture the human spirit continually re-kindle these patterns of resistance in women's everyday lives.

Women's work. Women's survival. Women's resistance. "In this city," Adrienne Rich said, speaking of New York, "where so many cultures struggle to persist, to hang onto their vitality . . . women are, as every-where, the linchpin of the economy . . . the strength of women is the deep undercurrent of all life. . . ."[63] Many of us from our radical and liberal lodgings and from sundry academic and professional posts have been outraged by these conditions through which women have been forced to propel the undercurrent of all life. We have spun theories, waged protests, conducted research, exposed and condemned, beseeched authorities for funds and legislation and relief. But until and unless that relief comes, and when it does it is almost always eventually subverted, life must be pro-pelled in practical ways, every day. That propulsion is women's resistance, driven deep underground, affected by but frequently impervious to the vagaries of power and politics, often disguised by design, and simulta-neously marginalized or made invisible by the underpinnings of social theories we have ourselves endorsed. Yet, "women's daily resistance [is] like water on a boulder,"[64] as the anthropologist Karen Brodkin Sacks truly put it, that grounds the life of the planet, a relentless, restorative cascade.[65]

THE WOMEN in my grandmother's generation made giving an art form/ "Here, gal, take this pot of collards to Sister Sue"; "Take this bag of pecans to school for the teacher"; "Stay here while I tend Mister Johnson's leg." Every child in the neighborhood ate in their kitchens. They called each other sister because of feeling rather than as a result of a movement. They supported each other through the lean times, sharing the little they had. The women of my grandmother's generation in my home town trained their daughters for womanhood.
   —Assata Shakur (1978)

We were so poor we couldn't pay our bills, and a man came to our house to turn off the meter for electricity. He told us he was going to do it, and Mama said, "No, you can't cut it off."

He said, "Yes, I'm going to have to."

"No, I can't let you. Just me and these children are here; you can't."

"Well, I'm gonna have to climb the pole to cut it off."

"No, I've got a gun." She had a shotgun. She said, "You climb the pole and you're gonna come down faster than you got up. I can't let you do that. I told you I'd pay when I got the money. But we don't have it."

. . . She talked him out of it, the rough way, but she did it.
   —Darlene Leache (1981)

When I was twelve I told my mother I was going to be a writer. When I was fifteen, she was still working long hours for low pay, and there were four kids to feed instead of two, and money was more scarce than ever, my mother managed to save enough to buy me a typewriter. "You can't be a writer without one," she said.
   —Anne Cameron (1986)

Mother was born and raised in Toishan district in the city of Canton. Her marriage was arranged by her parents through a matchmaker. She did not know her future husband until her wedding day. When she was but a child, her mother had bound her feet. Footbinding was a prerequisite to marriage; thus, her tiny, slender feet assured her of a husband. . . . In 1909, a short time after her marriage . . . she embarked on her voyage to America with her first-born daughter. . . . Mother's ocean voyage was long, tedious, and rough. Steerage quarters were crowded, the foreign food was not to her liking, and she did not understand or speak English. Upon her arrival in San Francisco, she was transferred to a small steamer, and taken to Angels Island where she was detained for a month. . . . Mother accepted her life in America with great courage and tenacity. She raised three sons and six daughters. . . . I look back and recall her life with pride, knowledge, and understanding.
   —Ruth Wong Chinn (1987)

When I come along the older ones was all gone and Papa was depressed because we had lost a lot of property during the Depression. It was taken from him. He had a nervous breakdown from it. He really got down. But Mama was his strength, she was the rock of the family. She would never, never, never give up. She would always say, "Well it could be worse. Let's get over this hurdle because there's another one coming."

—Corine Lytle Cannon (1984)

Bedrock.

Toward a Gathering of Women

This is the earth,
skin stretched bare
like a woman who teaches her daughters to
plant
     —Linda Hogan, "Desert"

Over the rubble
I crawl into dawn
corn woman bird girl sister
calls from the edge of a desert
where it is still night
to tell me her story
survival.

Rock speaks   a rooster language
and the light is broken
clear.
     —Audre Lorde, "Naming the Stories"

For my mother*

We speak
Of self hate and of love that breaks
through silences.
          We are lightning and justice
          Our souls become transparent like glass
revealing tears for war-dead sons
red ashes for Hiroshima
jagged wounds from barbed wire.
          We must recognize ourselves at last
          We are a rainforest of color
and noise
          We hear everything.
          We are unafraid.

          Our language is beautiful.
     —Janice Mirikitani, "Breaking Silence"

*"After forty years of silence about the experience of Japanese Americans in World War II
concentration camps, my mother testified before the Commission on Wartime Relocation
and Internment of Japanese American Civilians in 1981. These are excerpts from my
mother's testimony, modified with her permission."

N THE HIGH deserts of the Mohave and Colorado there grows a plant called creosote. It does not reproduce from seed. It reproduces itself through a vegetative or cloning method. The plant begins with what is called a stem-crown. New roots, stems, and branches grow from this central crown. "As drought comes and goes," a naturalist explains, "the inner branches die. . . . Eventually [the central crown] too, rots away, and the plant has developed into a clonal ring, a circle of individual, though genetically identical shrubs."[1] The process continues as young satellite shrubs grow around the outer edges of the ring. The original stem-crown will be completely gone, replaced by a patch of bare soil, but its identical genetic self will have been reproduced. One such clonal ring is estimated to be over nine thousand years old, making it the oldest single, living organism in the world. Life in the desert is like this, astonishing in its variety, adaptive ingenuity, and endurance. Many things that look dead are really alive, fingering the sand and rock, sinking roots, waiting, using an economy of opportunity to survive.

Kate and I took a trip one April weekend, driving eleven hundred miles roundtrip in a loop that took us through the heart of the Mohave and into Death Valley. We have been drawn back by the desert's beauty, the vastness, the expanse of night sky, and by the array of life we have seen—kit fox, jackrabbit, bobcat, coyote; the birds; the variety of flora: creosote, sage, ocotillo, teddybear cholla, barrel cactus, Mohave yucca, tamarisk, smoke tree, Joshua tree, elephant tree. From late February through April or May, depending on the year's rainfall, the desert floor is blanketed with a dazzling array of wildflowers. In the desert, time and space seem to merge, to become one idea instead of two, because of the vast distances and stillness. Being in this, one has the feeling of pausing indefinitely from the "normal" rush of life.

I began writing this chapter in the desert, at the time of the winter solstice. We were camped beside a dirt road in a state park a few miles from the Mexican border. It had been a very cold and unusually wet winter. Our water froze in the kettle; there was snow on the mountains around us; once it began to rain. It felt funny running around in the dusk, kicking up the dry desert sand and pulling everything inside our tent to keep it dry. The rain lasted only a few minutes, and there were only a few drops. The clouds drifted to the east and disappeared.

While I was there I read a story by Deena Metzger. The story was part of a novel in progress. She had been working out the problem of her name,

Deena. In the Old Testament it is spelled D-i-n-a-h. She is Jacob's daughter. In Metzger's retelling Dinah is given voice. The retelling is visioned at the top of Mount Sinai where Moses saw the burning bush and God delivered his ten commandments, and Metzger shivers in the high winds at dawn on the day of her pilgrimage. At the beginning of this retelling, Metzger writes: "The writer is always between the beginning and the end of the world and she must write in both directions at once, back and forth, so that the past and future coincide in one seed. And so I create and cancel time so we may meet in that desert where I hear the spirits can live."[2]

I thought: Metzger's place in the desert is a good one because the desert gives you such a powerful sense of the present; and Metzger's idea is that there is "one seed" in which past and future coincide as the present. And there is, after all, *only* the present. History is an invention that helps to hold the present in place; or it is an invention that helps to change it. This chapter is about change. However, it is not about politics in the conventional sense. It is not about spirituality in the metaphysical sense, conventionally speaking. It is about ways of thinking about ourselves as women, about the ways of knowing that come out of our experiences and that we share with other peoples, pivoting the class, cultural, and racial locations of our stories. It is about how to begin to act from those ways of knowing, and about how to begin to stand on our own grounds.

The desert is a metaphor. For how long women have endured. Like creosote. Waiting for the rains.

MANY contemporary women novelists are creating new ways of thinking by imagining cultures in which women and men are freed from different forms of colonialism and from racism, violence, pollution, famine, and the fragmentation so prevalent in the modern world. Their ideas are often drawn from an amalgam of tribal cultures, Eastern philosophy, especially the Tao, and the values so many women put into practice in their everyday lives. Such a novel has been written, for example, by Ursula K. Le Guin. It is called *Always Coming Home*. Riding a tension between past and future, the beginning and the end, "moving in both directions at once," as Metzger would have it, Le Guin proposes to create "an archaeology of the future." Le Guin asks: "Which is farther from us, farther out of reach, more silent—the dead or the unborn?"[3] She casts her line out to the unborn. They are the Kesh people and they inhabit the rich and fertile valley of the Na, tens of thousands of years from now.

Le Guin's novel is drenched in the dailiness of Kesh life replicating a process essential to women's ways of knowing. Values of friendship and connection, of relationship and context, of cycle and growth, of flowers and beauty, of ritual and a respect for the land, so common in women's ways of knowing, are central to the Kesh culture Le Guin has imagined. It is not the details of the Kesh culture alone that are important to us here, but the notion, so eloquently elaborated by Le Guin in this novel, that out of women's experiences and consciousness, values and knowledge, a viable ordering of the world is possible.

In this novel, Le Guin speaks in two distinct voices. She is first the ethnographer, the voice within the text, introducing, observing, transcribing all of the elements of the Kesh culture: language, music, poetry, drama, ritual, kinship, oral history, parable, myth, recipes, medical practices, economics, archives, maps, and so on. In this enterprise, Le Guin the ethnographer is assisted by the artist Margaret Chodos, whose imaginative sketches adorn the book, and by composer Todd Barton, whose representation of Kesh music is available on an accompanying tape.

Le Guin's second voice is that of the one whom she calls "Pandora," standing outside the text, in our own time, writing, self-consciously announcing the author's intentions and fears. Early, for example, "Pandora Worries About What She Is Doing . . .": "Pandora doesn't want to look into the big end of the telescope and see, jewel-bright, distinct, tiny, and entire, the Valley. She shuts her eyes, she doesn't want to see, she knows what she will see: Everything Under Control. The dolls' house. The dolls' country" (p. 53). This is Le Guin's warning to herself, and to us, as we read what she has written. We must not make a perfect picture, or she and we will have failed in her purpose. Her purpose was not to create a utopia but to point us toward a way of being, without wars and colonies and violence and rape and plundering. The point was to direct us toward a way of thinking about what it means to be a human being, drawn precisely from ways of knowing found in women's daily lives and found historically in many tribal cultures.

At the center of the novel is an oral history. It is given by Stone Telling. The significance of her story lies in the fact that she is a product of two cultures. Her mother is of the Kesh people, and Stone Telling is raised in the Kesh world. However, her father is of the Condors, a warrior people whose major city is located three hundred miles to the north of the Valley. Stone Telling is also the only person from the Valley to have left it to live among the Condor and to have successfully returned to it. She is able then both to elaborate the contrast of cultures and to describe the ways in which she survived.

Stone Telling meets her father for the first time when she is nine years old. Awed by him, enamored of his glory as a soldier and a commander, she imitates her father's ways. And, because she is the daughter of a commander, the Condor soldiers obey her orders also. Stone Telling remembers this scene from her childhood: "I heard my high, thin voice and saw ten strong men obey it, over and over. So I first felt the great energy of power that originates in imbalance, whether the imbalance of a weighted pulley or a society. Being the driver and not the pile, I thought it was fine" (p. 32).

This becomes a crucial experience for Stone Telling because she internalizes the imbalance, so that it replays itself out in many different forms in her life. When she falls in love, for example, she gives herself over completely to the man. He is the "driver" and she is the "pile." She describes the feelings she had: "The love in me loved everything he loved. My thoughts and feelings were swallowed up in that: I was the servant of my love, and served it as my father's soldiers served him; unquestioning" (p. 184). Being out of balance with herself, she became servant to another, this servitude defined as love.

Later, Stone Telling decides to leave the Valley and to live with her father among the Condor. In entering their world she exists in a society comparable in many ways to our own. The word "rape," for example, will enter her vocabulary as the women of peoples conquered by the Condor are brought back to the city for the pleasure of the warriors. She will learn the concept of "possession" as the Condor men act out of the belief that they own women, servants, buildings, the land.

Stone Telling lives by her wits, learns to manipulate the endless intrigues and power struggles of the empire's inner sanctum to her own advantage. She learns to lie. But most important, she clings to her memories of the Valley: "I tried to sing the Two Quail Song. . . . My voice sounded wrong, alone in that place. . . . I thought about the bowl of blue clay in my heyimas [prayer house] and about the spring of Sinshan Creek under the azalea and sweetshrub on the steep ridge of digger pines and dark firs and red madrone. . . . I went nearly crazy with grief" (p. 344). Eventually, with the collusion of her aging father, Stone Telling successfully flees the Condor city, taking her three-year-old daughter with her. She travels with a woman she had befriended from among the servants and they walk the three hundred miles back to the Valley of the Na. There is a moment in Stone Telling's story when she first understands the terrible mistake she has made in choosing to go with her father. She is en route to the City of the Condor. For the first half of the journey with her father she rides a sorrel mare to which she becomes very attached. The party stops for several days at South City. During this time Stone Telling is with the women and confined indoors. She does not yet know that is the normal regimen that will be required of her. Her father and his men are finally ready to resume their journey. Stone Telling recounts this scene:

> At last we left that house and that city and started north. I had missed the sorrel mare very much while I was trapped indoors, and had dreamed every day of riding her again. . . . when the women told me to get into a covered cart with them. I refused. One of the older Condor women ordered me to get into the cart. I said, "Am I dead? Am I a chicken?" . . . She got angry and I got angry. My father came and I began to tell him that I wanted to ride the sorrel mare. He said, "Get in the cart," and rode on by. He had looked at me as a woman among other women, a squawking hen among the poultry. He had changed his soul for his power. I stood a while taking this into myself as best I could while the other chickens peeped and squawked around me, and then I got into the cart. All that day travelling in that cart I thought, more than I had ever thought before, about how to be a human being. (P. 195)

At this moment, when the contrast of cultures is first visible to her, Stone Telling is finally able to ask herself the crucial question: What does it mean to be a human being? Le Guin's point has not been to answer it, but, through Stone Telling's voice, to create a space in which that question might be properly considered. In order to do that she must take us out of, place us above, give us an overview of the warrior society in which *we* are lodged *and* provide us with the outline of an alternative structure in which we could envision ourselves. Le Guin constructs such a culture from the fragments of human memory, from values embedded in women's lives. At the very beginning of her story Stone Telling says: "As a kitten does what other kittens do, so a child wants to do what other children do, with a wanting that is as powerful as it is mindless. Since we human beings have to learn what to do, we have to start out that way, but human mindfulness begins where that wish to be the same leaves off" (p. 29).

Stone Telling is Le Guin's emissary, bearing a gift of thought. It is crucial to Le Guin's purpose that the emissary be a woman, and not just any woman but one of Stone Telling's character and experience. Stone Telling's formative years are spent in a culture in which her femaleness is honored and respected; a culture in which balance and harmony, a respect for Earth and cycle, a passionate commitment to peace, are the prevailing values. Yet she is easily and fatally attracted to the power and the glory of the Condor. It is only when Stone Telling sees that her father perceives her "as a woman among women" that the seductive power of the warrior is stripped of illusion. And it is later still, when Stone Telling is subordinated within the bowels of the Condor empire, that she understands the infinite value of what she so impetuously and recklessly abandoned. It is then that the values of the Kesh culture reassert themselves in her, providing the grounding for her survival and escape. Even with this grounding, *established within her own lifetime*, Stone Telling must struggle to retain some semblance of her identity and integrity.

In entering the Kesh world we enter a reality dramatically different from our own. Elaborate in ritual and poetry, connected fundamentally to the land, Le Guin fuses what the poet and literary critic Paula Gunn Allen has called a "sacred hoop" of tribal belief: "The concept is one of a singular unity that is dynamic and encompassing, including all that is contained in its most essential aspect, that of life. . . . All movement is related to all other movement. . . . [All movement] must be harmonious and balanced and unified."[4]

Likewise, everything in the Kesh world is alive, the categories of animate and inanimate, natural versus supernatural are not applicable in this world view. Everything contains energy, which is simply exhibited in different forms. Again, Paula Gunn Allen's description of the tribal culture is helpful in understanding this concept of energy dispersal: "The closest analogy in Western thought is the Einsteinian understanding of matter as a special state or condition of energy. Yet even this concept falls short of the Native American understanding, for Einsteinian energy is essentially stupid, while energy in the Indian view is intelligence manifesting yet another way."[5]

In the Kesh world of Le Guin's imagination is the reality of Earth, conveying the quintessential meaning of the tribal view. Allen writes: "We are the land. To the best of my understanding, that is the fundamental idea that permeates American Indian life; the land (Mother) and the people (mothers) are the same."[6] The beauty of the land permeates the Kesh world as Le Guin expresses her understanding of the fusion of land and people. This poem, for example, is a gift from Stone Telling to her people:

> Old Stone, hold my soul.
> When I am not in this place
> face the sunrise for me.
> Grow warm slowly.
> When I am not alive any more
> face the sunrise for me.
> Grow warm slowly.
> This is my hand on you, warm.
> This is my breath on you, warm.
> This is my heart in you, warm.
> This is my soul in you, warm. (P. 254)

In surviving the Condor nightmare, Stone Telling is able to imagine herself as something other than a colonized subject. Wrapping herself in the fragments of the Kesh culture which she can still summon, she is sustained by the knowledge of another reality and heartened by the prospect of coming home to it. To excavate this reality, to protect these shards of knowledge, both female and tribal, to make of them patterns for everyday use, to elaborate their detail,

> cleaving to the timbre, the tones of what
> we are—even when all the texts describe
> it differently[7]

as Adrienne Rich wrote, is to engage in an archaeology of the present. It is to wrap ourselves in these ways of knowing as best we can. The point is not to go back to some mythical time but to ground ourselves, our survival, our everyday lives in principles congruent with our experience about what it means to be a human being, about what it means to sustain a life force. It is to launch ourselves into a world of our own making, believing in its viability, its durability, and *acting* out of these values every day, with simplicity, patiently culling, bearing gifts of plenty, and no matter how hard this is and how "impractical" we are told that it is to be this way in the "real" world. And from this ground, spreading ourselves, deepening our understandings, building carefully a different kind of cultural ensemble, moving toward a gathering of women.

Pieces of these ideas about what may be called the "web of life" mark the works of many other contemporary women writers from very diverse cultures, traditions, and histories. They have in common, however, an invocation of tribal values, a visioning of ancestral communities, and a centering in values associated with women's everyday lives. In searching for new ways of thinking, tribal cultures are particularly important because many of them, at least on the North American continent and before the European contact, were not structured by male supremacy, racism, or the private ownership of property. They are among the few examples we have of such existence. They provide a philosophical model of a system of thought in which there is a reverence for the female principle as the source of life, and a balance between women and men, a complementarity as it were, in the arrangement of human affairs. Significantly these cultures also seem not to have allowed for the institutionalized expression of hierarchy and domination. There was an essential valuing of individual human dignity, but there was not the sense of Western individualism. A tribal person could not exist apart from her tribespeople: "If the nation is shattered, the universe collapses. This is a tragedy which is beyond description in English, which has no word for what is destroyed."[8]

These ideas about the web of life drawn from tribal consciousness and from what are today associated with women-centered values are at the heart of the "dance cape of learning" protected by the Nootka women of British Columbia. They have been passed on in stories from one generation to the next, and they have been retold by Anne Cameron in her book *Daughters of Copper Woman.* "Torn and fragmented as it is," the women say, this dance cape "is still better than what the invader brought with him."[9] These are stories about how to live, about how to see beauty, about how to love, and about how to stand inside one's own experience and see out clearly and without fear. Above all else, these stories are about teaching women how to love themselves individually and collectively.

These ideas about the web of life are the magic that draws many women back to the images of the goddess, to the artistry in ancient caves, to what Merlin Stone has called "Ancient Mirrors of Womanhood," to the legends of Crete and the practice of Celtic ritual.[10] The most recent and apparently incontrovertible evidence gathered from archaeological excavations in Europe, the Middle and Near East, and North Africa establishes that matrilineal, matrifocal, agricultural, goddess-worshipping cultures existed throughout the Neolithic era. These early Neolithic cultures—before the Kurgan invasions from the north which ultimately destroyed them—gave no evidence of war or preparations for war. There were no fortifications, no weaponry, no artistic representations of war or a warrior caste. Metals were forged, such as gold and copper, but these were used for ornamentation and tools, not for weaponry. The Mother Goddess was believed to be the creatrix, and there was a belief that She was to be found everywhere and in all things. The Neolithic era lasted for ten thousand years. It was apparently characterized by egalitarian, peace-loving, and what are today viewed as women-centered principles. A substantial literature grounded in archaeology, anthropology, history, mythology, and art history exists confirming the existence of these cultures in many, many different parts of the world.[11]

These ideas about love and healing, balance and connection, about life and ritual inform the novel by Simone Schwarz-Bart called *The Bridge of Beyond*. This extraordinary tour de force is the life story of Telumee Lougandor, an elder, who is finally, at the end of her life, the beggar woman in the churchyard at the village of Fond-Zombie on the island of Guadeloupe. This is a story about colonialism and racism, and about cane fields owned by Europeans. It is about Africa and village life. It is about women's wisdom, about struggle and survival. But Telumee is not an object of pity and charity. She is the subject of her own life experience, and women's wisdom is passed on to her, and by her on to her adopted daughter, from the heritage of the elders: Queen Without A Name, Telumee's grandmother, and Mia Cia, the village witch and healer. African village life has been rekindled by these astonishing women, albeit adapted to the rigors of the New World, of the plantation system, having survived even the ravages of slavery. The meaning of this kindling is felt by Telumee as she sits under the plum tree in her front yard in the afternoon breeze, even as she cannot articulate what she feels. Queen Without A Name explains:

> Picking up a dry branch [the queen] started to draw a shape in the loose earth at her feet. It looked like a spider's web, with the threads intersecting to make ridiculously tiny little houses. Then, all around, she drew signs resembling trees, and, pointing with an ample gesture to her work, said, "That's Fond-Zombie."

Seeing my surprise, she explained tranquilly:

"You see, the houses are nothing without the threads that join them together. And what you feel in the afternoon under your tree is nothing but a thread that the village weaves and throws out to you and your cabin."[12]

This thread is spun into a web of resistance, a protective shield against the "fire of the cane" in which so many of the women and men of Fond-Zombie are forced to labor. The cane fields, of course, dominate the economy. The village sustains the life of the people, sustains the cultural sinews of women's invention, sustains and nurtures Telumee. The village embodies the web of life.

Drawing from an African tradition not unlike the village of Fond-Zombie (or the island of Carriacou in Paule Marshall's *Praisesong for the Widow*), Toni Cade Bambara propels a similar way of seeing women's resistance and survival in her novel *The Salt Eaters*. Drawn out of her experiences in the civil rights movement of the 1960s and set in the all-Black town of Claybourne somewhere in the deep South, the novel traces the healing of one Velma Henry, a former civil rights activist and community organizer who has fallen victim to the terrible and pervasive poisons of the system. An attempted suicide brings Velma Henry to the Southwest Community Infirmary "Established 1871 by the Free Coloreds of Claybourne," and delivers her into the hands of Minnie Ransom, holder of ancient wisdoms about the need for wholeness and roots, and the resident healer at the infirmary.

Flashbacks into Velma's memories of the sixties with its struggles and triumphs and pain and contradiction are woven into a series of contemporary still lifes in which Bambara paints a remarkable portraiture of community. Instructed in the fine art of organizing by Sophie Heywood, chapter president of the women's auxiliary of the Sleeping Car Porters, and held finally in the hands of the healer, Minnie Ransom, Velma Henry sees the moments of poisoning, steadily plotted in memory until the whole pattern is clear and recognizable. She is thinking to herself about protection against the bite of the serpent, otherwise known as capitalism, racism, patriarchy:

At some point in her life she was sure Douglass, Tubman, the slave narratives, the songs, the fables, Delaney, Ida Wells, Blyden, DuBois, Garvey, the singers, her parents, Malcolm, Coltrane, the poets, her comrades, her godmother, her neighbors, had taught her that [protection]. Thought she knew how to build immunity to the sting of the serpent that turned would-be cells, could-be cadres into cargo cults. Thought she knew how to build resistance, make the journey to the center of the circle, stay poised and centered in the work and not fly off, stay centered in the best of her people's traditions and not be available to madness, not become intoxicated by the heady brew of degrees and careers and congratulations for nothing done, not become anesthetized by dazzling performances with somebody else's aesthetic, not go under. Thought the workers of sixties had pulled the Family safely out of range of the serpents fangs. . . . But amnesia had set in anyhow. . . . Something crucial had been missing. . . . [13]

A snake bite is effectively neutralized by eating salt and by packing a salt poultice into the wound. This idea is announced in the title. Such a scene is enacted in the novel. This is Bambara's metaphor for healing the wounds of internalized racism, sexism, capitalism. The salt is already in us: it is in the mirror of one's self, and one's deepest fears of being and acting one's self; it is in African memory, in the connection to the center of light radiating from Minnie Ransom's ancient tree, and in the love of "Miz Ransom rocking that woman like the mothers of all times hold and rock however large the load, never asking whose baby or how old or is it deserving, only that it's a baby and not a stone."[14]

These ideas about the web of life inspired Annie Dillard's pilgrim at Tinker Creek;[15] they were what Marge Piercy saw under her sky "the color of pea soup";[16] and they were the source of Shug Avery's ecstasy in Alice Walker's novel *The Color Purple* when she told Celie: "One day when I was sitting quietly and feeling like a motherless child, which I was, it came to me: that feeling of being part of everything; not separable at all. I knew if I cut a tree, my arm would bleed. And I laughed and cried and run all around the house."[17] These ideas resonate in Ntozake Shange's choreopoem *For Colored Girls,* when the lady in purple speaks of "a layin' on of hands" and "the holiness of myself released" and the lady in red rejoins:

i fell into a numbness
til the only tree i cd see
took me up in her branches
held me in the breeze

made me dawn dew
that chill at daybreak
the sun wrapped over me like a million men
i waz cold/ i waz burnin up/ a child
& endlessly weavin garments for the moon
wit my tears

i found god in myself
& i loved her/ i loved her fiercely[18]

In a novel based upon the struggles of the Maori people of New Zealand to reclaim their land, Patricia Grace speaks of a poverty, the *pohara*, referring to the cultural death of a people. She contrasts this to the chosen poverty of her people farming again on their ancestral lands. They are resisting the European developers and restoring the ways of the ancestors. Central to this is the restoration of the elaborate wood carving of the *waiku*, the meeting place of community and prayer where the spirits of those who have passed join the spirits of those who live. In the ways of the ancestors the balance between women and men is restored, there is no sense of hierarchy, of inferiority, of women devalued, scorned, punished, hated. In the novel, alternating characters tell their own stories, each deepening our understanding of events, of history, of struggle. In this passage, the mother Roimata speaks of the hardship in the struggle to reclaim the land:

> There was money enough to pay for electricity, rates and petrol for the machines. There was enough for tea, flour, soap and cigarettes, but little more than that. Hemi's brother Stan [her husband's brother] sometimes said, "the gardens are great, the people are pohara," but it was only said so that we could laugh at ourselves. We are not *pohara*. Our whole family had known greater poverty. Some had survived, become whole again, and others had never mended.
> We were not *pohara*. Our chosen hardship was good and uplifting to all of us, a biting on the pebble that keeps an edge on the teeth. . . .[19]

Wrapping themselves in the spiritual wholeness of the ancestors, life is restored for this group of Maori people, however arduous their material existence.

Themes of spiritual wholeness, of the intricate balance of life, are presented by Leslie Marmon Silko in her beautiful novel *Ceremony*. In this story are layered many of the stories of the Laguna people of the south-western United States. Silko traces the subtle and intricate healing of a war veteran whose name is Tayo. He has been shattered by his experiences in the Pacific theater during World War II. The white doctors say he suffers from battle fatigue, and the Indian medicine man Ku'oosh explains the fracturing of a soul. Ku'oosh speaks in the Laguna language, "using the old dialect," explains Silko, "full of sentences that were involuted with explanations of their own origins, as if nothing the old man said were his own but all had been said before and he was only there to repeat." Ku'oosh says: "you know, grandson, this world is fragile. . . ."

> The word he chose to express "fragile" was filled with the intricacies of a continuing process, and with a strength inherent in spider webs woven across the paths through sand hills where early in the morning the sun becomes entangled in each filament of web. It took a long time to explain the fragility and intricacy because no word exists alone, and the reason for choosing each word had to be explained with a story about why it must be said this certain way. That was the responsibility that went with being human, old Ku'oosh said, the story behind each word must be told so there could be no mistake in the meaning of what had been said; and this demanded great patience and love. . . . [20]

In explaining this fragility, Ku'oosh is also explaining that if Tayo will choose to restore himself to balance he will help to restore the whole to balance.

Thousands of miles of land and ocean, continents, cultures, and centuries separate Stone Telling from Roimata from Shug Avery from Velma Henry from Telumee Lougandor and Queen Without A Name, from the Nootka women, from the Celtic women, from Ntozake Shange, Annie Dillard, Marge Piercy, and Leslie Marmon Silko. Yet there is a subtle something that connects them one to another in fiction, in history, and in life. The connection is in this idea, or rather in this consort of ideas, about growth and balance, family, and roots, and community. These ideas come from women generation after generation, and they have been passed on by women in the fragments of stories and old wives' tales, in memory, and in ritual, and now in the cogent and skilled retellings by consummate literary artists. These ideas emanate from women's labors, cast back over thousands of years, to create the conditions necessary for life, and to steadily improve the quality of their daily lives. Performed in many different cultures and contexts, these labors change in detail, but they are analogous in purpose and substance. In self-consciously representing these ideas now, women writers are providing us with what I have come to think of as a literature of ceremony. This idea was stimulated by the way in which Paula Gunn Allen explained her understanding of the role of ceremony in Native American culture. She wrote:

> The purpose of ceremony is to integrate: to fuse the individual with his or her fellows, the community of people with that of other kingdoms, and this larger communal group with the worlds beyond this one. A raising or expansion of consciousness naturally accompanies this process. The person sheds the isolated, individual personality and is restored to conscious harmony with the universe. . . . All ceremonies . . . create and support the sense of community that is the bedrock of tribal life.[21]

In general, this women's literature—unless by Native American women—is not intrinsically ceremonial in the same way that the writings of Native American people tend to be. However, much of this writing may be seen as ceremonial in purpose. Women writers coming from a womanist perspective are providing us with a way to integrate, a way to fuse our individualized, scattered experiences and feelings into a dance cape of learning which we might in some way wrap around ourselves, the way Stone Telling wrapped the fragments of the Kesh culture around herself. This literature of ceremony encourages us to heal, to love ourselves for who and how we are, to gather a sense of community, of struggle, of spiritual wholeness and sanity, of self-esteem. It allows us to honor and respect our cultural differences, while appreciating the many ways of women's invention. It is providing us with a way of validating our ways of knowing, making of them a more whole cloth, *un rebozo*, a shawl of memory and experience. Speaking of this process alive in the memory of her childhood, Mary TallMountain, Koyukon Athabascan, born in 1918 in Nulato, Territory of Alaska, tells us: "Despite loss and disillusion, I count myself rich, fertile, and magical. I tell you now. You *can* go home again."[22]

This is not to say that only women have or express these ideas and values. They are to be found in the writings and works of men, even though many of these men may also be affected by sexism. It is not to say that all women have these ideas or practice them. It is not to say that all mothers personally nurture, or nurture adequately, or succeed in providing their children with the best conditions for their growth. Women are not "essentially" virtuous, or more nurturing than men, or more loving, or caring, or "closer to nature." The point is that these ideas about life and about how to sustain it, about relationship and community and connection are generated by the nature of women's labors, and these labors, and the conditions under which they are enacted, inscribe a particular form of consciousness. This is true even when women are affected by racism, by class privilege, by homophobia, or crippled by the collision of oppressions to which they are subjected, or collude in their own oppression by engaging in the intrigues of those who hold power over them.

Ideas about this web of life, about creating the conditions for life, about improving the quality of daily life permeate many of the stories and poems told in this book. They inform in Ruth Winji's resistance to the purchase of the threshing machine with which to harvest the wheat. They are assumed in the integration of language and art by the women in the kitchen of Paule Marshall's childhood, and they are the values animating Avatara's resurrection in Marshall's praisesong. They are central to the imaginative encoding of the Ladáan language by Suzette Elgin's Nazareth, and to the search for the lost queen initiated by Judy Grahn. This idea of a web of life enables the conjuring by Betye Saar from the everyday artifacts of women's work and memory, inspires the ritual of survival of Nicholasa Mohr's mother, and the steady, grinding labors of Victoria Byerly's cotton mill workers. These ideas are in the garden of Alice Walker's mother, in the colored school of Bernice Johnson Reagon's childhood, and in the classroom created by Mary Tsukamoto to teach Japanese-American children a love for themselves, their parents, and grandparents. They propel the work at the Texas birth clinic run by Maria Elena Ortega's mother, and they are reflected everywhere in Judy Chicago's birth project. They make possible Maxine Hong Kingston's vision of an "icicle in the desert" in which paradox is finally held and applied as a way of being. In all of these stories there is an imaginative play drawn from women's everyday lives, of motion and sound, of rhythm and movement, of color and light, of earth and fabric, of cultural integrity and beauty and self-esteem, which swells in a day's work, a night's pain, an afternoon's sorrow. It is evidence of another way of knowing, of resistance re-visioned, of women gathering on their own ground. At the center of this ground is a lesbian connection sustaining a broad, rigorous, tough, and unconditional love for women, for their safety, their dignity, their wholeness.

This ground is also experienced as a crossroads. It is what Gloria Anzaldúa calls *la frontera*, the borderland. As a child growing up on many borders, racial, cultural, and religious, as a lesbian, a poet, a teacher of the children of migrant farm workers, Anzaldúa draws upon her experience to map out a way of seeing. Her work is an exemplar of how to interpret from experience, and it also directs our attention to a process of connection between ourselves as women, and across the many boundaries of difference.

In a beautifully crafted *historia* of essay and poem, symbol and legend, Anzaldúa relates her experiences as a Chicana, *una mestiza*, growing up in the mixture of cultures, the Indian and the Hispanic, in a context of Anglo domination:

> To live in the Borderlands means
>   the mill with the razor sharp teeth
>   wants to shred off your olive-red skin
>   crush out the kernel, your heart
>   pound you pinch you roll you out
>   smelling like white bread but dead[23]

The borderland becomes a powerful metaphor of physical location and spiritual place. There are three borders in Anzaldúa's conceptual framework. First there is the actual physical border marking the national boundaries between Mexico and the United States—"this thin edge of barbed wire"—traversed daily by hundreds of thousands of people, some "documented" and legal; some "undocumented" and illegal by virtue of "treaties" and "laws" and "papers" filed:

> In the Borderlands . . .
> you are at home, a stranger wherever you are
> the border disputes have been settled
> the volley of shots have shattered the truce
> you are wounded, lost in action
> fighting back, a survivor. (P. 194)

Anzaldúa traces historical patterns of migrations of the Indian peoples back and forth across this border for thousands of years and long before

European contact. We feel through her *historia,* her personal history, the linkages to the whole history, the craziness of borders invented, lands conquered.

Second, there are the cultural borders between the Indian, the Mexicano, and Anglo worlds, pitted in opposition by racism internalized, hierarchies codified, the Indian most despised, abandoned, definitions of womanhood entombed: "For a woman of my culture there used to be only three directions she could turn: to the church as a nun, to the streets as a prostitute, or to the home as a mother" (p. 17).

Third, there are the religious borders between the Aztec and the Catholic worlds, between the serpent *Coatlicue* and the Virgin Mary, the female archetypes: one powerful, transforming, "the incarnation of cosmic processes," the other frozen in purity, benign in her infinite compassion. Between these borders, Anzaldúa writes, she and her Chicana sisters must somehow exist:

> To survive the Borderland means
> you must live *sin fronteras* [without borders]
> be a crossroads (P. 195)

From this experience, out of this history, Anzaldúa proposes a way of thinking and of being which seeks to integrate oppositions, eliminate hierarchy, the either/or dualisms of Western thought. For Anzaldúa this is a necessity. As a lesbian, a Chicana, a feminist, the reconciliation of opposing definitions is essential in order for her to live a whole life. This way of thinking which Anzaldúa proposes is to *be* the crossroads herself. She finds the *symbol* of unification in *La Virgen de Guadelupe,* and the *process* of unification represented by *"la herencia* of *Coatlicue"* [the heritage of *Coatlicue*]. In explaining the history of *Guadelupe* Anzaldúa reveals the ways in which the Indian people themselves practically integrated the Indian and Spanish ways.

La Virgen de Guadelupe, Anzaldúa explains, first appeared on December 9, 1531, on the same spot where the Aztec goddess Tonatsi ("Our Lady Mother") had been worshipped. She quickly eclipsed all the other male and female religious figures in Mexico, Central America, and parts of the U.S. Southwest. Bowing to this popular absorption, integration, synthesis, and celebration, the Roman Catholic Church officially claimed her as "Mother of God" and as being "synonomous with la Virgen María" in 1660. Explaining the significance of this for herself as Chicana, and for

her people as a tactic of survival in sustaining the colonial onslaughts of
the Spaniards, the French, and finally the Anglos, Anzaldúa writes:

> Today, la Virgen de Guadelupe is the single most potent religious,
> political and cultural image of this Chicano/mexicano. She, like my
> race, is a synthesis of the old world and the new, of the religion and
> culture of the two races in our psyche, the conquerors and the con-
> quered. She is the symbol of the mestizo true to his or her Indian
> values. La cultura chicana identifies with the mother (Indian) rather
> than the father (Spanish). . . . Guadelupe unites people of different
> races, religions, languages. . . . She mediates between the Spanish and
> Indian cultures . . . between humans and the divine. . . . La Virgen de
> Guadelupe is the symbol of ethnic identity and of the tolerance for
> ambiguity that Chicano-mexicanos, people of mixed race, people
> who have Indian blood, who cross cultures, by necessity possess.
> (P. 30)

La Virgen de Guadelupe is the crossroads, the symbol of synthesis and
survival, the model of Anzaldúa's strategy of resistance and reclamation of
herself as a woman: "I want the freedom to carve and chisel my own face,
to staunch the bleeding with ashes, to fashion my own gods out of my
entrails. And if going home is denied me then I will have to stand and
claim my space, making a new culture—una cultura mestiza—with my
own lumber, my own bricks, and mortar and my own feminist architec-
ture" (p. 22). And later comes a poem of the woman alone:

> Raza india mexicana norteamericana, there's no-
> thing more you can chop off   or graft on me
> that will change my soul. . . .
> I am fully formed carved
> by the hands of the ancients   drenched with
> the stench of today's headlines.   But my own
> hands whittle   the final work   me. (P. 173)

The process of unification symbolized by Guadelupe is provided by
Coatlicue because she "depicts the contradictory. In her figure, all the
symbols important to the religion and philosophy of the Aztecs are integrated. . . . she is a symbol of the fusion of opposites: the eagle and the
serpent, heaven and the underworld, life and death, mobility and immo-
bility, beauty and horror" (p. 47).

For Anzaldúa the crossroad is the space between the borders. This space is symbolized by *Guadelupe* and enacted by *Coatlicue*. This is the ground upon which she, Anzaldúa, proposes to stand, "to whittle the final work" of herself. I think that she also invites all of us, as women, to consider the advantages of this place for ourselves. This space between borders is not a margin; on the contrary, it is our center. It is where we as women are in fact located because we live in a partriarchal, racially supremacist, class-conscious system. As women, *in relationship to each other*, if we are willing to stand that way, to abandon the "master's tools," we are all *mestizas*.[24] We traipse back and forth every day, sometimes several times a day between the cultures of our existence: the women's cultures, the men's cultures, the children's cultures, the work cultures, the class cultures, the lesbian cultures, the "straight" cultures, the racial cultures, the ethnic cultures, the church cultures. We *are* the crossroads: at work, at school, in community, with family, in church, with lovers, juggling, aching, arching. To successfully negotiate these crossroads we do not, in fact, see things in oppositions. We shift contexts, relate differences, make adjustments, integrate, synthesize, move with the spirit of a place. This is the work of what Anzaldúa calls our "mestiza consciousness," which is "indigenous like corn," already enacted (p. 81).

This is a strategy for *women's* coalition, for a politics of our own. The point then is not to find the lowest common denominator around which to unite (over our oppositions), but to abandon oppositional ways of thinking. The point is not so much to unite as to congeal—each element retaining its integrity and value, stuck together for a particular purpose, each of us using our skills to shift and relate, adjust and integrate. This is a strategy that comes out of the dailiness of our own lived experiences. We do this kind of politics every day. But, when we say the word "politics" it is freighted with historical, electoral, and factional references, and we are transported almost immediately back into the world of masculinist thought, shouting, denouncing, polemicizing, opposing.

Consider how we carry on debates in the women's movement, how our process mirrors masculinist forms, how we place ourselves in oppositional camps of radical, and lesbian, and separatist, and socialist. Consider how we carry on dialogues in our journals, in letters to the editor, in our "replies" and "rejoinders," defending our "positions" and correcting "misrepresentations." As women we are often taught to compete: with each other for men, with each other for male approval, at work, in university, in the professions.[25]

A lot of the ways in which we argue with each other in the women's movement and in women's studies comes out of this competition and the distrust that is its constant companion. It also comes out of our rage, our fire redirected at each other, hardened in frustration and fury at the system. When sexism, racism, homophobia are internalized, we spew that rage at convenient targets, the women who are reflections of parts of ourselves.[26]

I was born into the Old Left. I matured in the New Left, and in the civil rights and antiwar movements of the sixties. When I read ourselves now in the women's liberation movement, and in feminist scholarly journals, I have a sense of déjà vu. The content of our debates, the lines of demarcation, the contested versions of "truth" are different, but our *process* is the same as it was in all of those movements. And we factionalize and split just as they did.

I am reminded of a scene described by Vivian Gornick near the end of her book, *The Romance of American Communism*. Gornick also grew up in a Communist family, a generation before me. She described being at a meeting of the women's movement in Boston in the early seventies and making a statement in the course of a discussion which brought angry murmurs from those around her. Gornick recalled: "The speaker turned full face toward me. In a voice blazing with scorn she said to me: 'You're an intellectual and a revisionist.' I remained standing beside my seat, speechless. An intellectual and a revisionist. I hadn't heard those words used in this fashion since childhood. . . . What did she think those words meant?"[27] A decade later a mania for being "politically correct"—"p.c." in the jargon—had become central in many places within the women's movement.

This factionalizing and preoccupation with political line is not an inevitable by-product of politics. It is connected to a process, to a way of thinking. We have to stop thinking in oppositional categories. We have to stop thinking that one line is "correct" and that others must be "won over" to it, while those who disagree are "defeated." There are limits, of course. There are matters of principle which each of us define for ourselves as individuals and for ourselves as a movement. But we don't have to associate with that with which we disagree, and we also don't have to give energy to that with which we disagree by enacting opposition to it.

For example, when I read articles by women who call themselves lesbian separatists, I find that I am in agreement with many of the things they say. They are describing a slice of what is true for us as women, as lesbians. But when this becomes a "position" to which I must adhere in opposition to others, I find myself cut off. I find myself babbling "buts": but look at this, and what about that, and so on. And I find that the slice of what is true for us becomes distorted in the process of debate, in the process of making it an exclusive reality.

When I read essays by feminist scholars affirming that differences between women and men are not as significant and compelling as some have argued, I find myself moved to respectful acknowledgment. In one essay, for example, anthropologist Carol Stack talks about interviews she has conducted with Black women and men returning to the South after years (and sometimes generations) in northern cities. Stack proposes that these women and men have more in common with each other than not, and that these Black women have more in common with Black men than they do with white, middle-class women.[28] In another essay, anthropologist Judith Shapiro suggests that the emphasis on difference between women and men in feminist scholarship has reinforced and indeed created a kind of "gender totemism" in which gender differences are more symbolic than real.[29]

Both essays are persuasive. Both articulate a slice of what is true for us as women. But when this becomes a "position" in opposition to what is then called "cultural feminism," and when the works of Sara Ruddick, Carol Gilligan, and Nancy Hartsock are thus attacked because they are in a different "cluster," I find myself again cut off, babbling "buts." I find myself then, also, drawn to Catharine MacKinnon's eloquent "discourses on life and law," in which she argues that viewing gender as a matter of sameness and difference covers up the reality of gender as a system of power, hierarchy, and privilege, of imposed inequality.[30]

The point is that more than one thing is true for us at the same time. A masculinist process, however, at least as it has been institutionalized in Western society, accentuates the combative, the oppositional, the either/ or dichotomies, the "right" and the "wrong." What I have been about throughout this book is showing that the dailiness of women's lives structures a different way of knowing and a different way of thinking. The process that comes from this way of knowing has to be at the center of a women's politics, and it has to be at the center of a women's scholarship. This is why I have been drawn to the poetry and to the stories: because they are layered, because more than one truth is represented, because there is ambiguity and paradox. When we work together in coalitions, or on the job, or in academic settings, or in the community, we have to allow for this ambiguity and paradox, respect each other, our cultures, our integrity, our dignity.

As we have pressured against racial and sex discrimination, institutional doors have been opened, however tenuously and with whatever reluctance. Some of us have been allowed in, but nothing about the values of those institutions or their rules of success has changed, whether they be academic, corporate, ecclesiastic, political, medical, or juridical. The point is to change the values and the rules and to change the process by which they are established and enforced. The point is to integrate ideas about love and healing, about balance and connection, about beauty and growing, into our everyday ways of being. We have to believe in the value of our own experiences and in the value of our ways of knowing, our ways of doing things. We have to wrap ourselves in these ways of knowing, to enact daily ceremonies of life.

THE DESERT is a metaphor. For how long women have endured. Like creosote. Waiting for the rains.

We are the rains.

Notes

Dedication epigraph. Anryú Suharu, untitled poem, in *Women Poets of Japan,* ed. Kenneth Rexroth and Ikuko Atsumi (New York: New Directions, 1977), p. 73.

I. Conditions for Work

Epigraphs. Adrienne Rich, "Transcendental Etude" in Rich, *The Dream of a Common Language* (New York: Norton, 1978), p. 73; Sheila Rowbotham, *Woman's Consciousness, Man's World* (Middlesex: Penguin Books, 1973), p. 29; Leslie Marmon Silko, *Storyteller* (New York: Seaver Books, 1981), p. 7; Lucille Clifton, *Generations: A Memoir* (New York: Random House, 1976), p. 78.

1. Dorothy E. Smith, "A Sociology for Women," manuscript, 1979, p. 23. This paper was prepared for the conference, "The Prism of Sex: Toward an Equitable Pursuit of Knowledge," by the Women's Research Institute of Wisconsin, October 7–9, 1977. The proceedings were published under the conference title, and edited by Julia A. Sherman and Evelyn Torton Beck (Madison: University of Wisconsin Press, 1979). Smith's manuscript is in my possession. The printed version is somewhat revised, but the thrust of its argument remains intact.

2. Bettina Aptheker, *Woman's Legacy: Essays on Race, Sex, and Class in American History* (Amherst: University of Massachusetts Press, 1982).

3. For those interested in these debates, the following would be of use in supplying the major references: Annette Kuhn and AnnMarie Wolpe, eds., *Feminism and Materialism: Women and Modes of Production* (Boston: Routledge and Kegan Paul, 1978); Zillah R. Eisenstein, ed., *Capitalist Patriarchy and the Case for Socialist Feminism* (New York: Monthly Review Press, 1979); Lydia Sargent, ed., *Women and Revolution: A Discussion of "The Unhappy Marriage of Marxism and Feminism"* [by Heidi Hartmann] (Boston: South End Press, 1981); Sheila Rowbotham, *Woman's Consciousness, Man's World* (Middlesex, England: Penguin Books, 1973); Wally Seccombe, "The Housewife and Her Labour under Capitalism," *New Left Review* 83 (January–February 1973); Eli Zaretsky, "Socialist Politics and the Family," *Socialist Revolution* 19 (January–March 1974): 83–99, and his essay "Capitalism, the Family, and Personal Life," *Socialist Revolution* 18 (January–June 1973). It is important to note that the first discussion of the dual character of women's labor was initiated by the American Communist Mary Inman in two essays, "Woman-Power," published by the Committee to Organize the Advancement of Women, Los Angeles, 1942, and "The Two Forms of Production Under Capitalism," published by the author, Long Beach, Calif., March 1964. Both pamphlets are in my possession.

4. While the evidence of this partnership is abundant in the works cited

above, the scholarship on the exploitation of women's labor in the Third World by multinational corporations and capitalist enterprises indigenous to those countries is very significant. See, for example, June Nash and Maria P. Fernández-Kelly, eds., *Women, Men, and the International Division of Labor* (Albany: State University of New York Press, 1983); Maria Patricia Fernández-Kelly, *For We Are Sold, I and My People: Women and Industry in Mexico's Frontier* (Albany: State University of New York Press, 1980); Helen I. Safa and Eleanor Leacock, eds., *Development and the Sexual Division of Labor, Signs,* 7:2 (Winter 1981), a special issue; Aihwa Ong, *Spirits of Resistance and Capitalist Discipline: Factory Women in Malaysia* (Albany: State University of New York Press, 1987); Heleieth I. B. Saffioti, *Women in Class Society* (New York: Monthly Review Press, 1978). Also significant is the dissertation in progress by the Japanese scholar Yoshiko Miyake, "Women's Labor in Japan's Capitalist Society: *Joko Aishi,* or the Pitiful History of Mill Girls as the Product of the Union between Patriarchy and Capitalism" (January 1987), History of Consciousness Program, University of California, Santa Cruz.

    5. Sandra Harding, "The Instability of the Analytical Categories of Feminist Theory," *Signs* 11:4 (Summer 1986): 646. Of related interest are the following: Maria C. Lugones and Elisabeth V. Spelman, "Have We Got A Theory for You! Feminist Theory, Cultural Imperialism and the Demand for 'the Women's Voice,' " *Women's Studies International Forum* 6:6 (1983): 573–82; and Judith Stacey and Barrie Thorne, "The Missing Feminist Revolution in Sociology," *Social Problems* 32 (April 1985): 301–16.

    6. Adrienne Rich, *Of Woman Born: Motherhood As Experience and Institution* (New York: Norton, 1976), pp. 201–2.

    7. Rowbotham, *Woman's Consciousness, Man's World,* p. 27.

    8. These two assumptions, which provide the grounding for my work, retain elements of the Marxist philosophy in that they place significance on women's material conditions in terms of both the labor performed by women and the social, political, and economic structures that enforce women's subordination to men. The literature on this is vast and comprises the epistemological foundation for women's studies as a discipline. For those interested in more detailed analysis and sources I cite those works that particularly influenced my formulations: Sandra Harding and Merrill Hintikka, eds., *Discovering Reality: Feminist Perspectives on Epistemology, Metaphysics, Methodology, and the Philosophy of Science* (Boston: D. Reidel, 1983)—in this volume, the essays by Nancy Hartsock ("The Feminist Standpoint: Developing the Ground for a Specifically Feminist Historical Materialism") and Jane Flax ("Political Philosophy and the Patriarchal Unconscious") were particularly significant for me; Mary Vetterling-Braggin, Frederick A. Elliston, and Jane English, eds., *Feminism and Philosophy* (Totowa, N.J.: Rowman and Littlefield, 1977); Carol Gilligan, *In a Different Voice: Psychological Theory and Women's Development* (Cambridge: Harvard University Press, 1982); Candace West and Don H. Zimmerman, "Doing Gender," *Gender & Society* 1:2 (1987): 125–51; Barrie Thorne and Zella Luria, "Sexuality and Gender in Children's Daily Worlds," *Social Problems* 33:3 (1986): 176–90. I found several

anthropological and folkloric works helpful in making visible women's cultures, in particular, Rayna R. Reiter, ed., *Toward an Anthropology for Women* (New York: Monthly Review Press, 1975); Michelle Zimbalist Rosaldo and Louis Lamphere, eds., *Women, Culture & Society* (Stanford, Calif.: Stanford University Press, 1974); and Rosan A. Jordan and Susan J. Kalčik, eds., *Women's Folklore, Women's Culture* (Philadelphia: University of Pennsylvania Press, 1985). The work of physical anthropologists was also provocative in the formulation of these ideas. See, for example, Nancy Tanner and Adrienne Zihlman, "Women in Evolution, Part I: Innovation and Selection in Human Origins," *Signs* 1:3 (Spring 1976): 585–608; and Adrienne Zihlman, "Women in Evolution, Part II: Subsistence and Social Organization among Early Hominids," *Signs* 4:1 (Autumn 1978): 4–20. All of Joan Kelly's work has been extremely important to me. Her major feminist essays in historiography are contained in *Women, History & Theory: The Essays of Joan Kelly* (Chicago: University of Chicago Press, 1984).

9. Clifford Geertz, "From the Native's Point of View: On the Nature of Anthropological Understanding," in *Meaning in Anthropology,* ed. Keith H. Basso and Henry A. Selby (Albuquerque: University of New Mexico Press, 1976), p. 228.

10. Dorothy E. Smith, "A Peculiar Eclipsing: Women's Exclusion from Man's Culture," *Women's Studies International Quarterly* 1(1978): 282.

11. Clifford Geertz, *The Interpretation of Cultures: Selected Essays* (New York: Basic Books, 1973), pp. 5, 14. Geertz is centered on men in his description and analysis, but it seems to me that, stripped of its masculinist intentions, his semiotic approach—i.e., the concept of understanding cultural codes and of making them intelligible—is a useful one.

12. Virginia Woolf, *A Room of One's Own* (1929; New York: Harcourt, Brace & World, 1957), p. 68.

13. Rich, *Of Woman Born,* pp. 15–16.

14. Ibid., pp. 63–64.

15. Ibid., p. 64.

16. Akua-Lezlie Hope, untitled poem, in *Ordinary Women: An Anthology of Poetry by New York City Women,* ed. Sara Miles, Patricia Jones, Sandra Marie Esteves, Fay Chiang (New York Ordinary Women, P.O. Box 664, Old Chelsea Station, New York, N.Y., 10011, 1978). This book is out of print. A copy of it is in my possession.

17. Rich, *Of Woman Born,* p. 246.

18. This statement became the title of the first chapter of Jacqueline Jones's book *Labor of Love, Labor of Sorrow: Black Women, Work, and the Family from Slavery to the Present* (New York: Random House, Vintage Books, 1986), pp. 11–43. It was made by Janie Scott who said her mother was "strong and could roll and cut logs like a man, and was much of a woman" (p. 18).

19. Lorna Dee Cervantes, "Oaxaca, 1974" in her book *Emplumada* (Pittsburgh: University of Pittsburgh Press, 1981), p. 44.

20. Kitty Tsui, "It's in the Name," in her book, *The Words of a Woman Who Breathes Fire* (San Francisco: Spinsters, Ink, 1983), pp. 1–3.

21. Maxine Hong Kingston, *The Woman Warrior: Memoirs of a Girlhood Among Ghosts* (New York: Random House, Vintage Books, 1977). A detailed discussion of this novel will be found in Chapter 4.

22. Nessa Rapoport, "The Woman Who Lost Her Names," in *The Woman Who Lost Her Names: Selected Writings by American Jewish Women,* ed. Julia Wolf Mazow (San Francisco: Harper and Row, 1980), pp. 135–44; Nellie Wong, *Dreams in Harrison Railroad Park* (Berkeley, Calif.: Kelsey St. Press, 1977). This poem is read by the author in the film *Mitsuye & Nellie: Asian American Poets,* produced by Allie Light and Irving Saraf, 1979. Available from Light-Saraf Films, San Francisco, California.

23. Paule Marshall, *Praisesong for the Widow* (New York: Dutton, 1984). An excellent, critical essay on this novel which explores the significance of *nommo* is by Barbara Christian, "Ritualistic Process and the Structure of Paule Marshall's *Praisesong for the Widow,*" in her book, *Black Feminist Criticism: Perspectives on Black Women Writers* (New York: Pergamon Press, 1985), pp. 149–58. A more extensive discussion of this novel is in Chapter 4 of this book.

24. Michelle Cliff, *Claiming an Identity They Taught Me to Despise* (Watertown, Mass.: Persephone Press, 1980).

25. Sandra Cisneros, *The House on Mango Street* (Houston: Arte Publico Press, 1985), pp. 12–13.

26. Irena Klepfisz, "Secular Jewish Identity: *Yidishkayt* in America," *Sinister Wisdom,* no. 29/30 (1986): 46–47. This was a special issue of *Sinister Wisdom* entitled *The Tribe of Dina: A Jewish Women's Anthology,* with guest editors Melanie Kaye/Kantrowitz and Irena Klepfisz.

27. Janet Campbell [Hale], "Desmet, Idaho, March, 1969," in Fisher, *The Third Woman,* p. 107. These ideas about language are further explored in the novel by Janet Campbell Hale, *The Jailing of Cecelia Capture* (New York: Random House, 1985), pp. 68–69. The Random House edition is out of print. A revised paperback edition is available from the University of New Mexico Press, Albuquerque. This novel was nominated for a Pulitzer Prize.

28. These words were reproduced on a poster distributed widely by the Syracuse Cultural Workers, Syracuse, New York, beginning in 1985 to publicize the film *Broken Rainbow.* The poster was designed by Maria Florio. The film, which won the 1985 Academy Award for Best Documentary, was produced and distributed by Earthworks Films, Malibu, California.

29. An explanation of some aspects of Navajo language will be found in a review-essay by Harriet Desmoines, "Sweet Medicine," *Sinister Wisdom,* no. 13 (Spring 1980): 59. A useful laying-out of North American tribal concepts will be found in Paula Gunn Allen, "The Sacred Hoop: A Contemporary Perspective," in her book *The Sacred Hoop: Recovering the Feminine in American Indian Traditions* (Boston: Beacon Press, 1986), pp. 54–75.

30. Laura Balbo, "The Servicing Work of Women and the Capitalist State," manuscript, 1980. The information about the origins of the idea for this essay was the result of a conversation with the author when she was a visiting professor at

the University of California, Santa Cruz. Professor Balbo was elected in 1983 to the Italian Parliament.

31. Susan Griffin, *Woman and Nature: The Roaring Inside Her* (New York: Harper and Row, 1978). The earliest, sustained discussion of women's silences in literature is by Tillie Olsen, *Silences* (New York: Delta Books, 1978).

32. Adrienne Rich, "Origins and the History of Consciousness," in her book *The Dream of a Common Language: Poems 1974–1977* (New York: Norton, 1978), p. 7.

33. Woolf, *A Room of One's Own*, p. 80.

34. Lorna Dee Cervantes, "Para Un Revolucionario," in *The Third Woman: Minority Woman Writers of the United States,* ed. Dexter Fisher (Boston: Houghton Mifflin, 1980), pp. 381–83. The English translation of the Spanish is: *una liberación,* "a liberation"; *Pero . . . carnal,* "But . . . brother"; *tus hijos,* "your children"; *de la sala,* "from the room"; *para ti con manos bronces,* "for you with brown hands"; *mi espíritu,* "my soul"; *es la hamaca,* "is the hammock"; *Hermano Raza,* "blood brother"; *la revolución,* "the Revolution."

35. Kate Rushin, "The Bridge Poem," in *This Bridge Called My Back: Writings by Radical Women of Color,* ed. Cherríe Moraga and Gloria Anzaldúa (Watertown, Mass.: Persephone Press, 1981), pp. xxi–xxii.

36. One of the most powerful statements about the emotional and physical work of Black women in domestic service can be found in the novel by Alice Childress, *Like One of the Family . . . conversations from a domestic's life,* (1956; reprint ed., Boston: Beacon Press, 1987), with an introduction by the literary historian Trudier Harris.

37. Maxine Baca Zinn, Lynn Weber Cannon, Elizabeth Higginbotham, and Bonnie Thornton Dill, "The Costs of Exclusionary Practices in Women's Studies," *Signs* 11:2 (Winter 1986): 296.

38. Teresa Paloma Acosta, "My Mother Pieced Quilts," in *Festival de flor y canto,* ed. Alurista et al. (Los Angeles: University of Southern California, 1976), p. 38.

39. Paula Gunn Allen, "Woman/Work" in *That's What She Said: Contemporary Poetry and Fiction by Native American Women,* ed. Rayna Green (Bloomington: Indiana University Press, 1984), p. 29.

40. Alice Walker, "Women," in *Revolutionary Petunias and Other Poems* (New York: Harcourt Brace Jovanovich, 1973), p. 5. This poem is also included in Walker's essay "In Search of Our Mothers' Gardens," in her book by the same title (New York: Harcourt Brace Jovanovich, 1983), pp. 242–43.

41. Marge Piercy, "The seven of pentacles" from her book *Circles in the Water* (New York: Knopf, 1982), p. 128.

42. Meridel Le Sueur, "Rites of Ancient Ripening," in *Women and Aging: an anthology by women,* ed. Jo Alexander et al. (Corvallis, Oreg.: Calyx Books, 1986), p. 10.

43. Lorna Dee Cervantes, "Beneath the Shadow of the Freeway," in *Emplumada,* p. 12.

44. Hiroko B. Yamano, "Poems," manuscript, 1983 (in my possession). These poems were part of a final project for my class, "Introduction to Feminism," and given to me with permission to use.

45. Audre Lorde, "Poetry Is Not a Luxury," in her book *Sister/Outsider, Essays & Speeches* (Trumansburg, N.Y.: The Crossing Press, 1984), p. 37.

46. Norma Alarcón, "What Kind of Lover Have You Made Me, Mother?: Towards a Theory of Chicanas' Feminism and Cultural Identity Through Poetry," in *Women of Color: Perspectives on Feminism and Identity*, ed. Audrey T. McCluskey. Occasional Papers Series 1, Women's Studies Program, Indiana University (Bloomington, 1985), p. 85.

47. Aurora Levins Morales and Rosario Morales, *Getting Home Alive* (Ithaca, N.Y.: Firebrand Books, 1986), p. 40.

48. Quoted by Rochelle Ratner, "In Memoriam: Muriel Rukeyser 1913–1980," in Ratner's book *Trying to Understand What It Means to Be a Feminist: Essays on Women Writers* (New York: Contact II, 1984), p. 48.

49. Muriel Rukeyser, "Käthe Kollwitz," in *In Her Own Image: Women Working in the Arts*, ed. Elaine Hedges and Ingrid Wendt (Old Westbury, N.Y.: Feminist Press, 1980), p. 266.

50. Griffin, *Woman and Nature*, p. 209.

51. Walker, "The Nature of This Flower Is to Bloom," in *Revolutionary Petunias and Other Poems*, p. 70.

52. Rich, "Transcendental Etude," in *The Dream of a Common Language*, pp. 76–77.

53. Judy Grahn, *The Highest Apple: Sappho and the Lesbian Poetic Tradition* (San Francisco: Spinsters, Ink, 1985), p. 7.

54. Adrienne Rich, "When We Dead Awaken: Writing as Re-Vision," in her book *On Lies, Secrets, and Silence: Selected Prose, 1966–1978* (New York: Norton, 1979), pp. 37–38.

55. Michele Roberts, "Martha and Mary raise Consciousness from the Dead," in Zoë Fairbairns et al., *Tales I Tell My Mother* (Boston: South End Press, 1980), p. 72.

56. Rich, "Transcendental Etude," p. 74.

II. The Dailiness of Women's Lives

Epigraphs. Gwendolyn Brooks, *Maud Martha* in Brooks, *Blacks* (Chicago: The David Co., 1987); Michelle Cliff, *Claiming an Identity They Taught Me to Despise* (Watertown, Mass.: Persephone Press, 1980), pp. 41–42; E. M. Boner, *A Weave of Women* (1978; Bloomington: Indiana University Press, 1985), p. 213; Marguerite Ickis, quoting her great-grandmother, in Mirra Bank, *Anonymous Was a Woman* (New York: St. Martin's Press, 1979), p. 94.

1. Deena Metzger, "In Her Own Image," *Heresies* 1 (May 1977): 7.

2. The concept of a women's standpoint is elaborated theoretically in an essay by Nancy Hartsock, "The Feminist Standpoint: Developing the Ground for

a Specifically Feminist Historical Materialism," in *Discovering Reality: Feminist Perspectives on Epistemology, Metaphysics, Methodology, and Philosophy of Science,* ed. Sandra Harding and Merrill B. Hintikka (Dordrecht and Boston: D. Reidel, 1983). Hartsock's essay, which I originally read in manuscript in 1980, significantly influenced my ideas in the shaping of this book.

3. Susan Griffin, *Woman and Nature: The Roaring Inside Her* (New York: Harper and Row, 1978), p. 201.

4. Carol Christ, *Diving Deep and Surfacing: Women Writers on Spiritual Quest* (Boston: Beacon Press, 1980), p. 1. In a later book, Christ refers to herself as a *thealogian* in an effort to feminize the tradition. See *Reflections on a Journey to the Goddess* (San Francisco: Harper and Row, 1987), especially, "Introduction: Finding the Voices of Feminist Thealogy."

5. Leslie Marmon Silko, *Storyteller* (New York: Seaver Books, 1981), pp. 3– 4.

6. Ibid., pp. 4–5.

7. Ibid., p. 247.

8. Susanne Juhasz, "Towards a Theory of Form in Feminist Autobiography: Kate Millett's *Flying* and *Sita;* Maxine Hong Kingston's *The Woman Warrior,*" in *Women's Autobiography: Essays in Criticism,* ed. Estelle C. Jelinek (Bloomington: Indiana University Press, 1980), p. 223–24.

9. Fern L. Johnson and Elizabeth J. Aries, "The Talk of Women Friends," *Women's Studies International Forum* 6:4 (1983): 358.

10. Alice Walker, "In Search of Our Mothers' Gardens," in her book *In Search of Our Mothers' Gardens: Womanist Prose* (San Diego: Harcourt Brace Jovanovich, 1983), p. 239.

11. Gloria Wade-Gayles, *No Crystal Stair: Visions of Race and Sex in Black Women's Fiction* (New York: Pilgrim Press, 1984), p. 102. Wade-Gayles was referring specifically to Alice Walker's novel *The Third Life of Grange Copeland.*

12. Walker, "In Search of Our Mothers' Gardens," p. 241.

13. Alice Walker, "The Nature of This Flower Is to Bloom," in her book *Revolutionary Petunias and Other Poems* (New York: Harcourt Brace Jovanovich, 1973), p. 70.

14. Adrienne Rich, "Twenty-One Love Poems, #1," in her book *The Dream of a Common Language: Poems 1974–1977* (New York: Norton, 1978), p. 25.

15. Bernice Mennis, "Gardens, Growth, and Community," *Women: A Journal of Liberation* 5:2 (1977): 44.

16. Bernice Mennis, "The Miracle," *Sinister Wisdom,* no. 29/30 (1986): 175. This was a special issue of *Sinister Wisdom* entitled *The Tribe of Dina: A Jewish Women's Anthology,* with guest editors Melanie Kaye/Kantrowitz and Irena Klepfisz.

17. Paule Marshall, "The Making of a Writer from the Poets in the Kitchen," *New York Times Book Review,* January 9, 1983, p. 3.

18. Ibid., p. 34.

19. Beth Brant (Degonwadonti), *Mohawk Trail* (Ithaca, N.Y.: Firebrand Books, 1985), pp. 20–21.

20. Tillie Olsen, "I Stand Here Ironing," in her book *Tell Me A Riddle: A Collection* (Philadelphia: Lippincott, 1961), p. 75.

21. Ibid., pp. 75, 76.

22. Ibid., p. 88.

23. Alice Walker, "Everyday Use," in her book *In Love & Trouble: Stories of Black Women* (New York: Harcourt Brace Jovanovich, 1973), pp. 48, 50.

24. Ibid., pp. 53–54.

25. Ibid., p. 59.

26. A useful, highly theoretical discussion of the way in which the commodity structure shapes all aspects of the dominant culture is provided by the Marxist critic Fredric Jameson, "Reification and Utopia in Mass Culture," *Social Text* 1 (Winter 1979): 132 especially. For a discussion of women as sexual objects for male gratification see, for example, Robin Morgan, "Theory and Practice: Pornography and Rape," in *Take Back The Night: Women on Pornography,* ed. Laura Lederer (New York: William Morrow, 1980), pp. 134–40; Irene Diamond, "Pornography and Repression: A Reconsideration," *Signs* 5:4 (Summer 1980): 686–701; Catharine A. MacKinnon, "Pornography: A Feminist Perspective," transcript of a lecture at the University of California, Santa Cruz, October 28, 1983. Some of MacKinnon's arguments are published in her essay "Feminism, Marxism, Method, and the State: Toward Feminist Jurisprudence," *Signs* 8:4 (Summer 1983): 635–58. See also Kathleen Barry, *Female Sexual Slavery* (New York: Avon Books, 1979), and Andrea Dworkin, *Pornography: Men Possessing Women* (New York: G. P. Putnam's Sons, A Pengrie Book, 1981).

27. Susan Keating Glaspell, "A Jury of Her Peers," in *American Voices, American Women,* ed. Lee R. Edwards and Arlyn Diamond (New York: Avon Books, 1973), p. 372. The story was first published in *Everyweek,* March 5, 1917.

28. Annette Kolodny, "A Map for Rereading: Or, Gender and the Interpretation of Literary Texts," *New Literary History* 11 (1979/1980): 462.

29. Glaspell, "A Jury," p. 378.

30. Shelley Shepard, "Myrna," manuscript, 1981. This story was written as a term project for my class "Introduction to Feminism." A copy of it is in my possession, and is used with permission.

31. Sara Ruddick, "Maternal Thinking," *Feminist Studies* 6:2 (Summer 1980): 347, 352.

32. Ibid., pp. 347, 358.

33. Rayna Green, "Magnolias Grow in Dirt: The Bawdy Lore of Southern Women," *Southern Exposure* 4:4 (Winter 1972): 31, 32, 33.

34. Ana Castillo, *The Mixquiahuala Letters* (Binghamton, N.Y.: Bilingual Press/Editorial Bilingue, 1986), p. 44.

35. Wade-Gayles, *No Crystal Stair,* p. 82.

36. Gwendolyn Brooks, *Maud Martha,* collected in Brooks, *Blacks,* pp. 286.

37. Ibid., p. 287.

38. Ibid., p. 279.

39. Ibid., p. 281.

40. Ibid., p. 284.

41. I am grateful to Ann Jealous, a therapist and an instructor at Monterey Peninsula College, for her discussion of this story in her class "Black Women in America," September 1987.

42. Barbara Christian, "Nuance and the Novella: A Study of Gwendolyn Brooks's *Maud Martha*," in her book *Black Feminist Criticism: Perspectives on Black Women Writers* (New York: Pergamon Press, 1985), p. 139.

43. Ibid., p. 128.

44. Dexter Fisher, ed., *The Third Woman: Minority Women Writers of the United States* (Boston: Houghton Mifflin, 1980), p. 144.

45. Sandra Cisneros, *The House on Mango Street* (Houston: Arte Publico Press, 1985), p. 71.

46. Ibid., p. 89.

47. Ibid., pp. 100, 15, 63.

48. Ibid., pp. 73–75.

49. Ibid., p. 98.

50. Ibid., pp. 10, 28, 30, 32.

51. Elaine Hedges, "The Nineteenth-Century Diarist and Her Quilts," *Feminist Studies* 8:2 (Summer 1982): 295–97.

52. Patricia Cooper and Norma Bradley Buferd, *The Quilters: Women and Domestic Art* (Garden City, N.Y.: Doubleday, Anchor Press, 1978), p. 15.

53. Ibid., p. 48.

54. Ibid., p. 76.

55. Ibid., p. 75.

56. Elaine Hedges, "The Nineteenth-Century Diarist and Her Quilts," p. 294.

57. Audre Lorde, *A Burst of Light* (Ithaca, N.Y.: Firebrand Books, 1988), p. 102.

58. Linda Otto Lipsett, *Remember Me: Women & Their Friendship Quilts* (San Francisco: Quilt Digest Press, 1985), p. 113.

59. Ibid., p. 114.

60. Michelle Cliff, " 'I Found God In Myself And I Loved Her / I Loved Her Fiercely': More Thoughts On The Work of Black Women Artists," in *Women, Feminist Identity and Society in the 1980's: Selected Papers*, ed. Myriam Diaz-Diocaretz and Iris M. Zavala (Amsterdam and Philadelphia: John Benjamins, 1985), pp. 109–23.

61. Margot Carter Blair, "An Interview With Cuesta Benberry," *The Flying Needle*, February 1985, p. 11.

62. *Afro-American Women and Quilts*, Cuesta Benberry, 1979. Pieced and appliqued cotton, 80″ × 52″, reproduced in color in the catalog by Jane Benson and Nancy Olson, with Jan Rindfleisch, *The Power of Cloth: Political Quilts 1845–1986* (Cupertino, Calif.: Euphrat Gallery, DeAnza College, March 3 to April 19, 1987), p. 33. Each of the quilts detailed in this section is reproduced in the gallery catalog.

63. Moira Roth, "The Field and the Drawing Room," in *Faith Ringgold*,

Change: Painted Story Quilts (New York: Bernice Steinbaum Gallery, January 13 through February 7, 1987), p. 7. Many of the story-quilts are reproduced in full color in this gallery catalog, with an extensive explanatory text.

64. See *The Quilt: Stories from the Names Project*, written by Cindy Ruskin, Photographs by Matt Herron, Design by Deborah Zemke (New York: Pocket Books, 1988).

65. Marjorie Agosín is a Chilean poet and activist. She has written extensively on women in the Chilean resistance. See, for example, Marjorie Agosín, "The Association of Families of the Detained-Disappeared, Women of Chile," *Woman of Power*, no. 3 (Winter/Spring 1986): 30–33; "Women Organizing Against the Pinochet Dictatorship" ibid., no. 4 (Fall 1986): 78–79; and "A Challenge to Silence, Latin American Women Write," ibid., no. 7 (Summer 1987): 36–37, 74.

66. The catalog and bookworks were printed by MOCHA (Museum of Contemporary Hispanic Art, 584 Broadway, New York, N.Y. 10012). I am very grateful to the Santa Cruz artist Mary Warshaw for calling the exhibit to my attention. She was one of the participating artists.

67. Walker, "In Search of Our Mothers' Gardens," p. 237.

68. See the essay by Michelle Cliff, "The Resonance of Interruption," *Chrysalis*, no. 8 (Summer 1979): 29–37.

III. The Lesbian Connection

Epigraphs. Elsa Gidlow, "Making for Meditation" in Gidlow, *Elsa: I Come With My Songs* (San Francisco: Booklegger Press & Druid Heights Books, 1986), p. 329; Gloria Anzaldúa, "La Prieta" in *This Bridge Called My Back: Writings by Radical Women of Color*, ed. Cherríe Moraga and Gloria Anzaldúa (Watertown, Mass.: Persephone Press, 1981), p. 205; Emily Dickinson, "Wild Nights" (#249) in *The Complete Poems of Emily Dickinson*, ed. Thomas H. Johnson (Boston: Little, Brown, 1960), p. 114.

1. Marilyn Frye, *The Politics of Reality: Essays in Feminist Theory* (Trumansburg, N.Y.: The Crossing Press, 1983), p. 156.

2. Ibid.

3. Catharine R. Stimpson, "Zero Degree Deviancy: The Lesbian Novel in English," *Critical Inquiry* 8:2 (Winter 1981): 365.

4. Lillian Faderman, *Surpassing the Love of Men: Romantic Friendship and Love between Women from the Renaissance to the Present* (New York: William Morrow, 1981), p. 197.

5. Faderman's discussion of this pervades the book, but it is brought to effective conclusion in the last chapter, "Romantic Friendship and Lesbian Love," ibid., pp. 411–15. See, also, Michel Foucault, *The History of Sexuality*, trans. Robert Hurley, vol. 1: *An Introduction* (New York: Pantheon Books, 1978). Although Foucault had a quite different agenda—he was interested in reconstructing an archaeology of knowledge as expressed in language—this study shows how sexuality is socially constructed. By designating sexuality as something that has a history, and therefore changes, Foucault shows us that it is a human invention.

6. Faderman, *Surpassing the Love of Men,* p. 16.

7. Leila J. Rupp, " 'Imagine My Surprise': Women's Relationships in Historical Perspective," *Frontiers* 5:3 (1981): 67. Similarly, historian John D'Emilio, in a stimulating essay, "Capitalism and Gay Identity," also suggests that both lesbian's and gay men's identity, as a core sexual identity, is made possible by the particularity of capitalist development and its effects on the structure of the family—in particular, the potential autonomy of "free labor." D'Emilio, developing a Marxist perspective, proposes that gays and lesbians, as sexually defined in the twentieth century, have not "always existed." See his essay in *Powers of Desire: The Politics of Sexuality,* ed. Ann Snitow, Christine Stansell, and Sharon Thompson (New York: Monthly Review Press, 1983), pp. 100–13. D'Emilio's book, *Sexual Politics, Sexual Communities: The Making of a Homosexual Minority in the United States, 1940–1970* (Chicago: University of Chicago Press, 1983), is also significant in this regard.

8. Adrienne Rich, "Compulsory Heterosexuality and Lesbian Existence," *Signs* 5:4 (Summer 1980): 635. This essay has been widely reprinted. It will be most conveniently located in Adrienne Rich, *Blood, Bread, and Poetry: Selected Prose, 1979–1985* (New York: Norton, 1986), pp. 23–75. This version also includes a "foreword" contextualizing its original conception and an "afterword" of correspondence between Rich and Ann Snitow, Christine Stansell, and Sharon Thompson, Marxist-feminist activists and scholars.

9. Adrienne Rich, "The Meaning of Our Love for Women Is What We Have Constantly to Expand," in her book *On Lies, Secrets, and Silence: Selected Prose, 1966–1978* (New York: Norton, 1979), pp. 223–30.

10. Carrol Smith-Rosenberg, "The Female World of Love and Ritual: Relations between Women in Nineteenth-Century America," *Signs* 1:1 (Autumn 1975): 10.

11. Ibid.

12. Nancy F. Cott, *The Bonds of Womanhood: "Women's Sphere" in New England, 1780–1835* (New Haven: Yale University Press, 1977).

13. Dorothy Sterling, ed., *We Are Your Sisters: Black Women in the Nineteenth Century* (New York: Norton, 1984). This volume contains many personal letters, diaries, narratives, and stories that were never intended for publication. It is a moving testimony to the private world of hundreds of Afro-American women, slave and free, in the nineteenth century. For the Sarah Douglass–Sarah Grimké correspondence, see pp. 130 ff; for the Emma V. Brown–Emily Howland correspondence, see pp. 287 ff.

14. Other significant evidence of this homosocial world is provided by historian Judith Walzer Leavitt, "Under the Shadow of Maternity: American Women's Responses to Death and Debility Fears in Nineteenth Century Childbirth," *Feminist Studies* 12:1 (Spring 1986): 129–54.

15. See, for example, Karen Blair, *The Clubwoman as Feminist: True Womanhood Redefined, 1868–1914* (New York: Holmes and Meier, 1980); Gerda Lerner, "Community Work of Black Clubwomen," in Lerner, *The Majority Finds Its Past: Placing Women in History* (New York: Oxford University Press, 1979).

The feeling of this homosocial world in the club movement among Afro-American women can be readily seen in the outstanding oral history project by historian Darlene Clark Hine et al., *The Black Women in the Middle West Project: A Comprehensive Resource Guide, Illinois and Indiana. Historical Essays, Oral Histories, Biographical Profiles and Document Collections* (Indianapolis: Indiana Historical Bureau, 1986), and the accompanying publication by Darlene Clark Hine, *When the Truth Is Told: A History of Black Women's Culture and Community in Indiana, 1875–1950,* published by the National Council of Negro Women, Indianapolis Section, 1981. See also Ruth Bordin, *Woman and Temperance: The Search for Power and Liberty, 1873–1900* (Philadelphia: Temple University Press, 1981).

16. Nancy Sahli, "Smashing: Women's Relationships Before the Fall," *Chrysalis,* no. 8 (Summer 1979): 21, 20.

17. Judith Schwarz, "Yellow Clover: Katharine Lee Bates and Katharine Coman," *Frontiers* 4:1 (1979): 59–67.

18. Ibid., p. 59.

19. Judith Schwarz, *Radical Feminists of Heterodoxy: Greenwich Village, 1912–1940* (Norwich, Vt.: New Victoria Publishers, 1986). The quote from Elizabeth Gurly Flynn is on page 1.

20. Blanche Wiesen Cook, "Female Support Networks and Political Activism: Lillian Wald, Crystal Eastman, Emma Goldman, Jane Addams," in Cook, *Women and Support Networks* (New York: Out and Out Books, 1979). The essay originally appeared in *Chrysalis,* no. 3 (Autumn 1977). A related article by Cook is "A Utopian Female Support Network: The Case of the Henry Street Settlement," in *Women in Search of Utopia,* ed. Ruby Rohrlich and Elaine Hoffman Baruch (New York: Schocken Books, 1984), pp. 109–15.

21. See also the article by Kathryn Kish Sklar, "Hull House in the 1890's: A Community of Women Reformers," *Signs* 10:4 (Summer 1985): 658–77.

22. Estelle Freedman, "Separatism as Strategy: Female Institution Building and American Feminism, 1870–1930," *Feminist Studies* 5:3 (Fall 1979): 512–29.

23. Cook, "Female Support Networks," pp. 28, 20.

24. Sarah Schulman, "When We Were Very Young: A Walking Tour Through Radical Jewish Women's History On the Lower East Side, 1879–1919," *Sinister Wisdom,* no. 29/30 (1986): 241. This was a special issue of *Sinister Wisdom* titled *The Tribe of Dina: A Jewish Women's Anthology,* with guest editors Melanie Kaye/Kantrowitz and Irena Klepfisz.

25. Nancy MacLean, *The Culture of Resistance: Female Institution Building in the International Ladies' Garment Workers Union, 1905–1925,* Occasional Paper no. 21, Women's Studies, University of Michigan (Ann Arbor, 1982), p. 13.

26. See, for example, Rosemary Curb and Nancy Manahan, eds., *Lesbian Nuns: Breaking Silence* (Tallahassee: Naiad Press, 1985), and Judith C. Brown, *Immodest Acts: The Life of a Lesbian Nun in Renaissance Italy* (New York: Oxford University Press, 1985). There has been some speculation that the astonishing Mexican poet and philosopher Sor Juana Ines de La Cruz (1652–1695)

was a lesbian. This is based upon evidence of love poems to women. It is certain that she entered convent life in order to avoid marriage. Her views were radical and feminist and rooted in a religious humanism. Threats from the Inquisition ultimately silenced her. A good English-language account is *A Woman of Genius: The Intellectual Autobiography of Sor Juana Ines de la Cruz,* trans. and introduction Margaret Sayers Peden (Salisbury, Conn.: Lime Rock Press, 1982). An interesting interpretation of her life will be found in a play by Estela Portillo Trambley, *Sor Juana and Other Plays* (Ypsilanti, Mich.: Bilingual Press, 1983). A thorough interpretive biography with emphasis on her philosophical views is by Marie-Cécile Berassey-Berling, *Humanismo y religión en Sor Juana Inés de la Cruz* (México: Universidad Nacional Autónoma De Mexico, 1983), esp. "El feminismo Cristiano de Sor Juana," pp. 262–84.

27. This analysis is explored in detail and with particular emphasis on the literary and psychoanalytic traditions by Faderman, *Surpassing the Love of Men,* esp. pp. 233–53, 297–340.

28. An important analysis of this period is made by Jennifer Terry, "Purging the Perverts: A History of Hysteria and Homophobia in the Loyalty-Security Programs of Postwar America (1946–1960)," manuscript, History of Consciousness Program, University of California, Santa Cruz, March 1987. Also of related interest is the essay by Madeline Davis and Elizabeth Lapovsky Kennedy, "Oral History and the Study of Sexuality in the Lesbian Community: Buffalo, New York, 1940–1960," *Feminist Studies* 12:1 (Spring 1980): 7–26. The focus of this essay is on sexuality and "Butch-Fem" relationships, with additional references for an understanding of lesbian culture in the 1950s. See also Allen Berube and John D'Emilio, "The Military and the Lesbians during the McCarthy Years," *Signs* 9:4 (Summer 1984): 759–75. See also Joan Nestle, *A Restricted Country* (Ithaca, N.Y.: Firebrand Books, 1987), esp. "Butch-Femme Relationships: Sexual Courage in the 1950s," pp. 100–110.

29. Judy Grahn, "Perspectives on Lesbianism: Lesbians as Bogeywomen," *Women: A Journal of Liberation* 1 (Summer 1970): 36–38.

30. Ibid., pp. 37–38.

31. Excellent material on how property laws have historically enforced male ownership of women may be found in Lorenne Clark and Debra Lewis, *Rape: The Price of Coercive Sexuality* (Toronto: Women's Educational Press, 1981), esp. pp. 111–31, and in Susan Schecter, *Women and Male Violence: The Visions and Struggles of the Battered Women's Movement* (Boston: South End Press, 1982), esp. pp. 209–40.

32. A brief but good background piece on women in the electronics industry in the Santa Clara Valley will be found by Allan Bernstein et al., "Silicon Valley: Paradise or Paradox," in *Mexican Women in the United States: Struggles Past and Present,* Occasional Paper no. 2, Chicano Studies Research Center Publication, UCLA (Los Angeles, 1980), pp. 105–12.

33. Mary Bularzik, "Sexual Harassment at the Workplace, Historical Notes," *Radical America* 11:4 (1978): 30. The legal and political history of sexual harass-

ment litigation will be found in the book by attorney Catharine A. MacKinnon, *Sexual Harassment of Working Women* (New Haven: Yale University Press, 1979).

34. Carol Gilligan, *In a Different Voice: Psychological Theory and Women's Development* (Cambridge: Harvard University Press, 1982), p. 48.

35. While sex-role socialization and women's subordination are almost universal, the specific content of the ground rules differs between cultures. A good, preliminary overview of the socialization process in the United States with sensitivity to class and racial differences is provided by Lenore Weitzman, "Sex-Role Socialization: Focus on Women," in *Women: A Feminist Perspective,* ed. Jo Freeman, 3rd ed. (Palo Alto, Calif.: Mayfield 1984), pp. 157–237. For an interdisciplinary overview of female socialization and the family covering historical, psychological, anthropological, and sociological perspectives, see Barrie Thorne, with Marilyn Yalom, eds., *Rethinking the Family: Some Feminist Questions* (New York: Longman, 1982). For a classic study of Afro-American women's socialization, see Joyce Ladner, *Tomorrow's Tomorrow: The Black Woman* (Garden City, N.Y.: Doubleday, Anchor Books, 1972). Excellent material on Chicana socialization patterns will be found in Margarita B. Melville, ed., *Twice a Minority: Mexican-American Women* (St. Louis: C. V. Mosby, 1980). See also Alfredo Mirande and Evangelina Enriquez, *La Chicana: The Mexican-American Woman* (Chicago: University of Chicago Press, 1979), esp. the chapter titled "The Woman in the Family," pp. 96–117.

36. Audre Lorde, *Sister Outsider: Essays & Speeches* (Trumansburg, N.Y.: The Crossing Press, 1984), p. 112.

37. *Lesbian Herstory Archives Newsletter* 9, September 1986, p. 2, published by the Lesbian Herstory Educational Foundation, New York City.

38. Ibid., p. 11. For a wonderful story about Mabel Hampton see Beth Hodges, "An Interview with Joan and Deborah of the Lesbian Herstory Archives," *Sinister Wisdom,* no. 11 (Fall 1978): 3–13.

39. Jane Meyerding, ed., *We Are All Part of One Another: A Barbara Deming Reader* (Philadelphia: New Society Publishers, 1984), pp. 234–35.

40. Elsa Gidlow, "Memoirs," *Feminist Studies* 6:1 (Spring 1980): 105. See also *Elsa: I Come With My Songs: The Autobiography of Elsa Gidlow,* ed. Celeste West (San Francisco: a druid heights book, Booklegger Press, 1986).

41. Elsa Gidlow, "The Spiritual Significance of the Self-Identified Woman," *Maenad: A Woman's Literary Journal* 1 (Spring 1981): 75.

42. Gloria T. Hull, "Researching Alice Dunbar-Nelson: A Personal and Literary Perspective," in *All the Women Are White, All the Blacks Are Men, But Some of Us Are Brave: Black Women's Studies,* ed. Gloria T. Hull, Patricia Bell Scott, and Barbara Smith (New York: Feminist Press, 1982), p. 192.

43. Gloria T. Hull, " 'Under the Days': The Buried Life and Poetry of Angelina Weld Grimké," *Conditions: Five* 2: 2 (1979): 23. For a much fuller discussion of Angelina Weld Grimké, see Hull's book *Color, Sex, and Poetry: Three Women Writers of the Harlem Renaissance* (Bloomington: Indiana University Press, 1987). Hull's introductory essay also contains comments on the Black gay men of

the Renaissance. In addition to the essay on Grimké, there is one on Alice Dunbar-Nelson and another on Georgia Douglas Johnson.

44. Hull, "'Under the Days,'" pp. 24, 25.

45. Gloria T. Hull, ed., *Give Us Each Day: The Diary of Alice Dunbar-Nelson* (New York: Norton, 1984), p. 25.

46. Nancy Manahan, "Future Old Maids and Pacifist Agitators: The Story of Tracy Mygatt and Frances Witherspoon," *Women's Studies Quarterly* 10:1 (Spring 1982): 11.

47. Ibid., pp. 12–13. This erasure was unfortunately continued in the account of their lives given in Robert Cooney and Helen Michalowski, eds., *The Power of the People: Active Nonviolence in the United States* (1977; Philadelphia: New Society Publishers, 1986), p. 46. This is a wonderful book but it is marred by the failure to acknowledge the lesbian identity of many of the women whose stories it tells.

48. See Rupp, "'Imagine My Surprise.'" Rupp provides information on many of these lesbian couples. Also invaluable in this regard is the work of Judith Schwarz. See particularly her book on the Heterodoxy Club (n. 19). This information has been very important to me personally. The names of many of these women were known to me when I was a teenager because of their radical politics, but there was never a hint of their lesbian identity. Had I known of their sexual preference I think it would have helped me greatly in acknowledging my own.

49. Paula Gunn Allen, "Beloved Women," *Conditions: Seven* 3:1 (1981): 65.

50. Ibid., p. 82.

51. Ibid., pp. 80–81. A somewhat revised version of this essay, retitled "*Hwame, Koshkalaka,* and the Rest: Lesbians in American Indian Cultures," is published in Paula Gunn Allen, *The Sacred Hoop: Recovering the Feminine in American Indian Traditions* (Boston: Beacon Press, 1986), pp. 245–61. Additional information on lesbian practices within American Indian cultures will also be found in Walter Williams, *The Spirit and the Flesh: Sexual Diversity in American Indian Cultures* (Boston: Beacon Press, 1986). Most of Williams's book is focused on the *Berdaches,* who were homosexual men, but the book concludes with a discussion of the amazon and warrior-women traditions. The first documented history, which includes extensive references to Native Americans, is the classic study by Jonathan Katz, ed., *Gay American History: Lesbians and Gay Men in the U.S.A.: A Documentary* (New York: Avon Books, 1976). See also the beautiful work compiled by Gay American Indians, Will Roscoe, coordinating editor, *Living the Spirit: A Gay American Indian Anthology* (New York: St. Martin's Press, 1988).

52. Audre Lorde, "Scratching the Surface: Some Notes on Women and Loving," in Lorde, *Sister Outsider,* pp. 49, 50. The essay, with the same title, was originally published in *Black Scholar* 9:7 (1978). Literary critic Chinosole has made the point that in a number of the African cultures to which Lorde refers, lesbianism was not sanctioned; indeed, penalties, including execution, were exacted. Chinosole concluded that such severity suggested the need for widespread suppression (Lecture at University of California, Santa Cruz, February 13, 1987).

For a fine discussion of Lorde's "biomythography" *Zami*, see Chinosole, "International Perspective on Black Autobiographical Writing: A Comparative Approach" (Dissertation in Comparative Literature, University of Oregon, Eugene, 1985). This dissertation has been accepted for publication by the University of California Press, Berkeley.

53. Lorde, "Scratching the Surface," pp. 49–50. This story was originally published in Iris Andreski, *Old Wives Tales: Life-Stories of African Women* (New York: Schocken Books, 1970).

54. Agnes Smedley, *Portraits of Chinese Women in Revolution*, ed. and with an introduction by Jan MacKinnon and Steve MacKinnon (Old Westbury, N.Y.: Feminist Press, 1976), pp. 105, 107. Smedley also includes a wonderful account of an evening she spent with these women in their residence, which culminated in an exchange of songs.

55. Two scholarly essays on the Chinese women's sisterhoods are Emily Honig, "Burning Incense, Pledging Sisterhood: Communities of Women Workers in the Shanghai Cotton Mills, 1919–1949," *Signs* 10:4 (Summer 1985): 700–714; and Marjorie Topley, "Marriage Resistance in Rural Kwangtung," in *Women in Chinese Society*, ed. Margery Wolf and Roxane Witke (Stanford, Calif.: Stanford University Press, 1975). Neither of these essays discusses the lesbian component of the sisterhoods.

56. Cherríe Moraga, *Loving in the War Years: lo que nunca paso por sus labios* (Boston: South End Press, 1983), pp. 55–56.

57. Ibid., p. 61.

58. Cherríe Moraga and Gloria Anzaldúa, eds., *This Bridge Called My Back: Writings by Radical Women of Color* (Watertown, Mass.: Persephone Press, 1981), p. 204.

59. Ibid., p. 141.

60. Kitty Tsui, *The Words of A Woman Who Breathes Fire* (San Francisco: Spinsters, Ink, 1983), pp. 4–5.

61. Barbara Smith, ed., *Home Girls: A Black Feminist Anthology* (New York: Kitchen Table. Women of Color Press, 1983), p. xxxii.

62. Elly Bulkin, "*from,* Hard Ground: Jewish Identity, Racism, and Anti-Semitism," *Conditions: Ten* 3:4 (1984): 117. This is part of a dialogue published in its entirety by Elly Bulkin, Minnie Bruce Pratt, and Barbara Smith, *Yours in Struggle: Three Feminist Perspectives on Anti-Semitism and Racism* (Brooklyn: Long Haul Press, 1985). Another dialogue may be found with Beverly Smith, Judith Stein, and Priscilla Golding, "The Possibility of Life Between Us: A Dialogue Between Black and Jewish Women," *Conditions: Seven* 3:1 (1981): 25–46. A related essay by Afro-American poet June Jordan is particularly relevant to this subject. See "The Blood Shall Be A Sign Unto You: Israel, and South Africa, April, 1985," in June Jordan, *On Call: Political Essays* (Boston: South End Press, 1985), pp. 107–16.

63. Evelyn Torton Beck, ed. *Nice Jewish Girls: A Lesbian Anthology* (Watertown, Mass.: Persephone Press, 1982), pp. xxxiv–xxxv.

64. Aurora Levins Morales and Rosario Morales, *Getting Home Alive* (Ith-

aca, N.Y.: Firebrand Books, 1986). The prose-poem is by Aurora and is called "If I Forget Thee, Oh Jerusalem," pp. 197–209.

65. Melanie Kaye, "Some Notes on Jewish Lesbian Identity," in Beck, *Nice Jewish Girls,* pp. 39–40.

66. *The Blatant Image,* A Magazine of Feminist Photography, no. 1 (1981) was published from Sunny Valley, Oregon, by coeditors Caroline Overman, Jan Phillips, Jean Mountaingrove, and Ruth Mountaingrove. A wide range of photography and essays marked this first and subsequent issues, which included lesbian and nonlesbian contributors.

67. Tee Corinne's photograph appeared on the front cover of *Sinister Wisdom,* no. 3 (Spring 1977). Its availability as a poster was announced in the fifth issue (Winter 1978).

68. See Judy Grahn, "Butches, Bulldogs, and the Queen of Bulldikery," in her book *Another Mother Tongue: Gay Words, Gay Worlds* (Boston: Beacon Press, 1984), pp. 133–61. The information on the Celtic queen Boudica was originally published by Grahn in "The Queen of Bulldikery," *Chrysalis,* no. 10 (1979): 35–41.

69. Mary Daly, *Gyn/Ecology: The Metaethics of Radical Feminism* (Boston: Beacon Press, 1978), pp. 14–15.

70. Joyce Trebilcot, "Conceiving Women: Notes on the Logic of Feminism," *Sinister Wisdom,* no. 11 (Fall 1978): 47. This essay is reprinted in Marilyn Pearsall, ed., *Women and Values: Readings in Recent Feminist Philosophy* (Belmont, Calif.: Wadsworth Publishing Co., 1986), pp. 358–63.

71. Monique Wittig and Sande Zweig, *Lesbian Peoples: Materials for A Dictionary* (New York: Avon Books, 1976), pp. 71, 81, 165.

72. Adrienne Rich, *The Dream of a Common Language: Poems 1974–1977* (New York: Norton, 1978), p. 76. The poem is called "Transcendental Etude."

73. Faderman, *Surpassing the Love of Men,* p. 84.

74. This poem was shared privately with me and the author asked to remain anonymous. It is excerpted with her permission.

75. Terry Baum and Carolyn Myers, "Dos Lesbos," in *Places Please! The First Anthology of Lesbian Plays,* ed. Kate McDermott (San Francisco: Aunt Lute/Spinsters, Ink, 1985), pp. 10–12.

76. Charlotte Bunch, *Passionate Politics: Feminist Theory in Action* (New York: St. Martin's Press, 1986), pp. 182, 184–85. Bunch's discussion is very useful; this book is a collection of essays from the early 1970s through 1986 and records the evolution of her thinking and of lesbian-separatist politics in this period.

77. Ibid., p. 185.

78. Ibid., p. 186–87.

79. Sarah Lucia Hoagland, "Lesbian Separatism: An Empowering Reality," *Sinister Wisdom,* no. 34 (Spring 1988): 29–30. Another essay of importance here is by Marilyn Frye, "Some Reflections on Separatism and Power," in her book *The Politics of Reality: Essays in Feminist Theory* (Trumansburg, N.Y.: The Crossing Press, 1983), pp. 95–109. See also the book edited by Sarah Lucia Hoagland and

Julia Penelope, *For Lesbians Only: An Anthology of Separatist Writing* (London: Onlywomen Press, forthcoming).

80. Adrienne Rich, "Women and Honor: Some Notes on Lying," in her book *On Lies, Secrets, and Silence: Selected Prose, 1966–1978* (New York: Norton, 1979), pp. 185–94.

81. Judy Grahn, "A Woman is Talking to Death," in her book *The Work of a Common Woman: The Collected Poetry 1964–1977* (New York: St. Martin's Press, 1978), pp. 124–25.

82. Sarah Lucia Hoagland, "Vulnerability and Power," *Sinister Wisdom*, no. 19 (Winter 1982): 13–23.

83. Audre Lorde, *The Cancer Journals* (Argyle, N.Y.: Spinsters, Ink, 1980), pp. 53, 57.

IV. In the Mind's Eye

Epigraphs: Alla Renée Bozarth, "Water Women" in Bozarth, *Womanpriest: A Personal Odyssey* (1978; San Diego, Calif.: Lura Media, 1988); Kim Chernin, "The Second Story My Mother Tells (1914–1920)" in Chernin, *In My Mother's House: A Daughter's Story* (New York: Ticknor and Fields, 1983), p. 46; Virginia Woolf, *The Letters of Virginia Woolf*, ed. Nigel Nicolson and Joanne Trautmann, vol. 3: *1923–1928* (New York: Harcourt Brace Jovanovich, 1977), p. 247; Paula Gunn Allen, "The Trick is Consciousness" in Allen, *Coyote's Daylight Trip* (Albuquerque: La Confluencia, 1978).

1. Maxine Hong Kingston, *The Woman Warrior: Memoirs of a Girlhood Among Ghosts* (New York: Random House, Vintage Books, 1977), p. 243. Subsequent citations of this book within this chapter will be given parenthetically within the text.

2. Ch'iu Chin, "The Narcissus by the River, II," in *Women Poets of China*, ed. and trans. Kenneth Rexroth and Ling Chung (1972; New York: New Directions, 1982), p. 82. The information about Chi'iu Chin is from the poster and accompanying text prepared by the Organization for Equal Education of the Sexes, Inc., 438 Fourth Street, Dept. 101, Brooklyn, N.Y. 11215, published in 1985.

3. "Princess Pari," *Korea Journal* 18:6 (1978): 52–57. Two prose versions are abridged and translated by Professor Lee Tae-dong at Sugang University, from *The Collection of Shamanastic Narratives*, vol. I (Won Kwang University, Iti, 1973).

4. See, for example, Anne Cameron, *Daughters of Copper Woman* (Vancouver, B.C.: Press Gang Publishers, 1981), especially the stories called "The Woman's Society," pp. 60–63; and "The Warrior Women," pp. 130–38.

5. Maria Herrera-Sobek, "Mothers, Lovers, and Soldiers: Archetypal Representation of Women in the *Corrido*," manuscript, University of California, Irvine, 1986, pp. 13, 310. I am grateful to the author for sharing her work with me.

6. Ibid., pp. 313–24; pp. 330–34. Herrera-Sobek authenticates the historical record of the role of these soldaderas and includes many remarkable photo-

graphs, and other memorabilia in this study. She summons a wide representation of lyrics from the *Corrido* popularizing the legend of these women warriors.

7. Judy Grahn, *Another Mother Tongue: Gay Words, Gay Worlds* (Boston: Beacon Press, 1984), pp. 170–72, 168, 169.

8. Michelle Cliff, *Abeng: A Novel* (Trumansburg, N.Y.: The Crossing Press, 1984), p. 14.

9. For those interested in a more detailed discussion of the maroons, see Herbert Aptheker, "Slave Guerrilla Warfare," in his book *To Be Free: Studies in Negro History* (1948; New York: International Publishers, 1968), pp. 11–30; and the study of Eugene D. Genovese, *From Rebellion to Revolution: Afro-American Slave Revolts in the Making of the New World* (1979; New York: Random House, Vintage Books, 1981), especially "Black Maroons in War and Peace," pp. 51–81. For a particularly gripping fictionalized account of maroon rebellion in the southern United States see the short story by Sherley Anne Williams, "Meditations on History," in *Midnight Birds: Stories of Contemporary Black Women Writers,* ed. Mary Helen Washington (Garden City, N.Y.: Doubleday, Anchor Press, Anchor Books, 1980), pp. 200–248.

10. See Basil Davidson, *Black Mother: The Years of African Slave Trade* (Boston: Little, Brown, 1961), especially his chapter "Mani-Congo: From Alliance to Invasion," pp. 144–52. The specific reference to Queen Zhinga is on pp. 151–52.

11. A fascinating reference to the origins of the Black Moses as a deity of the Dahomey peoples will be found in an essay by Michelle Cliff, " 'I Found God In Myself And I Loved Her/I Loved Her Fiercely': More Thoughts On The Work of Black Women Artists," in *Women, Feminist Identity and Society in the 1980's,* ed. Myriam Diaz-Diocaretz and Iris M. Zavala (Amsterdam and Philadelphia: John Benjamins, 1985), pp. 116–17. I also mean that the Moses of the Jewish people was undoubtedly dark given his North African–Middle East origins.

12. Rosalyn Terborg-Penn, "Black Women in Resistance: A Cross-Cultural Perspective," in *In Resistance: Studies in African, Caribbean, and Afro-American History,* ed. Gary Y. Okihiro (Amherst: University of Massachusetts Press, 1986), pp. 188–209.

13. Paula Gunn Allen, *The Sacred Hoop: Recovering the Feminine in American Indian Traditions* (Boston: Beacon Press, 1986), p. 214.

14. Paule Marshall, *Praisesong for the Widow* (New York: Dutton, 1984), pp. 37–39. Subsequent citations in this chapter to this book will be given parenthetically within the text.

15. There is an extensive literature on women and fairy tales, much of it in the field of child psychology, and not all of it by any means supports the viewpoint I have articulated. There is a helpful review-essay by Kay F. Stone, on "Misuses of Enchantment: Controversies on the Significance of Fairy Tales," in *Women's Folklore, Women's Culture,* ed. Rosan A. Jordan and Susan J. Kalčik (Philadelphia: University of Pennsylvania Press, 1985), pp. 125–45. See also Rosemary Minaid, ed., *Womenfolk and Fairy Tales* (Boston: Houghton Mifflin, 1975).

16. See Diana Dull and Candace West, "The Price of Perfection: A Study of

the Relations between Women and Plastic Surgery," a paper presented at the Annual Meeting of the American Sociological Association, Chicago, August 1987. Cited with permission of the authors who are on the Sociology Board, University of California, Santa Cruz. This paper is extremely helpful in showing the distinction between reconstructive and cosmetic surgery, in contextualizing the history of plastic surgery in the United States, and in illuminating the feelings of women patients about the cosmetic surgery they have had. The paper also explores physician attitudes.

17. Adrienne Rich, "Turning the Wheel: 4. Self-Hatred," in her book *A Wild Patience Has Taken Me This Far: Poems, 1978–1981* (New York: Norton, 1981), p. 55.

18. See "Spider Woman" and "Changing Woman" in Merlin Stone, *Ancient Mirrors of Womanhood: A Treasury of Goddess and Heroine Lore from Around the World* (Boston: Beacon Press, 1984), pp. 289–90, 291–92; and Anne Cameron, *Daughters of Copper Woman*, pp. 56–58.

19. Judy Grahn, *The Queen of Wands* (Trumansburg, N.Y.: The Crossing Press, 1982), pp. xii, 12.

20. Michele Murray, "Creating Oneself from Scratch," in *The Writer on Her Work: Contemporary Women Writers Reflect on Their Art and Situation*, ed. Janet Sternburg (New York: Norton, 1980), p. 83.

21. Kingston, *Woman Warrior*, p. 57.

22. Murray, "Creating Oneself from Scratch," p. 81.

23. Langer's remark was made at a Reed College Symposium, Portland, Oregon, Fall 1978, while introducing Tillie Olsen. It is cited by Deborah Rosenfelt, "From the Thirties: Tillie Olsen and the Radical Tradition," *Feminist Studies* 7:3 (Fall 1981): 380.

24. Alice Walker, "In Search of Our Mothers' Gardens," in her book of the same title (San Diego: Harcourt Brace Jovanovich, 1983), p. 233.

25. Honor Moore, "Introduction," to her edited book, *The New Women's Theatre: Ten Plays by Contemporary American Women* (New York: Random House, Vintage Books, 1977), p. xxvi.

26. Suzette Haden Elgin, *Native Tongue* (New York: Donald A. Wollheim, DAW Books, 1984). Elgin published a sequel, *Native Tongue II. The Judas Rose* (New York: DAW Books, 1987).

27. The distinction between feminist consciousness and female sensibility is important. A feminist consciousness is a *political* consciousness that refers to an explicit understanding of women's oppression and assumes a set of critical factors about women's history, economics, culture, and so on. A female sensibility is informed by women's *experience*, as distinguished from the experience of men. This experience is socially constructed (not biologically inherent) and varies from culture to culture. I first saw this distinction between consciousness and sensibility drawn by Judy Chicago in an interview with Lucy Lippard in Lippard's book, *From the Center: Feminist Essays in Women's Art* (New York: Dutton, 1976), p. 229. The issue is further explored in a useful essay by Julia Penelope Stanley and

Susan J. Wolfe (Robbins), "Toward a Feminist Aesthetic," *Chrysalis*, no. 6 (1978): 57–71.

28. Erica Jong, "The Artist as Housewife," in *In Her Own Image: Women Working in the Arts*, ed. Elaine Hedges and Ingrid Wendt (Old Westbury, N.Y.: The Feminist Press, 1980), pp. 118, 119.

29. Nan Elsasser, Kyle MacKenzie, and Yvonne Tixier Y Vigil, eds., *Las Mujeres: Conversations from a Hispanic Community* (Old Westbury, N.Y.: The Feminist Press, 1980), pp. 112, 112–13.

30. Renita Weems, " 'Artists without Art Form': A Look at One Black Woman's World of Unrevered Black Women," *Conditions: Five. The Black Women's Issue* 2:2 (1979): 48.

31. Kalamu Ya Salaam, "Searching for the Mother Tongue: An Interview with Toni Cade Bambara," *First World* 2:4 (1980): 48. A working paper by the literary critic Gloria T. Hull is extremely illuminating on the subject of form in writings by women of color. Her paper is *Reading Literature by U.S. Third World Women*, Working Paper no. 141 (Wellesley, Mass.: Wellesley College, Center for Research on Women, 1984), pp. 3–4 and 24–25 in particular. This essay provided me with a model of interracial analysis of poetic, oral, historical, and literary tradition which was extremely valuable in helping me to think about the shape of this book.

32. Lippard, *From the Center*, p. 48.

33. Quoted in Hedges and Wendt, *In Her Own Image*, pp. 71–72. A discussion of Schapiro's evolution as an artist and her struggle for self-expression will be found in Eleanor Munro, *Originals: American Women Artists* (New York: Simon and Schuster, Touchstone Book, 1982), pp. 272–81.

34. Discussion of *Womanhouse* and of the Woman's Building in Los Angeles will be found in Lippard, *From the Center*, pp. 96–100, 214–30. See also Gayle Kimball, ed., *Women's Culture: The Women's Renaissance of the Seventies* (Metuchen, N.J.: Scarecrow Press, 1981), pp. 17–18; and an interview with Judy Chicago called "A Female Form Language," pp. 60–71. A more comprehensive review of "The Feminist Art Movement" will be found in Charlotte Streifer Rubinstein, *American Women Artists: From Early Indian Times to the Present* (New York: Avon Books, 1982), pp. 374–437.

35. Cindy Nemser, "Conversation with Betye Saar," *Feminist Art Journal*, Winter 1975–76, p. 19.

36. Gretchen Erskine Woelfle, "On The Edge. Betye Saar. Personal Time Travels," *FiberArts*, July/August 1982, p. 56.

37. Nemser, "Conversations," p. 21. I am very grateful to Betye Saar for sending me slides of her work and catalogs of her 1987 exhibits so that I could include these in my discussion of her work.

38. My discussion is based upon the information, descriptions of the work process, and the reproductions of the china plates provided by Judy Chicago in *The Dinner Party: A Symbol of Our Heritage* (Garden City, N.Y.: Doubleday, Anchor Press, Anchor Books, 1979).

39. This comment was made just after the San Francisco opening of *The Dinner Party* at the Museum of Modern Art and was reported in the *San Francisco Chronicle*, March 18, 1979.

40. Judy Chicago, *The Birth Project* (Garden City, N.Y.: Doubleday, 1985), p. 7.

41. Ibid., pp. 4, 7.

42. Ibid., pp. 42, 85.

43. A further useful discussion of birth images in art will be found in Joellyn A. Snyder-Ott, *Women and Creativity* (Millbrae, Calif.: Les Femmes, 1978), especially in chapters "500 Years of Birth in Art Forms—No One Gives a Damn!" pp. 83–98, and "Creativity-Procreativity," pp. 109–18.

44. Chicago, *The Birth Project*, p. 39.

45. Walker, "One Child of One's Own: A Meaningful Digression Within the Work(s)," in her book *In Search of Our Mothers' Gardens*, p. 373. It is important to add here that there is one other plate that is not in the butterfly (vaginal) motif, and that is the one for Ethel Smythe, the British pianist who lived openly as a lesbian, also noted by Walker.

46. Chicago, *The Birth Project*, p. 188.

47. An essay that is culturally sensitive to Arab-Muslim women and that offers excellent medical and political information on genital mutilation, sexual practices, women's resistance, and the general status of Egyptian women has been written by Angela Davis, "Sex-Egypt," in *Women: A World Report*, A New Internationalist Book (New York: Oxford University Press, 1985), pp. 325–48.

48. Mayumi Oda, *Goddesses* (1981; Volcano, Calif.: Volcano Press/Kazan Books, 1988), p. 8. Subsequent citations to this work within this chapter will be given parenthetically within the text.

49. This comment was made during a guest lecture that Oda gave to my class in women's culture, University of California, Santa Cruz, Winter 1987.

50. "Art as Activism," a special issue of *Woman of Power, a magazine of feminism, spirituality, and politics*, no. 6 (Spring 1987): 62–63, displays the work of Karen Lee Robins. Gayle Kimball, "Goddess Imagery and Ritual: Interview with Mary Beth Edelson," in Kimball, *Women's Culture*, p. 91. See also Rubinstein, *American Women Artists*, p. 377: "Mary Beth Edelson . . . created a photo montage *Goddess, The Sister Chapel* (1978)—a group project in which eleven women painted eleven female heroes larger than life, ranging from Joan of Arc to artist Frida Kahlo—in a counterattack against the patriarchal worldview expressed in Michelangelo's Sistine Chapel frescoes."

51. I am indebted to University of California, Santa Cruz, student Noelle Remington for this information about Ana Mendieta. Remington's senior thesis in women studies (June 1988) is a comparative study of the performance art of Cindy Sherman, Faith Ringgold, and Ana Mendieta (who died in 1985).

52. Jacinto Quirarte, *Mexican American Artists* (Austin: University of Texas Press, 1973), pp. 44, 45. Due to impoverishment, Amezcua had no formal art training, and she uses very inexpensive pens and paper in her work. The color is

spectacular, and the overall effect is astonishing in its detail. Amezcua's figures are both male and female, among them saints from the Catholic influence.

53. Information on the reproductions of Elizabeth Catlett's work will be found in Arna Alexander Bontemps, Jacqueline Fonvielle-Bontemps, and David C. Driskell, *Forever Free: Art by African-American Women, 1862–1980* (Alexandria, Va.: Stephenson, 1980); in Elton C. Fax, *Seventeen Black Artists* (New York: Dodd Mead & Co., 1971), pp. 14–31; and, the most extensive, a retrospective by Samella Lewis, *The Art of Elizabeth Catlett,* published in collaboration with the Museum of African American Art, Los Angeles (Claremont, Calif.: Hancraft Studios, 1984).

54. Lewis, *The Art of Elizabeth Catlett,* p. 102. Subsequent citations to this work within this chapter will be given parenthetically within the text.

55. Michelle Cliff, "Object into Subject: Some Thoughts on the Work of Black Women Artists," *Heresies,* no. 15 (1982): 34–40.

56. Michelle Cliff, "The Resonance of Interruption," *Chrysalis,* no. 8 (Summer 1979): 30.

V. "Get over This Hurdle"

Epigraphs: Susan Dambroff, "Skeletons without Country" in Dambroff, *Memory in Bone* (San Francisco: Black Oyster Press, 1984), n.p.; Toni Morrison quoted by Dexter Fisher, " 'Intimate Things in Place': A Conversation with Toni Morrison," in *The Third Woman: Minority Woman Writers of the United States,* ed. Fisher (Boston: Houghton Mifflin, 1980), p. 168; Mitsuye Yamada, *Camp Notes and Other Poems* (Berkeley: Shameless Hussy Press, 1976), dedication; Ricky Sherover-Marcuse, "Liberation Theory: Axioms and Working Assumptions about the Perpetuation of Social Oppression," mimeographed, 1982; revised 1988 (available from Unlearning Racism Workshops, 6501 Dana, Oakland, Calif. 94609).

1. The poet is Dambroff, *Memory in Bone.* An essay by the historian Temma Kaplan helped me crystallize these ideas about a women's resistance although ultimately I worked out the issue in a somewhat different way. See Temma Kaplan, "Female Consciousness and Collective Action: The Case of Barcelona, 1910–1918," *Signs* 7:3 (Spring 1982): 545–66.

2. See, for example, Vera Laska, *Women in the Resistance and in the Holocaust* (Westport, Conn.: Greenwood, 1983); Linda Atkinson, *In Kindling Flame: The Story of Hannah Senesh 1921–1944* (New York: Lothrop, Lee and Shepard, 1985). A two-volume study of the German resistance movement was published in the German Democratic Republic and includes many women. See Institut für Marxismus-Leninismus beim Zentral Komitee der SED, *Deutsche Widerstandskampfer 1933–1945, Biographien und Briefe* (Berlin, GDR: Dietz Verlag, 1970).

3. A good essay providing a theoretical perspective on this process is by

Catharine A. MacKinnon, "Feminism, Marxism, Method, and the State: An Agenda for Theory," *Signs* 7:3 (Spring 1982): 515–44.

4. Lenore J. Weitzman, *The Divorce Revolution: The Unexpected Social and Economic Consequences for Women and Children in America* (New York: Free Press, 1985), p. 215.

5. For details on women's economic situation, see, for example, the outstanding study by the Women's Economic Agenda Project (518 17th Street, Oakland, Calif. 94612) called *Women's Economic Agenda a call to action by & for California women,* May 1987. The specific statistics on the incomes of divorced women and women were reported by Weitzman, *The Divorce Revolution,* p. 323. An excellent detailed analysis of child support and the economic consequences is provided by Carol S. Brunch and Norma J. Wikler in *Juvenile & Family Court Journal* 36:3 (Fall 1985): 5–26.

6. Fran Leeper Buss, *Dignity: Lower Income Women Tell of Their Lives and Struggles. Oral Histories* (Ann Arbor: University of Michigan Press, 1986), p. 195. This observation was made by "Lee" in her oral history. More of her story is recounted later in this chapter.

7. This phrase was used by Mamie Garvin Fields, with Karen Fields in their memoir *Lemon Swamp and Other Places: A Carolina Memoir* (New York: Free Press, 1983), p. xiv.

8. Louise Lamphere, "On the Shop Floor: Multi-Ethnic Unity against the Conglomerate," in *My Troubles Are Going to Have Trouble with Me: Everyday Trials and Triumphs of Women Workers,* ed. Karen Brodkin Sacks and Dorothy Remy (New Brunswick, N.J.: Rutgers University Press, 1984), pp. 248, 258–59.

9. Patricia Zavella, "'Abnormal Intimacy': The Varying Networks of Chicana Cannery Workers," *Feminist Studies* 11:3 (Fall 1985): p. 544.

10. Ibid., pp. 550, 553. This article was subsequently incorporated into a book by Patricia Zavella, *Women's Work and Chicano Families: Cannery Workers of the Santa Clara Valley* (Ithaca, N.Y.: Cornell University Press, 1987).

11. Kathleen C. Miller, "Through A Woman's Eyes: The Life Story of A Mexican-American Woman," (Master's thesis, Department of Social Science, San Jose State University, May 1976), pp. 2–3.

12. Ibid., pp. 45, 52.

13. Adrienne Rich, "Introduction" to *Ordinary Women/Mujeres Comunes,* ed. Sara Miles, Patricia Jones, Sandra Maria Esteves, Fay Chiang (New York: Ordinary Women, 1978), p. 7. Unfortunately this book is out of print. See also M. Brinton Lykes, "Discrimination and Coping in the Lives of Black Women: Analyses of Oral History Data," *Journal of Social Issues* 38:3 (1983): 79–100, for a scholarly analysis of "coping" strategies, many of which I am redefining as resistance. The essay is written from the point of view of social psychology.

14. This autobiographical statement appears on the back cover of a collection of poems by Meridel Le Sueur. See *Rites of Ancient Ripening* (Minneapolis: Vanilla Press, 1975).

15. The description was offered by Patricia Hampl and quoted by John

Crawford in his "Publisher's Note," to Meridel Le Sueur, *Harvest* (Cambridge, Mass.: West End Press, 1977).

16. Meridel Le Sueur, "Harvest," in ibid., p. 37.

17. Ibid., pp. 35, 31.

18. Ibid., p. 29.

19. Ibid., pp. 38–39.

20. Arlene Avakian, "Culture and Feminist Theory: An Armenian-American Woman's Perspective" (Dissertation, School of Education, University of Massachusetts, May, 1985). The oral history of Elmas Tutuian permeates many parts of the dissertation. The essential facts are recounted on pp. 123–26.

21. Arlene Avakian, "Elmas Tutuian—Lion Woman." Manuscript and transcript of oral history, p. 4. This unpublished work is cited with permission of the author.

22. Ibid., p. 5.

23. Ibid., p. 8.

24. Ibid., p. 10.

25. Avakian, "Culture and Feminist Theory," pp. 565–74.

26. Esther Katz and Joan Miriam Ringelheim, *Women Surviving the Holocaust: Proceedings of the Conference*. Published by the Institute for Research in History, 432 Park Avenue South, New York, N.Y. 10016, 1983, p. 29.

27. Ibid., p. 30.

28. Ibid., p. 33.

29. Ibid., p. 55.

30. Ibid., pp. 42–43.

31. Deborah Gesensway and Mindy Roseman, *Beyond Words: Images from America's Concentration Camps* (Ithaca, N.Y.: Cornell University Press, 1987), p. 66.

32. Valerie Matsumoto, "Japanese American Women during World War II," *Frontiers* 8:1 (1984): 8.

33. Gesensway and Roseman, *Beyond Words*, p. 84.

34. Ibid., p. 71.

35. Matsumoto, "Japanese American Women," p. 7.

36. Gesensway and Roseman, *Beyond Words*, p. 140.

37. Timothy J. Lukes and Gary Y. Okihiro, *Japanese Legacy: Farming and Community Life in California's Santa Clara Valley*, Local History Studies, volume 31 (Cupertino, Calif.: California History Center, 1985), pp. 115–26. The specific figures quoted are on pp. 118–19.

38. Matsumoto, "Japanese American Women," p. 8.

39. Ibid., p. 10.

40. Ibid.

41. Ibid., p. 13.

42. Isabel Miller, *The Love of Good Women* (Tallahassee: Naiad Press, 1986).

43. Ibid., p. 103.

44. Ibid., pp. 82–83.

45. Victoria Byerly, *Hard Times Cotton Mill Girls: Personal Histories of Womanhood and Poverty in the South* (Ithaca, N.Y.: I L R Press, New York State School of Industrial and Labor Relations, Cornell University, 1986). Clara Thrift's story is on pp. 110–22. Subsequent citations to this work within the chapter will be given parenthetically within the text.

46. Elsa Barkley Brown, "To Catch the Vision of Freedom: African American Women Struggle for Peoplehood and Community," a paper presented at the conference "Afro-American Women and the Vote: 1837 to 1965," University of Massachusetts, Amherst, November 14, 1987. Professor Brown is in the Department of Sociology, State University of New York, Binghamton. This unpublished paper is cited with permission of the author.

47. Ibid., p. 25.

48. Jacqueline Jones, *Labor of Love, Labor of Sorrow: Black Women, Work, and the Family from Slavery to the Present* (New York: Random House, Vintage Books, 1986), p. 3.

49. Ibid., 111, 131.

50. An early, definitive study of this period, for example, is by Rayford W. Logan, *The Betrayal of the Negro: From Rutherford B. Hayes to Woodrow Wilson* (New York: Collier Books, 1970; orig. pub. 1954). The original, 1954 title was *The Nadir*.

51. Fran Buss, *Dignity*, p. 16. Citations to this book within the rest of this chapter will be given parenthetically within the text.

52. Marcy Adelman, ed., *Long Time Passing: Lives of Older Lesbians* (Boston: Alyson Publications, 1986), pp. 14, 15.

53. Mitsuye Yamada, "Asian Pacific American Women and Feminism," in *This Bridge Called My Back: Writings By Radical Women of Color*, ed. Cherríe Moraga and Gloria Anzaldúa (Watertown, Mass.: Persephone Press, 1981), pp. 73–74.

54. Nicholasa Mohr, "A Thanksgiving Celebration," in her collection of short stories called *Rituals of Survival: A Woman's Portfolio* (Houston: Arte Publico Press, 1985), pp. 75–88.

55. Ibid., pp. 87–88.

56. Bernice Johnson Reagon, "My Black Mothers and Sisters, Or On Beginning: A Cultural Autobiography," *Feminist Studies* 8 (Spring 1982): 85–86.

57. Enedina Casarez Vasquez, "House of Quilts," *Third Woman* 3:1 & 2 (1986): 70.

58. Barbara Myerhoff, *Number Our Days* (New York: Simon and Schuster, Touchstone Book, 1978), p. 22.

59. Anna Lee Walters, *The Sun Is Not Merciful: Short Stories* (Ithaca, N.Y.: Firebrand Books, 1985). The story of the same title is on pp. 109–33.

60. Ibid., p. 116.

61. Ibid., p. 130.

62. Ibid., p. 132.

63. Adrienne Rich, "North American Tunnel Vision (1983)" in her book

Blood, Bread, and Poetry: Selected Prose, 1979–1985 (New York: Norton, 1986), p. 161.

64. Sacks and Remy, *My Troubles*, p. 10.

65. The succeeding quotes are from the following sources:

Assata Shakur, "Women in Prison: How We Are," *Black Scholar*, April 1978, pp. 13–14. Quoted by Michelle Cliff, "The Resonance of Interruption," *Chrysalis*, no. 8 (Summer 1979): 36.

Buss, *Dignity*, p. 131.

Anne Cameron, "Foreword" to her book *Dzelarhons: Myths of the Northwest Coast* (Madeira Park, B.C.: Harbour Publishing, 1986), p. 20.

Ruth Wong Chinn, "Square and Circle Club of San Francisco: A Chinese Women's Culture" (Senior thesis, Women's Studies, University of California, Santa Cruz, June 1987), pp. 2–3. This 137-page senior thesis provides an outstanding history of Chinese women in California, and includes nine oral histories.

Byerly, *Hard Times*, p. 145.

VI. Toward a Gathering of Women

Epigraphs: Linda Hogan, "Desert" in Hogan, *Seeing through the Sun* (Amherst: University of Massachusetts Press, 1985), p. 44; Audre Lorde, "Naming the Stories" in Lorde, *Our Dead Behind Us* (New York: Norton, 1986), p. 31; Janice Mirikitani, "Breaking Silence" in Mirikitani, *Shedding Silence* (Berkeley: Celestial Arts, 1987), p. 36.

1. Elna Bakker, *An Island Called California: An Ecological Introduction to Its Natural Communities* (1971; Berkeley: University of California Press, 1984), p. 311.

2. Deena Metzger, "The Tree on the Mountain," in *Hear the Silence: Stories by Women of Myth, Magic & Renewal*, ed. Irene Zahava (Trumansburg, N.Y.: The Crossing Press, 1986), p. 181.

3. Ursula K. Le Guin, *Always Coming Home* (New York: Harper and Row, 1985), p. 4. Subsequent citations to this work within this chapter will be given parenthetically within the text.

4. Paula Gunn Allen, *The Sacred Hoop: Recovering the Feminine in American Indian Traditions* (Boston: Beacon Press, 1986), p. 56.

5. Ibid., p. 60.

6. Ibid., p. 119.

7. Adrienne Rich, "Transcendental Etude," in Adrienne Rich, *The Dream of a Common Language: Poems 1974–1977* (New York: Norton, 1978), p. 74.

8. Gayle High Pine, "The Non-Progressive Great Spirit," p. 5. This is an unpublished manuscript. I am indebted to Rosa Maria Zayas for making it available to me in the fall of 1982.

9. Anne Cameron, *Daughters of Copper Woman* (Vancouver, B.C.: Press Gang Publishers, 1981), p. 63.

10. See Merlin Stone, *Ancient Mirrors of Womanhood: A Treasury of Goddess and Heroine Lore from Around the World* (Boston: Beacon Press, 1984).

Stone's work is informed by a cross-cultural, internationalist perspective that is particularly refreshing.

11. An excellent, well-documented synthesis of this material will be found in the first third of the book by Riane Eisler, *The Chalice & the Blade* (San Francisco: Harper and Row, 1987).

12. Simone Schwarz-Bart, *The Bridge of Beyond*, translated from the French by Barbara Bray (London: Heineman, 1982), pp. 84–85.

13. Toni Cade Bambara, *The Salt Eaters* (New York: Random House, Vintage Books, 1981), pp. 258–59.

14. Ibid., p. 110.

15. Annie Dillard, *Pilgrim at Tinker Creek* (1975; New York: Bantam Books, 1982). A Book-of-the-Month Club selection and described as "a mystical excursion into the natural world," Dillard's meditations convey precisely the sense of connection, balance, harmony, and life that are represented here.

16. This is in the poem that I quote in Chapter 1 (n. 41) by Marge Piercy, "The seven of pentacles," in her book *Circles on the Water* (New York: Knopf, 1982), p. 128.

17. Alice Walker, *The Color Purple* (New York: Harcourt Brace Jovanovich, 1982), p. 167.

18. Ntozake Shange, *for colored girls who have considered suicide / when the rainbow is enuf* (New York: Macmillan, 1977), pp. 62, 63.

19. Patricia Grace, *Potiki* (New York: Penguin Books, 1986), p. 105.

20. Leslie Marmon Silko, *Ceremony* (1977; New York: Penguin Books, 1986), pp. 35–36. An excellent critical review of this novel is provided by Paula Gunn Allen, "The Feminine Landscape of Leslie Marmon Silko's *Ceremony*" in her book *The Sacred Hoop*, pp. 118–26.

21. Allen, *The Sacred Hoop*, pp. 62–63.

22. Mary TallMountain, "You Can Go Home Again," in *I Tell You Now, Autobiographical Essays by Native American Writers*, ed. Brian Swann and Arnold Krupat (Lincoln: University of Nebraska Press, 1987), p. 13.

23. Gloria Anzaldúa, *Borderlands / La Frontera, The New Mestiza* (San Francisco: Spinsters / Aunt Lute, 1987), p. 195. Subsequent citations to this book within this chapter will be given parenthetically in the text.

24. In saying this I do not wish in any way to mitigate the realities specific to Chicanas or to underestimate the history and reality of racial oppression they have experienced. I am borrowing the concept to illuminate women's realities in a different sense.

25. See the very useful essay by Evelyn Fox Keller and Helene Moglen, "Competition and Feminism: Conflicts for Academic Women," *Signs* 12:3 (Summer 1987): 493–511. The essay is included in the work edited by Helen Longino and Valerie Miner, *Competition among Women: A Feminist Analysis* (New York: Feminist Press, 1988).

26. Audre Lorde identifies and elaborates this process in her essay: "Eye to Eye: Black Women and Anger" in her book *Sister Outsider: Essays & Speeches* (Trumansburg, N.Y.: The Crossing Press, 1984).

27. Vivian Gornick, *The Romance of American Communism* (New York: Basic Books, 1977), p. 261.

28. Carol B. Stack, "The Culture of Gender: Women and Men of Color," *Signs* 11:2 (Winter 1986): 321–24.

29. Judith Shapiro, "Gender Totemism," in *The Dialectics of Gender: Antropological Approaches,* ed. Richard Randolph, David Schneider, and May Diaz (Boulder, Col.: Westview Press, 1988).

30. Catharine A. MacKinnon, *Feminism Unmodified: Discourses on Life and Law* (Cambridge: Harvard University Press, 1987).

Small Press Publishers

CRUCIAL to the contemporary women's cultural renaissance has been the burgeoning of small presses. These are often staffed by only a few people, and exist on a minimal (or nonexistent) margin of profit. To encourage access to works cited in this book and published by such presses, the following listing is provided.

Arte Publico Press
University of Houston
4800 Calhoun 429AH
Houston, Tex. 77004

Aunt Lute/Spinsters
P.O. Box 410687
San Francisco, Calif. 94141

Black Oyster Press
c/o Lisa Kellman
821 Hampshire Street
San Francisco, Calif. 94110

Booklegger Publishing
555 29th Street
San Francisco, Calif. 94131

CALYX Books
P.O. Box B
Corvallis, Oreg. 97339

Celestial Arts Publishing
P.O. Box 7327
Berkeley, Calif. 94707

Crossing Press
P.O. Box 1048
Freedom, Calif. 95019

Feminist Press
City University of New York
311 E. 94th Street
New York, N.Y. 10128

Firebrand Books
141 The Commons
Ithaca, N.Y. 14850

Kitchen Table: Women of Color Press
P.O. Box 2753
Rockefeller Center Station
New York, N.Y. 10815

Lesbian Herstory Educational
Foundation
P.O. Box 1258
New York, N.Y. 10116

Long Haul Press
Box 592 Van Brunt Station
Brooklyn, N.Y. 11215

Naiad Press
P.O. Box 10543
Tallahassee, Fla. 32302

New Society Publishers
P.O. Box 582
Santa Cruz, Calif. 95061

New Victoria Publishers
7 Bank Street
Lebanon, N.H. 03766

Organization for Equal Education of
the Sexes, Inc.
438 Fourth Street
Brooklyn, N.Y. 11215

Press Gang Publishers
603 Powell Street
Vancouver, British Columbia
Canada V6A 1 H2

Seal Press
312 S. Washington
Seattle, Wash. 98104

Shameless Hussy Press
P.O. Box 5540
Berkeley, Calif. 94703

Sinister Wisdom Books
P.O. Box 1308
Montpelier, Vt. 05602

South End Press
300 Raritan Center
Edison, N.J. 08837

Volcano Press/Kazan Books
P.O. Box 270
Volcano, Calif. 95689

West End Press
P.O. Box 291477
Los Angeles, Calif. 90029

Women's Press, Ltd.
124 Shoreditch High Street
London E1 England

Index

abolitionists, 71–72, 83, 98, 99. *See also* civil rights movement; racism; slavery

abortion, 57, 96, 216. *See also* contraception

Acosta, Teresa Paloma, 29

Addams, Jane, 84, 85, 86, 100; and Mary Rozet Smith, 85, 86

Adelman, Marcy: *Long Time Passing,* 219–20

African-American women. *See* Afro-American women

African women, 70, 103–4, 132–33, 153–54, 241–42

Afro-American women, 12, 19, 22, 27–28, 47, 49–50, 52–54, 60–65, 83, 91, 95, 96–97, 98–100, 132–33, 134–35, 152–54, 201–2, 203–5, 241–44, 247, 253; as artists, 45–46, 71–73, 74, 142, 143–44, 145–48, 161–66; dialogue between Jewish women and, 108–10; history of, 8–10, 71, 207–10. *See also* lesbianism and women of color; racism; slavery; women of color

Agosín, Marjorie, 73

AIDS, 73, 118

Alarcón, Norma, 32

Allen, Paula Gunn, 29–30, 102–3, 133, 238–39, 246

American Indians. *See* Native American peoples

Amézcua, Chelo González, 161

Anthony, Katharine, 101

anti-Semitism, 23, 26, 64, 108–11, 114, 228; in the Black community, 108; resistance to, 108–9, 110–11, 188–90, 224 (*see also* resistance against Nazis)

antiwar movements, 100–101, 169–70

Anzaldúa, Gloria, 106, 248–51

Aries, Elizabeth, 44–45

Armenian-American women, 184–87

Arnold, June, 114

Asian-American women, 12, 106–7; Chinese-American women, 21–22, 107, 126–30, 137–38, 229, 247 (*see also* Chinese women); Japanese-American women, 156–61, 220–21, 232, 247; Japanese-American women, internment of, 31–32, 190–95, 214–15, 232; Korean-American women, 106; Pilipinas, 90. *See also* women of color

assault against women. *See* domestic violence; rape; violence against women

Avakian, Arlene, 184, 185, 187

balance, 7, 24, 47, 60, 160, 183–84, 194–95, 197–98, 236, 238, 241, 244–45, 251, 254. *See also* healing; Native American peoples; spirituality, web of life

Balbo, Laura, 24

Bambara, Toni Cade, 65, 144; *The Salt Eaters,* 242–43

Barnes, Djuna, 79

barrio. *See* ghettos, barrio

Barton, Todd, 235

Bates, Katharine Lee, 83–84, 85; and Katharine Coman, 83–84, 85

battered women. *See* domestic violence; violence against women

Baum, Marianne Cohn, 169

Baum, Terry, 114

Beck, Evelyn Torton: *Nice Jewish Girls,* 108–9, 110–11

Benberry, Cuesta, 71–72

Bethune, Mary McLeod, 99

birth control. *See* contraception

Black liberation. *See* civil rights movement

Black women. *See* African women; Afro-American women; women of color

Boston Marriage, 80, 85

Boudica, 112, 131

Brant, Beth, 50

Brooks, Gwendolyn, 60, 64, 67; *Maud Martha,* 60–65

Brown, Elsa Barkley: "To Catch the Vision of Freedom," 207–8

Brown, Emma V., 83

Rosario Morales, "Sugar Poem," in Aurora Levins Morales and Rosario Morales, *Getting Home Alive* (Ithaca, N.Y.: Firebrand Books, 1986), lines reprinted by permission of the publisher. Copyright © 1986 by Aurora Levins Morales and Rosario Morales.

Marge Piercy, "The Seven Pentacles," in "To Be of Use," in Marge Piercy, *Circles in the Water* (New York: Knopf, 1982), lines reprinted by permission of the publisher. Copyright © 1977 by Marge Piercy.

Bernice Johnson Reagon, "My Black Mothers and Sisters, Or On Beginning A Cultural Autobiography," *Feminist Studies* 8 (Spring 1982), lines reprinted by permission of the author. Copyright © 1981 by Bernice Johnson Reagon. First published in *Black Women and Liberation Movements*, ed. Virginia A. Blandford, Institute for the Arts and the Humanities, Howard University, Washington, D.C., 1981.

Adrienne Rich, "Self Hatred," in Adrienne Rich, *A Wild Patience Has Taken Me This Far: Poems 1978–1981* (New York: Norton, 1981), lines reprinted by permission of the publisher and the author. Copyright © 1981 by Adrienne Rich.

Adrienne Rich, "Origins and History of Consciousness" and "Transcendental Etude," in Adrienne Rich, *The Dream of A Common Language: Poems 1974–1977* (New York: Norton, 1978), lines reprinted by permission of the publisher and the author. Copyright © 1978 by W. W. Norton & Co.

Kate Rushin, "The Bridge Poem," in *This Bridge Called My Back: Writings By Radical Women of Color*, ed. Gloria Anzaldúa and Cherríe Moraga (Watertown, Mass.: Persephone Press, 1981), lines reprinted by permission of Gloria Anzaldúa and the author. Copyright © 1981 by Donna K. Rushin.

Ntozake Shange, *For Colored Girls Who Have Considered Suicide When the Rainbow is Enuf* (New York: Macmillan, 1977), lines reprinted by permission of the publisher and Methuen. Copyright © 1975, 1976, 1977 by Ntozake Shange.

Leslie Marmon Silko, "I always called her Aunt Susie" and "The Storyteller's Escape," in Leslie Marmon Silko, *Storyteller* (New York: Seaver Books, 1981), lines reprinted by permission of the publisher. Copyright © 1981 by Leslie Marmon Silko.

Leslie Marmon Silko, *Ceremony* (New York: Viking Penguin, 1986), excerpt reprinted by permission of the publisher. Copyright © 1977 by Leslie Marmon Silko. A Seaver Book.

Anryu Suharu, untitled poem, in *Women Poets of Japan*, ed. Kenneth Rexroth and Ikuko Atsumi (New York: New Directions, 1977), lines reprinted by permission of the publisher. Copyright © 1977 by Kenneth Rexroth and Ikuko Atsumi.

Kitty Tsui, "It's In the Name" and "Kwan Ying Lin: Kwan Yuen Sheung," in Kitty Tsui, *The Words of a Woman Who Breathes Fire* (San Francisco: Spinsters/Aunt Lute, 1983), lines reprinted by permission of the publisher. Copyright © 1983 by Kitty Tsui.

Alice Walker, *In Search of Our Mother's Gardens: Womanist Prose* (San Diego: Harcourt Brace Jovanovich, 1983), excerpts and lines of poetry reprinted by permission of the publisher and the author. Copyright © 1983 by Alice Walker.

Alice Walker, "The Nature of This Flower Is to Bloom," in Alice Walker, *Revolutionary Petunias & Other Poems* (New York: Harcourt Brace Jovanovich, 1973), lines reprinted by permission of the publisher and the author. Copyright © 1970 by Alice Walker.

Anna Lee Walters, "The Sun Is Not Merciful," in Anna Lee Walters, *The Sun is Not*